SNOWDONIA,
A HISTORICAL ANTHOLOGY

For Jennifer, Vivien and Christopher

SNOWDONIA,
A HISTORICAL ANTHOLOGY

by
David Kirk

Gwasg Carreg Gwalch

ISBN: 0-86381-270-8

First published in 1994, second edition in 2003.
Gwasg Carreg Gwalch, 12 Iard yr Orsaf, Llanrwst,
Wales LL26 0EH
☎ 01492 642031   ▤ 01492 641502
✆ books@carreg-gwalch.co.uk   website: www.carreg-gwalch.co.uk

Printed and published in Wales

"Well, what have we got here?" says the snarling critic,
"more tours, more trash, more plagiarism.
If a man walks a few miles,
he now publishes his observations
and cannot keep it a secret
that he has moved out of the place where he was born:
thus are the public inundated
with what are called descriptions and remarks."

Softly, splenetic Sir, suspend your ire,
description is not necessary
and our remarks I hope will not displease you.

Daniel Webb
'Observations and Remarks
During Four Excursions
Made to the Various Parts of Great Britain
in the Years 1810 and 1811'

Acknowledgements

*Specific thanks to Will Aaron, Edryd Gwyndaf
and Phil Lacey for their help and encouragement
in the preparation of this book.
Thanks also to the staff of Gwynedd Archives,
the British Library
and the National Library of Wales.*

Contents

Introduction

The subjects of this book are a great grey granite octopus of a mountain and, on a smaller scale, various members of humanity who have botanised upon it, burrowed in it, camped on it, climbed it, dangled from it, fortified it, guided others up it, mapped and measured it, painted it, steamed along it, peregrinated round it, or waxed poetic from its summit.

Snowdon's eight winding tentacles embrace a rocky wilderness of great scenic beauty and geological complexity. Add in the variations of temperature, of wind strength and direction, of cloud level and thickness and all the attendant details collectively termed 'weather', and the reasons for Snowdon's immense popularity become obvious: no two ascents ever present the same experience.

There are other reasons for the attraction Snowdon and its neighbouring peaks have exerted on outsiders. No other region of southern Britain has been more resistant to man's exertions. Agriculture, forestry, grazing, road-building, copper-mining, slate-quarrying, railway development, tourism, all have left their mark on the mountains yet none has managed to dominate or erase its predecessors.

Few visitors to Snowdonia had a stronger knowledge than George Borrow of Welsh history. First published in 1862, Borrow's *Wild Wales* can be found on the shelves of almost every bookseller in Britain. The author's genius stems from his recognition that the people of Snowdonia, be they inhabitant or itinerant, were even more fascinating than their surrounding scenery:

> 'I was overtaken by an old fellow with a stick in his hand, walking very briskly. He had a crusty and rather conceited look. I spoke to him in Welsh, and he answered in English, saying that I need not trouble myself by speaking Welsh, as he had plenty of English, and of the very best. We were from first to last at cross purposes. I asked him about Rhys Goch

and his chair. He told me that he knew nothing of either, and began to talk of Her Majesty's ministers and the fine sights of London. I asked him the name of a stream which, descending a gorge on our right, ran down the side of the valley, to join the river at its bottom. He told me that he did not know and asked me the name of the Queen's eldest daughter. I told him I did not know, and remarked that it was very odd that he could not tell me the name of a stream in his own vale. He replied that it was not a bit more odd than that I could not tell him the name of the eldest daughter of the Queen of England. I told him that when I was in Wales I wanted to talk about Welsh matters, and he told me that when he was with English he wanted to talk about English matters. I returned to the subject of Rhys Goch and his chair, and he returned to the subject of Her Majesty's ministers, and the fine folks of London. I told him that I cared not a straw about Her Majesty's ministers and the fine folks of London, and he replied that he cared not a straw for Rhys Goch, his chair or old women's stories of any kind.'

Borrow was one of the most talented writers to portray Wales and the Welsh but very far from being the first; he was indeed criticised for the unoriginality of his chosen theme. Yet the writings of Borrow's predecessors are almost forgotten. With isolated exceptions such as Gerald de Barri's *Itinerary through Wales* [1188], Daniel Defoe's *Tour through the Whole Island of Great Britain* [1724] and Joseph Hucks' *Pedestrian Tour through North Wales*, nearly all the travelogues, diaries, histories and guidebooks written of Wales prior to the present century have long been out of print. This is regrettable since they illuminate different facets of a landscape which is one of the most beautiful in Britain.

Borrow's wilderness had been tamed in part by the steam railway engine; his own journey to Wales had begun by train:

'With dragon speed, and dragon noise, fire, smoke, and fury, the train dashed along its road through beautiful meadows, garnished here and there with pollard sallows; over pretty streams, whose waters stole along imperceptibly; by venerable old churches, which I vowed I would take the first opportunity of visiting: stopping now and then to recruit energies at places whose old Anglo-Saxon names stared me in the eyes from station boards, as specimens of which, let me only dot down Willy Thorpe, Ringsted, and Yrthling Boro. Quite forgetting everything Welsh, I was enthusiastically Saxon the whole way from Medeshamsted to Blissworth, so thoroughly Saxon was the country, with its rich meads, its old churches and its names.'

What had the earlier visitors to say of their journeys before the age of railways and, further back in time, before Thomas Telford had completed his line of toll roads between London and Holyhead? Why did they come? How did they travel? Where did they stay? What did they see? The first recorded travellers were Roman invaders attempting to cement their hold on a newly conquered but rebellious province of Rome. Viewing Anglesey from the coast between Caernarfon and Bangor, it is easy to visualise Tacitus' account of the Roman assault across the Menai Straits in AD 61 under the newly appointed military governor of Britain, Gaius Suetionius Paulinus. Writing *The Annals of Imperial Rome* about AD 100, Tacitus refers to the island by a Latin derivative of its British title, *Mon*:

'Suetonius prepared to attack Mona, an island rendered formidable by large population and numerous refugees. Flat-bottomed boats were constructed to carry the infantry over the shallow river. The cavalry crossed at fords or swam with their horses.

'Large numbers of the enemy stood in opposition on the shore, among them black-dressed women with dishevelled hair running up and down and bearing torches before them after the manner of the furies. The Druids uttered the most dreadful curses, with hands uplifted to heaven. The sight so astonished and terrified the invading soldiers that they became fixed to the spot where they stood and were at risk of wounding from their enemy. Then, encouraged by the general, and encouraging each other not to be intimidated by fanatical females, they advanced their standards, overthrowing all who opposed them, and plunged the Britons into their own fires.

'Suetonius ordered the defeated island to be garrisoned and the altars of the Druids destroyed. It had been their religion to daub these alters in the blood of their prisoners and read the will of their gods in human entrails.'

After Tacitus, the shadows close in again until AD 430. The hill fortress of Dinas Emrys, near Beddgelert, may once have echoed to the voice of 'Myrddin-Emrys' immortalised by Thomas Malory as Merlin. The valleys of Snowdonia, heavily forested, were the ultimate refuge of Neolithic Man from Bronze Age Celts, shielding the latter in turn from the Iron Age Celts who later defied with outstanding success Roman and Saxon invaders before falling to the Normans under Edward I. It was from the conflicts between Celts and Saxons and among the Celts themselves that the legends of Arthur, Merlin and Uther Pendragon arose to be clothed by later writers in the medieval dress finally depicted by Malory's *Morte d'Arthur*.

Nennius, a British cleric, completed his *History of the Britons* in AD 796. Dinas Emrys [which has long been in private ownership but was purchased in 1993 by the National Trust for England and Wales] is accepted by many historians as being the location Nennius refers to in his account of a gradual retreat by the British leader Vortigern from Saxon invaders. The year is around AD 430. Unravelling a tangle of folklore, a British chieftain named Emrys emerges from Nennius' history as an opponent of Vortigern or 'Gwrtheyrn' [both names meaning simply 'high king']. The wooded surface of Dinas Emrys can have changed little in the past

1,500 years apart from the intrusion of a 12th century tower, now ruined, near its summit:

'But soon after, calling together his twelve wise men, to consult what was to be done, they said to him "Retire to the remote boundaries of your kingdom; there build and fortify a city to defend yourself".

'Having, to no purpose, travelled far and wide, they came at length to a province called Guenet [Gwynedd] and, having surveyed the mountains of Eryri, they discovered, on the summit of one of them, a site adapted to the construction of a citadel. Upon this, the wise men said to the king "Build here a city; for in this place it will ever be secure against the barbarians".

A. G. Bradley brings this story alive very vividly in his book *Highways and Byways in North Wales*, published in 1894:

'Let us salute with due awe Dinas Emrys, whither Vortigern, in despair of making further head against the Saxons whom he had invited to Britain, retired to brood upon his folly and his sorrows, and the remains of the ramparts and walls he raised are still to be seen upon the summit. He had tried in vain, says the old Welsh legend, to found this last fortress of his upon the morass below, and at last the wise men having consulted their oracles assured him the foundations would never stand till they had been sprinkled with the blood of a child born of a pure virgin. This was perhaps a roundabout way of suggesting that a more reasonable building site should be looked for. The much harassed king, however, took it literally and had what was left of his realm ransacked for the prodigy.

'Superstition could meet any demand in those days but, as a matter of fact, the lady who came forward to oblige his majesty in this particular case had so patent an object in view it seems strange that even fifth century credulity could swallow it. This was a vestal virgin who had born a child to a noble Roman. The child had grown into a youth but even thus late in the day his mother, it seems, thought she could do something to save her honour and was quite prepared to sacrifice her offspring and concoct a monstrous tale of total innocence and art magic. The youth was no less a personage than the afterwards famous Merlin, "Merddin Emrys", and he was ordered to be sacrificed.

'But when the boy was confronted with Vortigern's wise men, he showed such superhuman sagacity in discourse with them that they deemed it wise to let him alone and his life was spared. He it was who persuaded the king to remove his castle to yonder giddy summit of Dinas Emrys, and himself supplanting all the old wizards in Vortigern's confidence became his chief comfort and support, and began that career of prophecy which has made his name far the greatest of ancient British bards.'

From Dinas Emrys, Vortigern progressed to the massive hill fortress of Tre'r Ceiri near the west coast of the Llŷn Peninsular, perhaps with the aim of escaping his collapsing kingdom altogether and taking refuge in Brittany or Ireland. He was followed during subsequent centuries by an army of antiquarians, notably the Welsh-born writer, historian and topographer Thomas Pennant whose *Journey to Snowdon* was published in 1781:

'Ascend from Nefyn for a considerable way up the side of the high hill and, after a short ride on level ground, quit our horses in order to visit Nant y Gwytheyrn, or Vortigern's Valley, the immense hollow to which Vortigern is reported to have fled from the rage of his subjects, and where it was said that he and his castle were consumed with lightning. Nennius places the scene in Teivi [Teifi] in Caermarthenshire; but I believe that the historian not only mistakes the spot but even the manner of his death. His life had been profligate; the monks therefore were determined

13

that he should not die the common death of all men and accordingly made him perish with signal marks of the vengeance of Heaven. Fancy cannot frame a place more fit for a retreat from the knowledge of mankind, or better calculated to inspire confidence of security from any pursuit. Embosomed in a lofty mountain, on two sides bounded by stony steeps on which no vegetables appear but the blasted heath and stunted gorse; the third side exhibits a most tremendous front of black precipice with the loftiest peak of the mountain Eifl soaring above; and the only opening to this secluded spot is towards the sea (a northern aspect!) where that chilling wind exerts all its fury and half freezes during winter the few inhabitants. The glen is tenanted by three families who raise oats and keep a few cattle, sheep and goats; but seem to have great difficulty in getting their little produce to market.

'Just above the sea is a high and verdant mount, natural but the top and sides worked by art; the first flatted, the sides marked with eight prominent ribs from top to bottom. On this might have been the residence of the unfortunate prince, of which time has destroyed every other vestige. Till the beginning of the last century, a tumulus, of stone within and externally covered with turf, was to be seen here; it was known by the name of Bedd Gwrtheyrn; tradition having regularly delivered down the report of this having been the place of his interment. The inhabitants of the parish, perhaps instigated by their then minister, Mr Hugh Roberts, a person of curiosity, dug into the carn and found in it a stone coffin containing the bones of a tall man. This gives a degree of credibility to the tradition, especially as no other bones were found near the carn; nor were there any other tumuli on the spot: which affords a proof at least of respect to the rank of the person and that the place was deserted after the death of the royal fugitive, about the year 465.

'After emerging out of this cheerless bottom, I found fresh and amazing matter of speculations. I got into a bwlch or hollow between two summits of the Eifl mountains; a range that makes a most distinguished figure with the sugar-loaf points from various and distant parts of the country. They range obliquely and separate Llŷn from the hundred of Arfon, and jut into the sea near Vortigern's Valley.

'Across this hollow, from one summit of the Eifl to the other, extends an immense rampart of stones or perhaps the ruins of a wall which effectually blocked up the pass. On the Eifl is the most perfect and magnificent, as well as the most artfully constructed, British post I ever beheld. It is called Tre'r Caeri [Tre'r Ceiri] or The Town of the Fortresses. This, which was the accessible side, was defended by three walls; the lowest is very imperfect, the next tolerably entire and has in it the grand entrance. This wall in one part points upwards towards the third wall, which runs round the edges at the top of the hill. The second wall unites with the first which runs into a point, reverts and joins the highest in a place where the hill becomes inaccessible. The facings on the two upper walls are very entire, especially that of the uppermost. They are lofty and exhibit from below a grand and extensive front. The space on the top is an irregular area; part is steep, part flat, in most parts covered with heath, giving shelter to a few red grouse. The whole is almost filled with cells. To be seen to advantage, the station should be taken from the summit, about which the cells are very distinct and disposed with much art. About the middle is a square place fenced with stones, a sort of praetorium, surrounded with two rows of cells; numbers are also scattered about the plain and others again are contiguous to the wall along the inside.

'The cells are mostly perfect, of various forms: round, oval, oblong, square. Some of the round were fifteen feet in diameter. Of the oblong, thirty feet in length with long entrances regularly faced with stone. All of them, when inhabited, were well protected from the weather by roofs of thatch or sod.

'The upper wall was in many places fifteen feet high on the outside, and often sixteen feet broad. It consisted of two parallel and contiguous parts, one higher than the other, serving as a parapet to the lower which seemed to have had its walk like that on the walls of Chester. There was in one place a cell in the thickness of the wall, or perhaps a sally-port, in part stopped by the falling-in of the stones.'

In the 5th century, Tre'r Ceiri must have been one of the most formidable fortifications in the entire British isles. It remains today substantially as Pennant saw it, vast, rocky and ruinous, though no part could be described as 'perfect'. It is easily explored with the assistance of a 1:50,000 Ordnance Survey map. The gloom of its neighbouring valley, Nant Gwrtheyrn, has been relieved in recent years by the rescue of its former quarry village, Porth y Nant, at the foot of one of the steepest roads in Europe. The village has been developed into a visitor-centre with an emphasis on teaching the Welsh language.

The Welsh annal *Brut y Tywysogion* [The Chronicle of the Princes] notes briefly for the year AD 816:

'The Saxons ravaged the mountains of Eryri and took Rhufoniog [a region east of Snowdonia, around Denbigh] by force.'

A later incursion, this time by Normans in 1095 AD, is recorded by another Welsh chronicle *Brenhinedd y Saesson* [The Kings of the Saxons]:

'William marched into Wales at Michaelmas and dispersed his army and traversed all the country so that all the army came together at All Saints' at Snowdon. But the Welsh always went ahead into the mountains and moors so that they could not be reached; and the king then turned homewards because he saw that he could do nothing more there that winter.'

In 1188, an ambitious priest named Gerald de Barri accompanied Baldwin, archbishop of Canterbury, through Wales to raise support for an invasion of Palestine. Gerald compiled a written record of all he saw, penned in Latin under the name Giraldus Cambrensis. Baldwin died two years later and the work was dedicated to his successor at Canterbury, Stephen Langton. Both the earliest and for many centuries the most thorough of its kind, *Journey through Wales* details a clockwise circular itinerary commencing at Hereford in early March:

'I must not pass over in silence the mountains called by the Welsh Eryri and by the English Snowdon or Mountains of Snow which, gradually increasing from the land of the sons of Conan and extending themselves northwards near Deganwy, seem to rear their lofty summits even to the clouds when viewed from the opposite coast of Anglesey. They are said to be of so great an extent that, according to an ancient proverb, "As Mona could supply corn for all the inhabitants of Wales, so could the Eryri mountains afford sufficient pasture for all the herds, if collected together."

'On the high part of these mountains are two lakes worthy of notice. The one has a floating island in it which is often driven from one side to the other by the force of the winds; and the shepherds behold with astonishment their cattle, whilst feeding, carried to the distant parts of the lake. A part of the bank naturally bound together by the roots of willows and other shrubs may have been broken off and increased by the alluvion of the earth from the shore; being continually agitated by the winds which in so elevated a situation blow with great violence, it cannot reunite itself firmly with the banks. The other lake is noted for a wonderful and singular miracle. It contains three sorts of fish: eels, trout and perch, all of which have only one eye, the left being wanting. But, if the curious reader should demand of me the explanation of so extraordinary a circumstance, I cannot presume to satisfy him.

'According to vulgar tradition, these mountains are frequented by an eagle who, perching on a fatal stone every fifth holiday, in order to satiate her hunger with the carcases of the slain, is said to expect war on that same day and to have almost perforated the stone by cleaning and sharpening her beak.'

Interesting though floating islands, one-eyed fish and prophetic birds may be, the most informative feature of Gerald's *Journey through Wales* and *Description of Wales* is their description of the Welsh, as in the following account of their hospitality:

'Visitors who arrive in the morning are entertained till evening by the conversation of young women and music of the harp, for each house has its young women and harps allotted to this purpose. In each family, the art of playing on the harp is held preferable to any other learning. In the evening, when no more guests are expected, the meal is prepared according to the number and dignity of the persons assembled and according to the wealth of the family who entertains; the kitchen does not supply many dishes nor high seasoned incitements to eating. The house is not adorned with tables, cloths and napkins. They study nature more than splendour, for which reason they place all the dishes together upon mats with large platters or trenchers full of sweet herbs; they also make use of a thin and broad cake of bread, baked every day, which in old writings was called Lagana (Bara Llech or griddle-bread) and they sometimes add chopped meat with broth.

'A bed made of rushes and covered with a coarse kind of cloth manufactured in the country, called Brychan, is then placed along the side of the room, and they all in common lie down to sleep. Nor is their dress at night different from that by day, for at all seasons they defend themselves from the cold only by a thin coat and waistcoat. The fire continues to burn by night as well as by day, at their feet, and they receive much comfort from the natural heat of the persons lying near them. When the under side begins to be tired with the hardness of the bed, or the upper one to suffer from cold, they immediately leap up and go to the fire, which soon relieves them from both inconveniences. Returning to their couch, they then expose their sides alternately to the cold and to the hard bed.'

The Welsh king Llywelyn ap Iorwerth, though married to a daughter of the Norman king John, attempted to assert his independence early in the 13th century and retreated into Snowdonia when the rebellion failed. The *Brut y Tywysogion* entry for AD 1211:

'John, king of England, gathered a mighty host and made for Gwynedd, planning to dispossess Llywelyn and to destroy him utterly, princes with him. Llywelyn ap Iorwerth moved to the wilderness of Eryri.'

The same source records for AD 1284:

'A year after Edward of Caernarfon [Edward II] was born, the king held a fair at Moel-yr-Wyddfa [the Snowdon summit]. And he had a tournament held at Nefyn in Llŷn. And thereupon the king went towards England, exultantly happy with victory. After that there were four years of continued peace at a stretch, without anything to be recorded for that length of time.'

Memories of Llywelyn ap Iorwerth still haunt Snowdonia. He is pictured to visitors as a thoughtless rogue who murdered his hound, Gelert, thinking it had made an unscheduled meal of his son. This miserable story was exploited at Llywelyn's expense by David Prichard who was the proprietor of Beddgelert's Goat Hotel from 1802 to 1821. If anything is buried in the dog's alleged grave, it is Prichard's honesty along with a few bones contemporary with

Prichard himself. David Jenkin's outlines the fraud in *Bedd Gelert, Its Facts, Fairies and Folk-lore* [1899]:

> 'It had no place at all in the folklore of this part until it was brought to the parish by the late David Prichard, of the Goat Hotel, who was a native of South Wales. It was he, along with William Prichard, the parish clerk, and Richard Edwards of Pen y Bont Fach, who raised the stone that is exhibited today on the spot that was afterwards called "the Dog's Grave".
>
> 'It seems that a very excellent dog of the name of Gelert has been buried in the grave, and the comely spinsters who owned the dog spoke of its virtues as many and wonderful.'

If a Llywelyn merits criticism, it is Llywelyn ap Gruffydd for imprisoning his rebellious brother Owain for 23 years in Dolbadarn castle though this was fairly gentle behaviour compared with the family strife within England's Norman monarchy.

A small detail needs to be addressed before proceeding and that is the matter of pronouncing Welsh placenames and personal names. The language combines great beauty with antiquity, deriving from the Roman-British conglomerate spoken in much of Britain before the Anglo-Saxon invasions around AD 450. Welsh spelling has greater phonetic logic than 20th century English. The key points are few and quite easy to memorise:

The letter 'w' is used as a vowel in examples such as cwm [a small valley, like the English coombe] but always pronounced with a very short 'oo'. Many Welsh words are much younger than cwm: driving too quickly along the narrow roads of Snowdonia can result in a detour by ambiwlans.

The letter 'y' is also employed as a vowel. It usually has the same sound as the short u of 'sun' unless in the last syllable of a word when it becomes the i of 'ink'. Thus the place-name Betws-y-coed sounds as bet-oos-a-koed and mynydd [mountain] as munith. Yr Wyddfa [the Welsh name for Snowdon's summit, meaning The Conspicuous] sounds as a-roo-ithva.

The vowel 'u' is pronounced as the i of ink, thus Curig sounds as 'kirrig' and Trum as 'trim'.

The 'dd' of Beddgelert is always pronounced 'th' as in 'the' [not as the aspirated 'th' of 'think'].

The letters 'g' and 'c' are always hardened, thus Gelert as in 'get' and Carnedd as in 'cairn'.

The 'ch' of Crib Goch [literally Ridge Red] is the same partial throat-constriction used by the Scots in 'loch' . . . often hardened by English-speakers into 'lock'. This sound once existed in English and is preserved in the otherwise illogical spelling of 'through' and 'borough'. The sound is halfway between h and k and was probably killed off in England by a surfeit of winter coughs. Note also the Welsh mountain name Cnicht: the initial hard c is sounded, so too is the later soft ch. The equivalent English word [knight] has changed drastically in sound but again preserves its written form.

The 'Ll' and 'll' of Llanberis, Llanrwst and Llangollen are the same as the above 'ch' but with a concluding l. Thus llan ['ch-lan'] sounds halfway between hlan and clan.

A single 'f' always hardens into v, thus fawr [large] and fach [small] are pronounced vawr and vach. The soft English f is achieved in Welsh using 'ff', hence Ffestiniog. [The Festiniog Railway lost its Ff due to a registration error by an English clerk.]

All clear? Then proceed with confidence through Llanfairpwllgwyngyllgogerychwyrndrobwllllantysiliogogogoch. This is the Victorian-contrived name of a small village in Anglesey, in fact two neighbouring village names joined together, just beyond Thomas Telford's suspension bridge across the Menai Straits. A. G. Bradley claimed in 1894 that 'the Englishman has never yet lived who could say it from memory correctly and without halting'; the trick is to deliver it in a single breath. Its romantic meaning is 'The church of Mary in a hollow [pwll] under a white hazel close to the rapid whirlpool [drobwll] near Tisilio's church by the red cave'. A more accurate modern description might be 'A fairly dull village on the road to Holyhead near the railway station with the second longest name in Britain'. The longest was contrived much more recently, in 1984, for Mawddach station on the Fairbourne narrow-gauge railway near Dolgellau.

As for the origin of 'Beddgelert', if not the grave of a four-legged

Gelert then perhaps a two-legged one? Welsh literature has kept a reasonably good record of the country's early saints but makes no reference to anyone of this or similar name. David Jenkins prefers an alternative explanation:

> 'One of the earliest orders of monks in Celtic countries was called Ceile De, or Keledei, which name means "a servant of God". Kurtz, in his *Church History* (London, 1891) says that to the old Celtic priests "was given the Celtic name Kele-de, Latinised as Colidei, and in the modern form Culdees". It is quite possible for Bethkele [quoted by Thomas Pennant from a 1531-dated priory seal] to be a corruption of Bwth Celei (the Hut of the Culdees) and for the name of Bedd Gelert to be thus derived.'

Welsh family names show different but distinct patterns as can easily be discovered by inspecting the Evans, Hughes, Jones, Parry, Price or Powell pages of any telephone directory in the United Kingdom. There will be found the sons of Evan, of Hugh, of John, of Harry, of Rhys and of Hywel. Thomas Pennant's 1773 tour explains:

> 'I must take notice that Thomas ap Richard ap Howel ap Jevan Vychan, Lord of Mostyn, and his brother Piers, founder of the family of Trelacre, were the first who abridged their name; and that on the following occasion. Rowland Lee, bishop of Lichfield and president of the marches of Wales, in the reign of Henry VIII sat at one of the courts on a Welsh cause and, wearied with the quantity of aps in the jury, directed that the panel should assume their last name, or that of their residence; and that Thomas ap Richard ap Howel ap Jevan Vychan, should for the future be reduced to the poor dissyllable Mostyn; no doubt to the great mortification of many an ancient line.'

Two particular themes emerge from these collected writings:

Firstly, the broad similarity in outlook between observers across the many centuries which they span, confirming that human character and inquisitiveness have changed little during the past 2,000 years.

Secondly, the value of personal letters, diaries and journals in recording aspects of contemporary life more detailed than any historical summary compiled long after the events it endeavours to describe. This book will have served its purpose if it encourages its readers to recognise the value of their own observations, be they the economics of feeding a horse [often as costly as feeding the rider] or the details of refuelling what will certainly prove a much more transient aid to human transport: the petrol-driven motor car. Today's commonplace is tomorrow's history, particularly when recorded in the form most readily accessible to succeeding generations: the written word.

Chapter One

In August 1485, a Welshman succeeded in overthrowing the English king, Richard III, and established himself firmly on the throne of England and Wales as Henry VII. Rather than transfer the English court to Wales, Henry Tudor and his supporters transferred themselves to London. With England and Wales now united to Welsh as well as English satisfaction, travel between the two countries could proceed without hindrance. Snowdonia was open to outsiders, if they could but find a road.

One of the earliest travellers to enjoy this freedom was John Leland, appointed by Henry VIII as King's Antiquary. He was charged with searching out Britain's literary and artistic treasures, in particular those held by the church. Leland's *Itinerary in Wales* [1536 to 1539] consequently reads more like a catalogue than a journal:

'In Cairarvonshire [Caernarfonshire] in Huwchurvay [Uwch Gwyrfai] commote is Llin edwarchen [Llyn y Dywarchen] with the Swimming Island, and thereof it has its name of a swimming swarth of earth.

'All Cregeeryri [Craig Eryri] is forest. The best wood of Cairarvonshire is by Glinne Kledder [Glyn Lledr], and by Kapel Kiryk [Capel Curig], and at Llanperis [Llanberis]. Meatly good wood about Conwey Abbay, and Penmachno, and about Cotmore, and Coiteparke by Bangor [Cortmore and Coed y Park, near Bethesda], and in many other places.

'In Llene and Iuionith [Llŷn and Eifionydd] is little wood.

'Cairarvonshire about the shore has reasonably good corn, as about a myle upland from the shore onto Cairarvon. Then more upward by Eryri Hilles, and in them is very little corn, except oats in some places, and a little barley and scant rye. If there were, the deer would destroy it.

'Dolebaterne [Dolbadarn] on a rock betwixt two linnys [llyns – lakes]. There is yet a piece of a tower where Owain Goch, brother to Lleulen (Llywelyn), last prince, was in prison.

'The ground all about the Tyue [Teifi], and a great mile toward Stratfler [Strata Florida], is horrid with the sight of bare stones, as Cregeryri Mountains be.'

In 1610, a map of Caernarfon was published by the cartographer John Speed showing the town to have expanded eastward of the walls which remain substantially intact today. An accompanying description of Snowdonia repeats the myth that the mountains remain under snow throughout the year:

'These Mountains may not unfitly be termed the British Alps, as being the most vaste of all Britaine, and for their steepnesse and cragginesse not unlike to those of Italy, all of them towring up into the Aire, and round encompassing one farre higher than all the rest, peculiarly called Snowdon-Hill, though the other likewise in the same sense, are by the Welsh termed Craig Eriry, as much as Snowy Mountains, taking their name as doth (by Plinies testimony) Niphates in Armenia, and Imaus in Scythia: For all the yeare long these lye mantelled over with Snow hard crusted together, though otherwise for their height they are open and liable both to the Sunne to dissolve them, and the windes to over-sweepe them.'

Thomas Johnson, a Yorkshire-born apothecary with a professional interest in botany, arrived in Snowdonia some 30 years after Speed. 'Glynn-lhivon', where Johnson stayed while visiting its owner, still exists on the east side of the Pwllheli road six miles south of Caernarfon, albeit surrounded since by a high stone wall built at enormous cost. Glynllifon later became an agricultural college and, more recently still, a wildlife park. In 1623, Johnson issued the first catalogue of local plants ever published in England. This was followed in 1633 by his enlargement of John Gerard's *The Herball*. In 1634 Johnson completed a botanical guide based on a tour of Oxford, Bath,

Bristol, Southampton and the Isle of Wight. A similar work on Wales followed in 1641, entitled *Itinerary of a Botanist*.

'Leaving Chester, and entering Wales at Flint Castle (by which there is a small town of the same name), we arrived at the sacred fountain of Holiwell. There we saw a well worshipped in ancient religion on account of the murder of the virgin Wenefrid and, among other plants decorating the surround hills, we picked up the Erica Vulgaris and the Tennifolia, both variegated, with little white flowers. Having dined here, we were this night hospitably entertained at Ruthlande [Rhuddlan].

'On the following morning we pursued our journey. Six miles ahead there is a mountain called Garthgogo [Cefn yr Ogof] by the natives. On the side of the mountain there is under a great precipice a mighty cave called by the terrible name of Ogo-Gumbyd [ogof – cave] with a difficult steep approach. This we went into. We saw the Polytrichus, the Saxifraga aurea, the Phyllitis etcetera, in the cave itself. On the approach we saw the Brassica sylvestris growing freely in the fissures of the stones, and not far from here we dug up also the Phyllitis multifida.

'Eight miles from here we were on the point of crossing the river at Aber Conwey when a manservant of the distinguished man Thomas Glynne came to us and told us that his master was expecting us not far from where we were. So we turned aside to the house of Bodskalan belonging to the noble Robert Wynne, famed for his hospitality. There we spent the rest of the day and also the night.

'The next day, having thanked our generous host for his kindness, we stayed awhile at Conovium, or Aber Conwey, which town is pleasantly situated and was, even of old, strongly fortified by walls and a castle. Then, before we had gone five miles, we went through two passes full of horror — Pen-maen-behan and Pen-maen-mawre, that is, the smaller and the greater promontory. Here huge rocks hanging over

26

the sea admit of a narrow and dangerous path for travellers for, on the one side, stones threaten to fall from the rocks and, on the other side, the sea roaring fearfully at the foot of the huge precipice promises death to him who slips. The greater of these passes is about a mile in length.

'Leaving this behind us at last, Bangor, the seat of a bishopric, and Carnarvon, a pretty little town, delayed us a little. Entering the castle, which was of old very strongly fortified, we visited the place made famous through being the birthplace of Edward II who was called Edward of Carnarvon.

'Having travelled four miles from here, we at last reached Glynn-lhivon, the mansion of the truly generous man Thomas Glynne. This seat is very pleasantly situated: there are dark groves, brooks murmur gently as they flow over the pebbles, there are gardens on this side and that, beautified by many flowers and plants. The higher of them, sloping gently, presents a very pleasing view: on one side St George's Channel can be seen and, not far off, the island of Mona and even Ireland can be seen in fine weather. On the other side our British Alps, the highest mountains in the whole island, rear themselves up so that, wherever you go, there is something worth seeing.

'Not to be idle in this picturesque spot, on the following morning we went to the sea shore, which is not further than a mile from the house, and there we dug up the Soldonella and the Gnaphalium marinum. The Roman soldiers had a station here, on the very edge of the sea, the remains of which are still to be clearly seen [Dinas Dinlle]. Leaving the shore, we spent the rest of the day in visiting gardens, woods and pastures.'

Johnson ascended Snowdon via what is now termed the Snowdon Ranger path or possibly via the southern ridge of Bwlch Main. The latter seems the most likely, given the reference to 'rough rocky precipices on either hand':

'After the 3rd of August had dawned, we got on horseback and betook ourselves to our British Alps. The highest of all these is called Snowdon by the English and Widdfa by the Britons.

'Captivated by the desire to visit this mountain, we hastened and obtained the help of a boy as a guide from a farmer (because not only the summit but the whole mass of our mountain was veiled in cloud). Then, leaving our horses and outer garments, we began to climb the mountain. The ascent at first is difficult but, after a bit, a broad open space is found, but equally sloping, great precipices on the left and a difficult climb on the right.

'Having climbed three miles, we at last gained the highest ridge of the mountain, which was shrouded in thick cloud. Here the way was very narrow and climbers are horror-stricken by the rough rocky precipices on either hand, and the Stygian marshes, both on this side and that, the greatest of which is called the "Abode of the Devil" by the inhabitants. But when we got to such a point on the ridge that we could not proceed any further, we sat down in the midst of the clouds and first of all we arranged in order the plants we had, at our peril, collected among the rocks and precipices, and then we ate the food we had brought with us.'

'Leaving the mountains, we returned to Glynn-lhivon by dusk and spent the next day there quietly. On the following morning Mr Glynne, with his relative, Mr Owen, conducted us towards Mona.'

Civil war broke out in Britain one year after the above was written. Johnson sided with the royalists and, on September 14 1644, was shot in the shoulder during a skirmish with a detachment of Sir William Waller's troops. He died a fortnight later.

Another echo of the civil war can be sensed in John Taylor's 'Short Relation of a Long Journey Encompassing the Principalitie of Wales'. Sir John Owen, whom Taylor claims to have visited, had been one of the strongest royalist supporters in Wales and is recorded as having participated in seven battles, nine sieges and 32 actions. In 1644, Owen was governor of Harlech Castle and vice-admiral of North Wales. In 1648, he led 400 men in an attack on Caernarfon. This was successful and led to the murder of William Lloyd, parliamentarian high sheriff of Merionethshire, for which Owen narrowly escaped execution. Seven years after Taylor's visit, Owen organised an unsuccessful rising against Cromwell and had his estates sequestered; in 1663, after the restoration of the monarchy, he received a grant of £20,970.

Taylor travelled through North and South Wales in 1652 and appears from his written account to have been the first true tourist in the sense of being motivated by general curiosity. He met the cost of this and other travels by encouraging subscribers to commit themselves to buy a printed summary of what he saw. The preface to Taylor's tour shows this method of financing to be not entirely trouble-free:

'A Taylor's Bill, with few or no items: by or for John Taylor.

'Now in the seventy fourth year of mine age,
I take an English and Welsh pilgrimage:
From London first I bend my course to Chester,
And humbly I to all men am requester;
That when I have past over hills and dales,
And compast with my travels famous Wales,
That when to you that I a book do give,
Relating how I did subsist and live,
With all my passages both here and there,
And of my entertainment every where,
Write but your names and dwellings in this bill,
I'le finde you, for the book give what you will,
Twelve voyages and journies I have past,
And now my age sayes this may be my last.
My travels story shall most pleasant be
To you that read, though painfull unto me,

'In this bill I did promise to give to my friends a true relation of my journey and entertainment (which I have done), and I do give to them more than I promised, which is a brief chronicle of Wales which I did not mention in my bill. I know there are foure or five sorts of adventurers with me in this wearisome journey, some of them have paid me already (before I went) and their paine is past; if all the rest do pay me (being near 3000) I am deceived; if none doe pay me I am miserably cousened; for those that have paid, or can and will pay, I thank them; for such as would if they could, or will when they can, I wish them ability to perform their wills for their own sakes, and mine both; but for those that are able to reward me and will not, I will not curse them, though I fear they are almost past praying for.'

Born and schooled in Gloucester, Taylor became apprenticed to a Thames boatman only to be press-ganged into the navy. He was present in 1596 at the Siege of Cadiz and 'seven times at sea . . . served Eliza queen' before retiring. He lived for the next few years as a Thames boatman and published several pamphlets during the reign of James I, complaining that too many fellow watermen were in competition. He also berated the increasing use of 'hired hackney hell carts' and the decline in ferry traffic caused by the closure of theatres south of the Thames.

Turning to rhyme as a source of extra income, Taylor styled himself the 'water poet' and offered to celebrate in verse (for a fee) birthdays, weddings and funerals. He presented copies of these works to Ben Johnson and other distinguished contemporaries, attracting many patrons with his 'boisterous insolence'. Taylor's actions were sometimes as boisterous as his words, notably when he commenced a voyage down-river from London in a brown paper boat with two fish tied to canes for oars. The paper must have been strong since he covered three miles before the vessel disintegrated. His Welsh travels were accomplished more conventionally, on horseback. Their full title is almost an essay in itself:

'A Short Relation of a Long Journey Made Round or Ovall by Encompassing the Principalitie of Wales, from London, through and by the Counties of Middlesex and Buckingham, Berks, Oxonia, Warwick, Stafford, Chester, Flint, Denbigh, Anglesey, Carnarvon, Merionith, Cardigan, Pembroke, Caermarden, Glamorgan, Monmouth, Glocester, &c.

'This painfull circuit began on Tuesday the 13th of July last, 1652 and was ended (or both ends brought together) on Tuesday the 7 of September following, being near 600 Miles.

'Performed by the Riding, Going, Crawling, Running and Writing of John Taylor, dwelling at the Sign of the Poets Head, in Phenix Alley, near the middle of Long Aker in Covent Garden. March 26, 1653.'

The tour is mostly in prose but introduced by a rhyming outline of Taylor's route from London to the Welsh border:

'Thus John upon Dun's back, were both Dun John.
And thus the tedious way we wand'red on.
Now to proceed in order duly, truly,
I London left the thirteenth day of July:
The wayes as faire as man could well desire,
Cause I had none to draw Dun out o'the mire:
I fifteen miles (to Rislip) that day went,
Baited at Edgeworth to give Dun content;
There my acquaintance, of good fame and worth,
Did welcome me: the next day I set forth,
With boots, sans spurs, with whip, and switch of burch,
I got on twenty miles to Stoken church:
The fifteen day, S. Swithin, I and Dun,
Did shuffle sixteen miles to Abington;
There till the Tuesday following I abode,
From thence I sixteen miles to great Ive rode,
There at the Swan mine host was free and kind,
He had but one eye, t'other side was blinde;
But surely he a right good-fellow was,
And there one night my dun did eat good grass.

On July's twenty one from Ive I went,
And unto Warwick straight my course I bent;
There did I find another signe o'th Swan,
Mine hostesse kind, mine host a gentile man.
And for your love to me, good Master Venner,
With humble thanks I am your praises penner.
My gratitude to Master Jacob Harmer,
His draper's shop could never make me warmer,
Then high and mighty Warwick's drink did there,
It made my brains to caper and careere,
It was of such invincible strong force,
To knock me (in five miles) twice from my horse:
And sure, I think, the drink was certainly
Infused with the conqu'ring ghost of Guy.
On July's two and twentieth day I came
Unto an ancient house call'd Hunningham,
There were two ladies of good worth and fame,
Whom for some reasons I forbeare to name;
Their son and grandson (John) I'le not forget,
He's nobly minded as a baronet;
Foure dayes they kept me with exceeding cheere,
And gave me silver because travels deare.
From thence my journey 5 miles I pursue,
To Coventry, most famous for true blew;
There the faire crosse, of ancient high renown,
Stands firme, though other crosses all are down.
Tis a dry city, and dry let it be,
Twas not made dryer one small drop for me:
Like a camelion, there I broke my fast,
And thence I twenty miles to Lichfield past;
There at the George I took my lodging up,
I well was lodg'd, and well did sup and cup,
When there, by chance, I cast my wandring eye on
The ruin'd church, with griefe I thought on Sion:
I sigh'd to see that sad confusion,
Like th' Hebrews by the brook of Babylon.

On July's twenty seventh I rode alone
Full sixteen miles unto a town call'd Stone.
Next day to Nantwich, sixteen long miles more,
From thence to Chester, near the Cambrian shore:
There was my welcome in such noble fashion,
Of which in prose I'le make some briefe relation.'

Taylor progressed from Chester through Flint to Holywell and onwards to Anglesey, making no mention of the notoriously dangerous river crossing to Beaumaris. The perils of this ferry were evidently of no concern to a retired boatman:

'Monday, the second of August, when the day began, I mounted my Dun, having hired a little boy (to direct me in the way) that could speak no English, and for lack of an interpreter, we travelled speechless eight miles to Rudland, where is an old ruined wind and war-shaken castle; from that town, after my horse and the boy, and my self had dined with hay, oats, and barrow causs, we horsed and footed it twelve miles further, to a fine strong walled town, named Aberconwy: there I lodged at the house of one Mr Spencer (an English man); he is a post-master there, and there my entertainment was good, and my reckoning reasonable. There is a good defensive castle which I would have seen, but because there was a garrison, I was loath to give occasion of offence, or be much inquisitive.

'The next day, when the clock struck two and foure,
I mounted Dun, Dun mounted Penmen Mawre;
And if I do not take my aime amisse,
That lofty mountain seems the skies to kisse:
But there are other hills accounted higher,
Whose lofty tops I had no mind t'aspire:
As Snowdon and the tall Plinnillimon,
Which I no stomak had to tread upon.
Merioneth mountains, and shire Cardigan
To travell over, will tire horse and man:

33

I, to Bewmaris came that day and din'd,
Where I the good lord Buckley thought to find:
But he to speak with me had no intent,
Dry I came into's house, dry out I went.
I left to Bewmaris, and to Bangor trac'd it,
Ther's a brave church, but time and war defac'd it:
For love and money I was welcome thither,
Tis merry meeting when they come together.

'Thus having travelled from Aberconwy to Benmorris [Beaumaris] and to Bangor, Tuesday 3 August, which in all they are pleased to call 11 miles, but most of the Welsh miles are large London measure, not any one of them but hath a hand breadth or small cantle at each end, by which means, what they want in broadness, they have it in length; besides the ascending and descending almost impassable mountains, and the break-neck stony ways, doth make such travellers as my self judge that they were no misers in measuring their miles; besides, the land is coarser than it is in most parts about London, which makes them to afford the larger measure: for coarse broad-cloth is not at the rate of velvet or satin.

'Wednesday the 4th of August, I rode 8 miles from Bangor to Caernarvon, where I thought to have seen a town and a castle, or a castle and a town; but I saw both to be one, and one to be both; for indeed a man can hardly divide them in judgement or apprehension; and I have seen many gallant fabrics and fortifications but, for compactness and completeness, of Caernarvon I never yet saw a parallel. And it is by art and nature so sited and seated, that it stands impregnable; and if it be well manned, victualled and ammunitioned, it is invincible, except fraud or famine do assault or conspire against it.

'I was five hours in Caernarvon, and when I thought that I had taken my leave for ever of it, then was I merely deceived; for when I was a mile on my way, a trooper came galloping after me and enforced me back to be examined by Colonel

Thomas Mason (the governor there) who, after a few words, when he heard my name and knew my occasions, he used me so respectfully and bountifully that (at his charge) I stayed all night and, by the means of him and one Mr Lloyd (a justice of the peace there), I was furnished with a guide and something to bear charges for one week's travel, for which courtesies, if I were not thankful, I were worth the hanging for being ungrateful.

'The 5th of August I went 12 miles to a place called Climenie [Clenenney, 12 miles south of Caernarfon] where the noble Sire John Owen did, with liberal welcome, entertain me.

'The 6th day I rode to a town called Harleck [Harlech], which stands on a high barren mountain, very uneasy for the ascending into, by reason of the steep and uneven stony way; this town had neither hay, grass, oats or any relief for a horse: there stands a strong castle but the town is all spoilt and almost uninhabitable for the late lamentable troubles.

'So I left that town (for fear of starving my horse) and came to a place called Bermoth [Barmouth] (12 miles that day, as narrow as 20). That place was so plentifully furnished with want of provision that it was able to famish 100 men and horses.'

The cynicism of John Taylor re-emerges on a greatly amplified scale in a satirical tour by William Richards. This was based on a business journey into Wales in June 1673 and was published under the initials W. R. in 1682 as *Wallography, or the Briton described*. Richards was born in 1643 at Helmdon, Northamptonshire. Following his father into the church, he was a preacher in Marston, Oxfordshire, at the time of his journey. The work was reprinted in 1741 as part of John Torbuck's *Collection of Welch Travels and Memoirs of Wales* with a thinly veiled attribution to Jonathan Swift: 'a pleasant relation of D--n S--t's journey'. There is certainly a similarity in style between the two writers but Swift was only 15 years of age when the work was penned:

'We stumbled upon an house, or a dunghill modelled into the shape of a cottage, whose outward surface . . . appeared to be not unlike a great blot of cow-turd. This structure straddled over about eight ells [1 ell – 45 inches] of ground, above the surface whereof the eves were advanced about two yards and the chimney peeped out about a foot above the eves. The light flowed in through the old circumference of a bottomless peck which, being struck in thatch, supplied the place of an orbicular casement. The doorway was a breach in the wall towards one end which being of a dwarfish size i.e. two foot lower in stature than an ordinary man, we were forced to abridge our dimensions and to creep in.

'The parlor, hall, kitchen i.e. one room within, was prettily adorned with the poetry of ballads; a crippled pipkin with a broken shin, near allied to a dish of the same matter; a vocal spoon with a whistle at the end; and a tipsy cradle reeling in the corner, methought, were a pretty sort of goods, and not unhandsome furniture. A whole litter of children was strew'd upon the floor; only one mop-headed boy was tripos'd on a cricket and blew the fire. The carved mantle-tree seemed to be defended by a little wooden fellow, furiously strutting in an oaken cloak, and we perceived the window was endorsed with the picture of a fly.

'We observed that the bulky cupboard was a nuisance to the whole family of household stuff, which it had mightily disobliged by entrenching on their liberties, they grudging it so much room; and indeed the table, bed, and other utensils have not suffered a little detriment by its injurious contiguity.

'We had a prospect of whole territories about this building which, though not large, yet were exceedingly well fortified; a little hedge being a pallisado on one side, and a narrow trench instead of a bulwark on the other. The continuity of the mound was violated by a notch in the corner to set a stile in over which, when we passed, we espied a bank like a little hybla capped with a hive of bees which this small Eden curiously carved and, as it were, quin-cunx'd into a knot, did feast with the moisture of its delicious flowers.

'The country is mountainous and yields pretty handsome clambering for goats and hath variety of precipice to break one's neck which a man may sooner do than fill his belly, the soil being barren and an excellent place to breed a famine in.

'The commodities of the nation are chiefly woollen clothes, as cottons, baize, etc, of which their tattered backs are an ill sign; for sure they are not so silly as to furnish other countries with raiment and to go naked themselves.

'As for the diet of the Britons, it is not very delicate, neither is he curious in it. And if he should, his appetite might curl his nicety and, by pleasing his palette, he may starve his belly. A good mess of flummery, a pair of eggs, he rejoices at it as a feast, especially if he may close his stomach with toasted cheese, a morsel of which he hath a great kindness for. You may feel him pictured sometimes with that crevice in his head, called a mouth, charged at both corners with a crescent of cheese, and himself a cock horse on a red herring and his hat adorned with a plume of leeks. Good edible equipage which, when hunger pinches, he makes bold to nibble. He first eats his cheese and leeks together and, for a second course, he devours his horse.

'The cattle we saw most legible on their mountains were goats and heifers of a dwarfish size but very hardy, of a flinty constitution calculated on purpose for the meridian of a rock on which, it seems, they can as heartily feed as an ostrich on an anvil. Great numbers of these are often disembogu'd into adjacent countries which after some time circulate home again in a stream of money which yields wonderful refreshment to the fainting dominion, almost sick for the comfort of such a cordial.

'That which we admired most of all amongst them was the virginity of their language, not deflowered by the mixture of any other dialect. The purity of Latin was debauched by the Vandals and was Hun'd into corruption by that barbarous people, but the sincerity of British remains inviolable. Tis a tongue (it seems) made for every mouth as appears by an instance of one in our company who, having got a Welsh polysyllable into his throat, was almost choked with consonants, had we not, by clapping him on the back, made him disgorge a gutteral or two and so saved him.'

'After we had crammed our budget with these few notices, we jogged on with our freight to the brink of the sea where, mounted on a pinnace, we rode to Bristol from whence with all possible speed we trudged in a few days to the metropolis of the nation called London.'

Chapter Two

Editing an edition of Camden's 'Britannia' in 1695, Edmund Gibson returned to the subject of Llyn y Dywarchen's floating island. More than 500 years had elapsed since its description by Gerald de Barri. Gibson reported seeing a small green patch 'which is all the occasion of the fable of the wand'ring Island.' Another Edmund, the astronomer Halley, visited the lake in May 1697 and contributed a contradicting report to the Royal Society's *Philosophical Transactions* for 1698:

> 'In one of these lakes I was on board a floating island, as it may be called; the lake is scarce half a mile about, environed with boggy, turfy soil, a piece of which, about six yards long and four broad, floats on the water, having broad-spreading funguous roots on its sides, the lightness of which buoys it up. It was driven on the lee shore, but I launched it off and swam it to be satisfied that it floated. This I take the more notice of, because it is denied to be true by the author of the additions to Camden lately published; but I myself saw it as described, and was told it had formerly been bigger, there being a lesser spot that they told us had been heretofore a part thereof, which floated likewise." [Richard] Wilson took this lake and island as the subject of one of his pictures, and of it the following story is told. "It is said that the artist was for a long time puzzled how to give a notion of the phenomenon in a painting, but at length he conquered the difficulty by depicting a man standing on the island in the act of wafting it nearer the shore with the aid of a long staff."

Halley ascended Snowdon on May 26 of his 1697 visit, describing the region as 'this horrid spot of hills':

> 'We saw Ireland plainly, and the mountains of Cumberland and Westmorland very faintly, but evidently in the north; and I think we saw as far as St David's head into the south.

39

Carnarvonshire and Anglesey lay under us like a map, affording a very pleasant prospect, were it not for the horrors of the neighbouring precipices. Hence we counted fifteen or sixteen lakes, great and small, where the cavities of the rocks are filled up with the rills that gleet from the hills. All these are said to abound with trouts, some of which we found to be especial good fish.'

As for the floating island, the *Gossiping Guide to Wales* would be able to add nearly 200 years later, in 1891:

'There is still, or was recently, a bit of turf — enough to swear by — cropping up out of the water. A retaining wall, which does not add to its beauty, has been built on one side of the lake by a Copper Mining Company, whose works we saw in the Nantlle Valley.'

Not until the early 18th century did the leisure-time tourists arrive in any quantity. The writer of *A Trip to North Wales by E.B.* was probably Edward Bysshe, journalist, self-styled gentleman and author of *The Art of Poetry* which was published in London in 1702. The exaggerated style of writing is typical of this period. The reference to churchyards being used as 'a dancing place, and that every Sunday' reflects a tradition which by 1700 had largely declined in England:

'Wales (antiently called Cimbria) is divided into North and South Wales. 'Tis the former of these I propose to say somewhat of. This consists of six entire (tho' small) counties, viz. Montgomery, Flint, Denbigh, Merioneth, Carnarvan and the Isle of Anglesea, and is separated from England by the Rivers Dee and Severn. The air is the best thing it has to boast of and will sooner procure you an appetite than furnish you with the means to supply it.

'The country here looks like the fag end of Creation, the very rubbish of Noah's Flood, and will (if any thing) serve to confirm an Epicurean in his creed that the world was made by chance.

'The highest hills that I ever saw in England, such as Penygent, Ingleburrough and the like, are mere cherrystones to the British Alps; and no more to be compared with them, for stature, than a grasshopper with Goliath. There is not in the whole world a people that live so near to, and yet so very far from, Heaven as the Welsh do.

'You cannot travel from town to town but you must needs take the clouds in your way, who so gratefully resent your civility in calling upon them that you will have no occasion to complain they send you away dry.

'A tree challenges as many lookers-on here as a blazing star or any African monster does elsewhere. And for green things (leeks only excepted) you might have seen as many in Egypt when the locusts had been rampaging the country.

'Coaches in many parts were never so much as heard of, nor can the natives form any ideas of them that are not as disproportioned to the truth as Montezuma's conception of the sea, who had never seen anything longer than a horse-pond. Carts are about the size (and somewhat the shape) of brewers' drays.

'Horses are no rarities but very easily mistaken for mastiff dogs, unless viewed attentively; they will live half a week upon the juice of a flint stone. Grass and hay they know as little as oats. And they will run upon the ridge of a mountain as thin as the back of a knife, with as much security and speed as an accomplished race-horse will exert upon Newmarket Heath or Salisbury Plain.

'They want not store of mutton, that is tolerably sweet for meat so lean, but goat's flesh (as more suitable to their own rank constitution) has the preference; this (forsooth) they call rock-venison. These goats are such excellent climbers that the only way to be familiarly acquainted with them is to tender your respects by musket ball.

'Little want is there of fish, such as trout, guinard, salmon, lobsters and the like, but no maids to be met with.

'Their beef is as tough as an artillery-man's coat upon a training day and requires a veritable ostrich's stomach to digest it.

'Their houses consist of one room but that plentifully stock'd with inhabitants; for besides the proprietors, their children and servants, you shall have two or three swine and black cattle under the same roof. These houses have holes dug in their sides that serve both to let in light and let out smoke; they represent both windows and chimneys. Should a man have a chimney, necessary on the top of his thatched mansion there, he would stand in great danger of being pricked down for High Sheriff.

'Wolves were formerly as plentiful amongst them as pick-pockets at a conventical 'til, their princes being obliged to pay a yearly tribute of 300, in a process of time none were left in the land.

'They are so well versed in the history of their descents that you shall hear a poor beggar woman derive her extraction from the first maid of honour to Nimrod's wife, or else she thinks she is a nobody. If they want a pewter spoon or porringer in their house, yet will they by no means be without a pedigree.

'Their church-yards serve the dead for a burying and the living for a dancing place, and that every Sunday, for there you shall see a blind harper mounted upon a grave stone, making admirable harmony, and surrounded by the long-ear'd tribe like another Orpheus amongst the Beasts.

'The first town we slept in was Welshpool in Montgomeryshire. We got early to bed in regard of our next day's journey which consisted of 12 Welsh (that is to say 36 English) miles; for every one of them was a complete Dutch League.

'I had not gone a third part of the way e're my horse lost a shoe, an ordinary misfortune in that rocky country. I desired the Judge to stay till he was shod but he told me he could not for he was oblig'd, by such an hour, to meet his brother at the city of Dinas Mouthaye [Dinas Mawddwy] (a place I shall no more forget than a Parliament Soldier Edge-Hill or Marston-moor) which (as he said) lay straight on and was but 6 miles distant. I ordered my man to book it down, to prevent mistakes, and expected to find a place at least twice as big as Shrewsbury. Well, I got my beast shod, with much ado, by a very beast as himself: a smith that could speak no more English than a Dromedary and who liv'd (like the antient Trogladites Herodotus and Strabo mention) at least three fathom underground.

'The town of Dolgethlie [Dolgellau] had several things very remarkable belonging to it of which the most memorable were these:

'First, it was walled with walls six miles high, meaning a ridge of rocks that environed it. And they were such, I'll assure you, as would have bid defiance to Hannibal and all his vinegar.

'Then we came to it under water and out of it over water. A boarded channel conveyed a small river over our heads, and we went out of it over a bridge.

'Then the steeple grew. There was but one bell, a mere tintinabulum, and that hung in a tree which, to do the country right, was the only tree I saw growing there, for, setting aside that, I did not see timber enough to make a whipping post of.

'Lastly, there were more ale-houses than houses in it, for every house was subdivided into divers little tenements, each of which sold drink apart.

'Surrounded by a vast tribe of the bare-footed regiment, we got at length into our lodgings, where I desired my landlady to show me a good room. "That you shall have," said she, "God knows, and such a one as Christ nor Saint David ever lodged in". And in that she spoke nothing but the truth for it was a ground chamber whose walls looked as if they had catched the leprosy. They were plastered with mortar of 20 different sorts of colours and at the bed's-head was a cranny through which the wind diluted with force enough to blow off a man's night-cap.

'No less than a whole cart-load of monumental timber was carved into my bedstead and it was to be ascended by a ladder of six or eight steps, so that it was highly necessary for a man to make his Will before he went into it, lest, if he had tumbled out in the night, he had awakened in another world the next morning, as infallibly he must have done.

'The ticking was so obdurate that it seemed to be quilted with flint stones instead of feathers and perfectly drew indentures in my flesh. Upon the teaster a whole race of Welsh spiders (descended, I presume, from the great Cadwalader) hung in clusters, ready to drop into my mouth if I slept with it open.

'My Man they crammed into a hole in the roof of the house, about the size of an English hen-roost, where not-withstanding, as he told me himself, he made a shift to enjoy a more comfortable repose than his master could meet with.

'But this was not all. Misfortunes rarely come single; in the middle of the night (wanting the usual fortifications of lock and bolt to my chamber door) in comes a great sow who, I suppose, had been Tenant in Possession there before, and came to claim a re-entry. With this grunting chamber-fellow I was obliged to pass over the night.

'When I got up I called for a basin of water, to see if the liquid element would contribute anything towards ameliorating my looks. The wench brings me no less than a pailful but so very dirty that I saw nothing likelier to turn a man's stomach.

'I next sent out for a barber and, in about half an hour's time, in comes a greasy fellow, swift to shed innocent blood, who in a trice pulls out a woollen night-cap and about two ells of toweling. After some fumbling, he pulls out a thing called a razor, but any man else would easily have mistaken it for a chopping knife; and, with pure strength of hand, in a short time, he shaved me so clean that not only the hairs of my face, but my very skin, was become invisible. I gave him a small piece bearing Caesar's image and superscription, at which he doffed me so low a bow that the very clay floor was indented with his knuckles, and so he reverently took his leave.'

Another early visitor was Daniel Defoe or one of his near-contempory editors. Born Daniel Foe in the London parish of St Giles, Cripplegate, he adopted in 1703 the surname by which he is remembered. He was educated in Stoke Newington for the Nonconformist ministry but became a hose merchant in Cornhill, manager of a Tilbury brick and tile works, a dealer in cloth, and a member of the Butchers' Company. He was several times forced into hiding from his creditors but repaid them when writing brought him prosperity.

Defoe is credited as the founder of English journalism, having started *The Review* while imprisoned at Newgate for a satirical work entitled *The Shortest Way with Dissenters*; evidently the dissenters had not recognised the satire. His *Tour through Great Britain* began to appear (anonymously . . . 'By a Gentleman') in 1724 and, when completed, became one of the finest topographical guides ever written of these islands:

'That side of the country of Carnarvon which borders on the sea is not so mountainous, and is both more fertile and more populous. The principal town in this part is Carnarvon, a good town, with a castle built by Edward I to curb and reduce the wild people of the mountains, and secure the passage into Anglesea. As this city was built by Edward I so he kept his Court often here, and honoured it with his presence very much; and here his eldest son and successor, though unhappy (Edward II), was born, who was therefore called Edward of Caernarvon. This Edward was the first Prince of Wales; that is to say, they first of the Kings of England's sons who was vested with the title of Prince of Wales. And here was kept the chancery and exchequer of the Princes of Wales.

'It is a small but strong town, clean and well built, and considering the place the people are very courteous and obliging to strangers. It is seated on the firth or inlet called Menai, parting the isle of Anglesea, or Mona, from the main land, and here is a ferry over to the island called Abermenai Ferry. And from thence a direct road to Holly Head, where we went for no purpose but to have another view of Ireland, though we were disappointed, the weather being bad and stormy.

'Whosoever travels critically over these mountains, I mean of S. Wales and Merionithshire, will think Stone-henge in Wiltshire and Roll-Rich ([Rollright] Stones in Oxfordshire no more a wonder, seeing there are so many such, and such like, in these provinces, but they were generally monuments of the dead, as also are the single stones of immense bulk any other, of which we saw so many that we gave over remarking them; some we saw from 7, 8, to 10, and one 16 foot high, being a whole stone, but so great, that the most of the wonder is, where they were found, and how dragged to the place; since, besides the steep ascents to some of the hills on which they stand, it would be impossible to move some of them, now, with 50 yoke of oxen. And yet a great many of these stones are found confusedly lying one upon another on the utmost summit or top of the Glyder, or other Hills, in Merionith and Carnarvonshire; to which it is next to impossible that all the power of art, and strength of man and beast could carry them, and the people make no difficulty of saying the devil set them up there.'

The perspective of Snowdon and its immediate neighbours, rising sharply from valley floors which are near to sea-level, tends to exaggerate both height and distance. Defoe, or the writer credited as Defoe, fancied North Wales more formidable than the Swiss Alps:

'I must confess, I that have seen the Alps, on so many

occasions, have gone under so many of the most frightful passes in the country of the Grisons, and in the mountains of Tirol, never believed there was any thing in this island of Britain that came near, much less that exceeded those hills, in the terror of their aspect, or in the difficulty of access to them. But certainly, if they are out done any where in the world, it is here: even Hannibal himself would have found it impossible to march his army over Snowden, or over the rocks of Merionith and Montgomery shires; no, not with all the help that fire and vinegar could have yielded, to make way for him.

'The only support we had in this heavy journey was (1) that we generally found their provisions very good and cheap, and very good accommodations in the inns. And (2) that the Welsh gentlemen are very civil, hospitable, and kind; the people very obliging and conversible, and especially to strangers; but when we let them know we travelled merely in curiosity to view the country, and be able to speak well of them to strangers, their civility was heightened to such a degree that nothing could be more friendly, willing to tell us every thing that belonged to their country, and to show us every thing that we desired to see.

They value themselves much upon their antiquity. The ancient race of their houses, and families, and the like; and above all, upon their ancient heroes: their King Caractacus, Owen ap Tudor, Prince Lewellin, and the like noblemen and princes of British extraction; and as they believe their country to be the pleasantest and most agreeable in the world, so you cannot oblige them more than to make them think you believe so too.'

By his own account, *Memoirs of the Secret Services of John Macky, Esq., During the Reign of King William, Queen Anne and King George I*, John Macky 'came early into the measures of the revolution' against King James. Macky carried to London in 1692 news of an intended French invasion of England and a year later was appointed inspector of the coast from Harwich to Dover, charged with preventing treasonable communication between England and France. In later years he fell under government suspicion and was imprisoned until the accession of George I. He subsequently established a packet boat service to Dublin but this proved more costly than anticipated and was soon abandoned.

Macky's *A Journey through England and Scotland* neglects Wales in its title but not in its content. It was published in 1732, six years after Macky's death:

> 'They speak all Welsh here, and if a stranger should lose his way in this country of Carnarvan, 'tis ten to one, if he meets with any one that hath English enough to set him right. The people are also naturally very surly and, even if they understand English, if you ask them a question their answer is "Dime Salsenach" [dim Saesneg] or "I cannot speak Saxon or English". Their bibles and prayer books are all printed in Welsh, in our character, so that an Englishman can read their language although he doth not understand a word of it. It hath a great resemblance of the Bas-Britons but they retain the letter and character as well as language, as the Scots and Highlanders do.

> 'They retain several Popish customs in North Wales for, on a Sunday after morning service, the whole parish go to Football till the afternoon service begins, and then they go to the ale-house and play at all manner of games; which ale-house is often kept by the parson, for their livings are very small.

> 'From Conway thro' the mountainous country of Carnarvan, I passed the famous mountain of Penmanmawr; so dreadfully related by passengers travelling to Ireland. It is a road cut out of the side of the rock seven foot wide; the sea lies perpendicularly down, about forty fathom on one side, and the mountain is about the same height above it on the other side; it looks dismal but not at all dangerous for there is now a wall breast high along the precipice, however there is

an ale-house at the bottom of the hill on the other side, with this inscription:

'Now your fright is over, take a Dram.'

At Penmaenmawr, between Bangor and Conwy, the mountains of Snowdonia present a near vertical face to the sea. The modern roadway avoids this obstacle by means of two tunnels blasted through the granite. John Wesley, the founder of Methodism, noted of Penmaenmawr in his Journal of August 13th 1756 that ' . . . the road runs so far above the beach that one could not venture to look down, but that there is a wall built all along, about four feet high. Meantime, the ragged cliff hangs over one's head, as if it would fall every moment.'

A later writer, Joseph Hucks, would observe in 1795:

'The pass of Penmaenmawr, that was once attended with so much danger to the wary traveller, is now perfectly safe.'

The eldest son of Sir Thomas Lyttelton, George Lyttelton was born at Hagley in Worcestershire. Educated at Eton and Christchurch, Oxford, he became equerry to Frederick, Prince of Wales, before entering the House of Commons at the age of 26 as MP for Okehampton. At 46 he was appointed chancellor of the exchequer but a year later retired and was made a baron. In 1756 he wrote his *Account of a Journey into Wales* as a series of letters addressed to a Mr Bower:

'Brynkir, Carnarvonshire, July 6, 1756
    'Nothing remarkable occurred in our ride until we came to Festiniog, a village in Merionethshire, the vale before which is the most perfectly beautiful of all we had seen. From the height of this village you have a view of the sea. The hills are green and well shaded with wood. There is a lovely rivulet which winds through the bottom; on each side are meadows

and above are cornfields which seemed placed there to guard this charming retreat against any invaders. With the woman one loves and the friend of one's heart and a good study of books one might pass an age there and think it a day. If you have a mind to live long and renew your youth, come with Mrs Bower and settle at Festiniog. Not long ago there died in that neighbourhood an honest Welsh farmer who was 105 years of age. By his first wife he had 30 children, 10 by his second, 4 by his third and 7 by two concubines. His youngest son was 81 years younger than his eldest and 800 persons descended from his body attended his funeral.

'When we had skirted this happy vale an hour or two, we came to a narrow branch of the sea which is dry at low water. As we passed over the sands, we were surprised to see that all the cattle preferred that barren place to the meadow. The guide said it was to avoid a fly which, in the heat of the day, came out of the woods and infested them in the valleys. The view of the said lands is terrible as they are hemmed in on each side with very high hills but broken into a thousand irregular shapes. At one end is the ocean, at the other the formidable mountains of Snowdon, black and naked rocks which seem to be piled one above the other. The summits of some of them are covered with clouds and cannot be ascended. They do altogether strongly excite the idea of Burnet of their being the fragment of a demolished world. The rain which was falling when I began to write this letter did not last long; it cleared up after dinner and gave us a fine evening which employed us in riding along the sea coast, which is here very cold. The grandeur of the ocean, corresponding with that of the mountain, formed a majestic and solemn scene. Ideas of immensity swirled and exalted our mind at the sight. All lesser objects appear mean and trifling so that we could hardly do justice to the ruins of an old castle situated on the top of a conical hill [Criccieth], the foot of which is washed by the sea and which has every feature that can give a romantic appearance.

'This morning, July 7, being fair, we ventured to climb up the top of a mountain, not indeed so high as Snowdon which is here called Moel Guidon, i.e. the nest of the eagle, but one degree lower than that of Moel Happock [Moel Hebog], the nest of the hawk, from whence we saw a phenomenon new to our eyes but common in Wales. On the one side was midnight, on the other bright day. The whole extent of the mountain of Snowdon on our left hand was wrapped in clouds from top to bottom but on the right the sun shone most gloriously over the sea coast of Carnarvon. The hill we stood upon was perfectly clear, the way we came up a pretty easy ascent, but before us was a precipice of many hundred yards and below a vale which, though not cultivated, has much savage beauty. The sides were steep and fringed with low wood. There were two little lakes, or rather pools, that stood in the bottom from which issued a rivulet that serpentined in view for two or three miles and was pleasing relief to the eyes. But the mountains of Snowdon, covered with darkness and thick clouds, called to my memory the fall of Mount Sinai with the Laws delivered from it and filled my mind with religious awe.

'This afternoon we propose going to Carnarvon and you may expect a continuation of my travels from Shrewsbury which is our last stage.

'Adieu my dear Bower. I am perfectly well, eat like a horse and sleep like a monk, so that I may, by this ramble, preserve a stock of health that may last all winter and carry me through my parliamentary campaign.'

Lyttelton's tour was first published seven years after his death as an appendix to Henry Penruddocke Wyndham's *A Gentleman's Tour Through Monmouthshire and Wales in June and July 1774*. This became one of the works most frequently quoted [though not always acknowledged] by later writers on North Wales. The Wyndham family was active in the political life of Salisbury, Henry having been elected mayor of that city in 1770. He served as sheriff of Wiltshire the following year and as MP for that county from 1795 until the 1812 dissolution. The first edition of Wyndham's tour was published anonymously in 1775. An enlarged edition based on a further visit to Wales through July and August 1777 appeared in 1781 with the author's name on the title page:

'We were induced by the cleanliness of our little inn and the attentive complacency of our landlady to sleep three nights at Tan-y-Bwlch. This is a single house in the parish of Festiniogg and about three miles below it. The river Dryryd divides the inn from the parish church of Maynturogg; it lies in a deep and narrow valley between the mountains which are but moderately clothed in wood excepting near the house where the sylvan walks amid the craggy precipices are extremely picturesque. At a little distance from the inn on a woody mountainside is a pleasant seat of a widow, Griffith, and here I cannot but confirm the remark of the author of the "Letters from Snowdon" [a short work published anonymously but sometimes attributed to Joseph Cradock] that the women of this county generally survive the men, who commonly fall an early sacrifice to intemperance. A heavy glutinous ale has charms enough to debauch the senses of the whole principality. In our journey we frequently found the most retired alehouses filled with middling gentry who count it unbecoming their character to retire sober.

'The poor through necessity reap the benefit of their climate and live to advanced ages while the richer heir seldom waits long for the possession of his estate, and seldom long enjoys it. Sir John Wynne, who wrote about the year 1600, complains against this vicious custom of his countrymen and, speaking of an ancient festival, says that "my ancestors spent the day in shooting, wrestling, throwing the sledge, and other acts of activity, and drinking very moderately withal, not according to the gluttonous manner of our days".

'We now travelled a desolate and cloud-capped country but, as it happened to be low water, we avoided some of these mournful mountains by descending on the sands of the Traeth Mawr which carried us to Pont Aberglaslyn which divides Merioneth from Carnarvonshire. This bridge is one wide stone arch and is built over a roaring waterfall from two perpendicular precipices. Here we paused; the grandeur of the scenery before us impressed a silent admiration on our senses. We at length moved slowly onward, contemplating the wonderful chasm. An impending craggy cliff at least 800 feet high projects from every part of its broken front stupendous rocks of the most capricious forms and shadows a broad and translucid torrent which rages like a cataract amid the huge ruins fallen from the mountain.

'The disjointed fragments of the opposite declivity, crushing their moldering props, seem scarcely prevented from overwhelming the narrow ridge which forms the road upon the brink of the flood. The romantic imagination of Salvator Rosa was never fired with a more tremendous idea, nor has his extravagant pencil ever produced a bolder precipice. Leaving with regret this sublime and unparalleled pass, which continues for nearly a mile, we pursued our route through the miserable town of Bethkelert, over a rocky desert at the foot of Snowdon and by the edges of two lakes, one of which commands attention from its size and the scenery around it, to Llyngwennyn bridge, near which is a picturesque waterfall.'

Joseph Cradock attracted early attention for being inoculated in the mid 18th century, at the enormous cost of £100. His father ['Joseph Cradock of Leicester and Gumley'] was threatened by a mob prejudiced against this then contentious form of treatment. Sent to Emmanuel College, Cambridge, after his father's death, Cradock left for London before completing his studies. A keen playgoer, he married and lived initially in Dean Street, Soho. The attractions of Gumley seem to have outweighed those of London's theatres, however, and the family moved there to an inherited estate. Cradock climbed to the summit of Snowdon either along what is now called the Snowdon Ranger Path or from the village of Rhyd-ddu, starting very late in the day with the evident hope of viewing the sunrise from the summit, and descending on the Llanberis side past the Ceunant Mawr waterfall. The ascent is described in his *Account of Some of the Most Romantic Parts of North Wales*, published in 1774:

'I passed my evening at a very good inn at Carnarvon and, having procured an intelligent guide, returned early next morning through Bettus [Bettws Garmon] to the foot of Snowdon. Having left my horses at a small hut, and hired a mountaineer to carry some cordials and provisions, with a spiked stick, but imprudently without nails in my shoes, about ten o-clock I began to ascend the mountain. The two first miles were rather boggy and disagreeable, but when the prospect opened, I soon forgot all difficulties. In the course of the two last I passed by six precipices, which I believe were very formidable, but as I was near the brink, and the wind very high, I did not venture to examine too narrowly.

'On the summit, which is a plain about six yards in circumference, the air was perfectly mild and serene, and I could with pleasure contemplate the amazing map that was unfolded to my view. From hence may be distinctly seen the Wicklow hills in Ireland, the Isle of Man, Cumberland, Lancashire, Cheshire, Shropshire, and part of Scotland; all the counties of North Wales; the Isle of Anglesea; rivers, plains, woods, rocks, and mountains, six-and-twenty lakes, and two seas.'

Chapter Three

Compared with his Hebridean tour, Samuel Johnson's *Diary of a Journey into North Wales in the year 1774* is lamentably sketchy. An edited version was prepared by R. Duppa, barrister at law, and published in 1841. Duppa notes: 'Dr Johnson commenced his journey into Wales, July 5, 1774, in company with Mr and Mrs Thrale and their daughter, now Lady Keith, and returned August 25. In the prosecution of this tour, whatever was his own gratification or disappointment, he appears but little to have gratified the curiosity of others; for Boswell says "I do not find that he kept any journal or notes of what he saw in his tour in Wales. All that I heard him say of it was that instead of bleak and barren mountains there were green and fertile ones; and that one of the castles in Wales would contain all the castles that he had seen in Scotland." '

Johnson and his companions left the Thrale's home in Streatham, described by Duppa as a village in Surrey about six miles from London, on Tuesday July 5 at 11 a.m. They reached Barnet in Hertfordshire at 1.40 p.m. having paid 2 shillings a mile for four horses:

'August 24. We went to Pwllheli, a mean old town, at the extremity of the country. Here we bought something, to remember the place.

August 25. We returned to Caernarvon, where we ate with Mrs Wynne.

August 26. We visited, with Mrs Wynne, Llyn Badarn, and Llyn Beris, two lakes, joined by a narrow strait. They are formed by the waters which fall from Snowdon and the opposite mountain. On the opposite side of Snowdon are the remains of a large fort [Dolbadarn], to which we climbed with great labour. I was breathless and harassed. The Lakes have no great breadth, so that the boat is always near one bank or the other. Queeny's goats, one hundred and forty-nine I think.' [Duppa: Mr Thrale was near-sighted and could not see the goats browsing on Snowdon, and he promised his daughter, who was a child of ten years old, a penny for every goat she would show him, and Dr Johnson kept the account; so that it appears her father was in debt to her 149 pence. Queeny was the epithet, which had its origin in the nursery, by which Mrs Thrale was always distinguished by Johnson.]

August 27. We returned to Bangor, where Mr Thrale was lodged at Mr Roberts', the Register.

August 28. We went to worship at the cathedral. The quire is mean, the service was not well read.'

Thomas Pennant's outstanding *Tours in Wales* was published in 1778 and became a model for many later visitors. Its three volumes remain a useful reference for any serious student of Wales. Pennant was undoubtedly motivated by Gerald de Barri's *Itinerary through Wales* of 1188 through his friendship with Sir Richard Colt Hoare who translated Gerald's Latin original into English. Though highly regarded as a naturalist, Pennant was not without his critics. Thomas Percy, bishop of Dromore and literary contemporary of Samuel Johnson, declared of Pennant's *Tour into Scotland* that 'A carrier who goes along the side of Loch Lomond would describe it better'. Johnson responded 'He's a whig, sir; a sad dog. But he's the best traveller I ever read; he observes more things than anyone else does.'

Pennant's first published writing was a description of an earthquake felt in April 1750 at Downing, the family's Flintshire home. Four years later he toured Ireland but found his travels too enjoyable to allow time for journalising. The artist and engraver Moses Griffith [1749 to 1809], born in Llŷn, entered into service with Pennant in 1769 and accompanied him on many of his travels to prepare supporting illustrations. Most of Pennant's travels were on horseback and it was to temperate living and abundant riding exercise that he attributed his health:

'On a lofty rock, above one of the lakes, stand the remains of Castell Dolbadern, consisting of a round tower, and a few fragments of walls. It was constructed with the thin laminated stones of the country, cemented with very strong mortar, without shells. The inner diameter of the tower is only twenty-six feet. This seems to have been built to defend the pass into the interior parts of Snowdonia; it was likewise used as a state prison.

'In this valley are two groups of wretched houses. The farthest is near the end of the upper lake, with its church, dedicated to St Peris, who was, we are told, a cardinal. Here is to be seen the well of the saint, inclosed with a wall. The sibyl of the place attends, and divines your fortune by the appearance or non-appearance of a little fish, which lurks in some of its holes.

'From hence I took a ride above the lakes, to their lower extremity. The upper is the least, but much the most beautiful piece of water. It is said to be in places a hundred and forty yards deep; to have abounded with char, before they were reduced by the streams flowing from the copper mines, which had been worked on the side of the hills. The lower lake is about a mile and a half long, narrows gradually into the form of a river called the Rythel [Afon Rhythallt], and flows in a diffused channel to Caernarvon, where it assumes the name of Seiont.

'Near the end of the lake lives a celebrated personage, whom I was disappointed in not finding at home. This is Margaret uch Evans, of Penllyn, the last specimen of the strength and spirit of the antient British fair. She is at this time about ninety years of age. This extraordinary female was the greatest hunter, shooter, and fisher, of her time. She kept a dozen at least of dogs, terriers, greyhounds and spaniels, all excellent in their kinds. She killed more foxes in one year than all the confederate hunts do in ten: rowed stoutly, and was queen of the lake: fiddled excellently, and knew all our old music: did not neglect the mechanic arts, for she was a very good joiner: and, at the age of seventy, was the best wrestler in the country; and few young men dared to try a fall with her. Some years ago, she had a maid of congenial qualities; but death, that mighty hunter, at last earthed this faithful companion of her's. Margaret was also blacksmith, shoe-maker, boat-builder, and maker of harps. She shoed her own horses, made her own shoes, and built her own boats, while she was under contract to convey the copper ore down the lakes. I must not forget, that all the neighbouring bards payed their addresses to Margaret, and celebrated her exploits in pure British verse. At length she gave her hand to the most effeminate of her admirers, as if predetermined to maintain the superiority which nature had bestowed on her.

'About half a mile farther, I visited the remains of Llys Dinorddwig, a house said to have been one of the palaces of prince Llewelyn ap Gryffydd [grandson of Llywelyn ap Iorwerth], the walls high and strong, the hall twenty-four yards long, and before the house is a deep ditch over which had probably been a draw-bridge. Not very far from hence is a spot, called Rhyw'r Cyrn, or The Brow of the Horns; where, according to old usage, an officer stood and blew his horn, to give notice to the household of the approach of their master, or to summon the vassals to assemble on all occasions of emergency.

'This is part of the woodless flat, between the mountains and the Menai. Its want of strength is supplied by several posts, fortified in the British manner. Dinas Dinorddwig, about half a mile south-east of the church of Llaneniolen, is the chief. The area is very large, surrounded with an agger of small stones, backed by another of very large ones, then succeeds a deep ditch, a rampart of earth, a second vast ditch, and a third rampart: within the area is a circle of stones, the post probably of the commander in chief.

'To the east is a strong chalybeate water, formerly in much repute. It is called Ffynon Cegin Arthur, or The Water of

Arthur's Kitchen, and is the source of Aber Cegin, which falls into the sea between Bangor and Penrhyn.

'In our way from hence, we passed by another post, called Pen y Gaer; and soon after, by a smaller, called Bryn y Castelau, surrounded with a single wall; and on an eminence on the other side of the Rythell, is another, named Caer Cwm y Glo, or Caer Carreg-y-Fran, from which had been (as we were informed) a paved way to Llys Dinorddwig. I may here add, that after the death of Llewelyn [ap Gruffydd], Edward I bestowed that palace on Sir Gryffydd Llwyd, the same gentleman who first brought him the news of the birth of his son Edward of Caernarvon.'

The following day, Pennant ascended Snowdon from Llanberis by an indirect route which took him southwest to join the path [nowadays called the Snowdon Ranger] which runs eastward from Llyn Cwellyn:

"After refreshing myself with a night's rest at Mr Close's, agent to the mines in Llanberis, early in the morning began our ascent to the highest peak of Snowdon, under the guidance of Hugh Shone, whom I beg leave to recommend as a most able conductor. Keep upon the side of the lake, for a considerable way; then turn to the left, and see, not far from the road, Ceunant Mawr, a noble cataract, precipitating over two vast rocks into two most horrible chasms. Near this place were found several beads; some of glass, and one of jet.

'The beads and a remarkable shell, that were found in the same place, are in the possession of the Reverend John Llwyd of Caerwys. The beads are known in Caernarvonshire by the name of Glain Neidr, and are worn as amulets against the chin-cough.'

'This mountainous tract scarcely yields any corn. Its produce is cattle and sheep, which, during summer, keep very high in the mountains, followed by their owners, with their families, who reside in that season in Hafodtai, or summer dairy-houses, as the farmers in the Swiss alps do in their Sennes. These houses consist of a long low room, with a hole at one end, to let out the smoke from the fire, which is made beneath. Their furniture is very simple: stones are the substitutes of stools; and the beds are of hay, ranged along the sides. They manufacture their own cloaths, and dye their cloths with Cenn du y Cerrig, or Lichen omphaloides; and another Cenn, the Lichen parietinus; native dyes, collected from the rocks. During summer, the men pass their time either in harvest work, or in tending their herds; the women in milking, or making butter and cheese. For their own use, they milk both ewes and goats, and make cheese of the milk, for their own consumption. The diet of these mountaineers is very plain, consisting of butter, cheese, and oat-bread, or Bara Ceirch; they drink whey; not but they have a reserve of a few bottles of very strong beer, by way of cordial, in illness. They are people of good understanding, wary and circumspect, usually tall, thin, and of strong constitutions, from their way of living. Towards winter, they descend to their Hen Dref, or old dwelling, where they lead, during that season, a vacant life.

'In the course of our ascent, saw on the left, above the Cwm, Moel y Cynghorion, or The Hill of Council. Pass through Bwlch y Maes-cwm, and skirt the side of Snowdon, till we reach Bwlch y Cwm Brwynog, where the ascent becomes very difficult on account of its vast steepness. People here usually quit their horses. We began a toilsome march, clambering among the rocks. On the left were the precipices over Cwm Brwynog with Llyn du yr Arddwy [Llyn du'r Arddu] at their foot. On our right were those over the small lakes Llyn Glas, Llyn-y-Nadroedd, and Llyn Goch [Llyn Coch]. The last is the highest on this side of the mountain; and, on whose margins, we were told, that, in fairy days, those diminutive gentry kept their revels. This space between precipice and precipice, formed a short, and not very agreeable isthmus, till we reached a verdant expanse, which gave us some respite, before we laboured up another series of broken crags: after these is a second smooth tract, which reaches almost to the summit, which by way of pre-eminence, is styled Y Wyddfa, or The Conspicuous. [Pennant's 1883 editor, John Rhys, suggests the meaning 'is more probably to be sought in the word gwydd, wood, which would connect the name with the mountain as a Royal Forest'.] It rises almost to a point, or, at best, there is but room for a circular wall of loose stones, within which travellers usually take their repast.

'The mountain from hence seems propped by four vast buttresses; between which are four deep Cwms, or hollows: each, excepting one, has one or more lakes, lodged in its distant bottom. The nearest was Ffynnon Llâs or The Green Well, lying immediately below us. One of the company had the curiosity to descend a very bad way to a jutting rock, that impeded over the monstrous precipice; and he seemed like Mercury ready to take his flight from the summit of Atlas. The waters of Ffynnon Llâs from this height appeared black and unfathomable, and the edges quite green. From thence is a succession of bottoms, surrounded by lofty and rugged hills, the greatest part of whose sides are perfectly mural, and form the most magnificent amphitheatre in nature. The Wyddfa is on one side; Crib y Distill, with its serrated tops, on another; Crib Goch, a ridge of fiery redness, appears beneath the preceding; and opposite to it is the boundary called the Lliwedd. Another very singular support to this mountain is Y Clawdd Goch, rising into a sharp ridge, so narrow as not to afford breadth even for a path.

'The view from this exalted situation is unbounded. In a former tour, I saw from it the county of Chester, the high hills of Yorkshire, part of the north of England, Scotland and Ireland; a plain view of the Isle of Man and that of Anglesey lay extended like a map beneath me, with every rill visible. I took much pains to see this prospect to advantage: sat up at a farm on the west till about twelve, and walked up the whole way. The night was remarkably fine and starry: towards morn, the stars faded away, and left a short interval of darkness, which was soon dispersed by the dawn of the day. The body of the sun appeared most distinct, with the rotundity of the moon, before it rose high enough to render its beam too brilliant for our sight. The sea which bounded the western part was gilt by its rays, first in slender streaks, at length glowing with redness. The prospect was disclosed like the gradual drawing up of a curtain in a theatre. We saw more and more, till the heat became so powerful, as to attract the mists from the various lakes, which in a slight degree obscured the prospect. The shadow of the mountain was flung many miles, and shewed its bicapitated form; the Wyddfa making one, Crib y Distill the other head. I counted this time between twenty and thirty lakes, either in this county or Meirioneddshire. The day proved so excessively hot that my journey cost me the skin of the lower part of my face, before I reached the resting-place, after the fatigue of the morning.'

The exact height of Snowdon was a subject of some dispute, as Pennant observes in the same tour:

'The reports of the height of this noted hill have been very differently given. A Mr Caswell, who was employed by Mr Adams, in 1682, measured it by instruments made by the directions of Mr Flamstead and asserts its height to be 1,240 yards: but for the honour of our mountain I am sorry to say that I must give greater credit to the experiments made of late years, which have sunk it to 1,189 yards and one foot, reckoning from the quay at Caernarvon to the highest peak.'

Later during his tour, Pennant made a partial ascent of Snowdon, climbing southwest of Llyn Llydaw before descending to Glaslyn. The preliminary approach on horseback from Nant

Peris up to Pen-y-pass and down into Nant Gwynant was evidently a scramble hardly meriting the word 'road':

'Near the end of Nant-beris, pass beneath Glyder Fawr, and observe the strata of a columnar form, high above our heads. At times, vast fragments of this tremendous rock tumble down, the ruins are scattered about the base, and exhibit awful specimens of the frequent lapses. One is styled the Cromlech, for having accidentally fallen on the other stones, it remains lifted from the earth, with a hollow beneath, resembling one of those Druidical antiquities. The length of the incumbent stone is sixty feet, the breadth forty-six: the thickness sixteen. The hollow is said once to have been occupied by an old woman; but now serves for a sheep pen.

'The ascent from hence is either over loose stones, or a solid stair-case, and is exceedingly steep. It is a singular road, lying in a stupendous chasm, bounded for above a mile by nearly equidistant precipices, of prodigious height; those of the Glyders being on one side, and on the other those of Snowdon.

'Refresh ourselves on a spot called Gorphwysfa, or The Resting Place. At a small distance from which is Bwlch y Gwyddyl, or The Pass of the Irishmen; from whence is a singular view of Dyffryn Mymbyr, the chasm we had left; and far below us, the picturesque vale of Nant Gwynan, the scene of many a bloody skirmish in the time of Edward IV, between William Earl of Pembroke, and the Welsh Lancastrians under Jevan ap Robert.

'Descend a very steep road, into that part called Cwm Dyli; where we quitted our horses, and began a most toilsome journey to visit the hidden vales lodged in the bosom of the mountains. We began with clambering up the rugged face of a rock, broken into a multitude of short precipices, and divided in the middle by a cataract, the discharge of the waters from the Alpine lakes. After about a quarter of a mile's labour, we reach Cwm Dyli, a flat tract of hay ground watered by a river and filled with hay makers; the farmer and his family being resident here in his Havodty for the summer season. After dining with them on curds and whey, we kept along the river's side and found opposed to us another front, rugged as the former and attended with a cataract. This was surmounted with equal difficulty. We found, on arriving at the top, an hollow a mile in length filled with Llyn Llydaw, a fine lake, winding beneath the rocks and vastly indented by rocky projections here and there jutting into it. In it was one little island, the haunt of black-backed Gulls which breed here and, alarmed by such unexpected visitants, broke the silence of this sequestered place by their deep screams.

'We continued our walk, ascending along a narrow path above the lake as far as the extremity; then descending, reached the opposite side in order to encounter a third descent as arduous as the preceding. This brought us into the horrible crater, immediately beneath the great precipice of the Wyddfa, in which is lodged Ffynnon Lâs [Glaslyn]. Its situation is the most dreadful, surrounded by more than three parts of a circle, with the most horrible precipices of the Wyddfa, Crib y Distill and Crib Goch, with the vast mural steeps of Lliwedd, continued over the other lake and Cwm Dyli. In the Lliwedd was a strange break, called Bwlch y Saethau or The Pass of the Arrows, probably a station for hunters to watch the wanderings of the deer.

'The margins of Ffynnon Lâs here appeared to be shallow and gravelly. The waters had a greenish cast; but what is very singular, the rocks reflected into them seemed varied with stripes of the richest colours, like the most beautiful lute strings, and changed almost to infinity.

'Here we observed the Wheat-ear, a small and seemingly tender bird, and which is almost the only small one, or indeed the only one, except the Rock Ouzel or Mwyalchen y Graig, that frequents these heights: the reason is evidently the want of food.

'We descended from this dreary scene, on the other side of

the hill, above Llyn Llydaw, having the tremendous red precipices of Crib Goch high above us, rising into a mere ridge, serrated its whole length. The faces of many of the rocks were marked with large veins of coarse white crystal; and others, especially Crib Goch, were varied with the deep green of the dwarf Alpine Juniper. On attaining the tops of the hills above the lower end of the lake, we descended to the Gorphwysfa where we found our horses and returned once more into Nant Gwynan.'

'From hence is a pleasant but short ride near the river to the village of Bedd Kelert, seated in a beautiful tract of meadows at the junction of three vales, near the conflux of the Glas Llyn and the Colwyn, which flows through Nant Colwyn, a vale that leads to Caernarvon. Its situation was the fittest in the world to inspire religious meditation amidst lofty mountains, wood and murmuring streams. The church is small, yet the loftiest in Snowdonia. The east window consists of three narrow slips. The roof is neat and there yet remains some very pretty fret-work. A side-chapel is supported by two neat pillars, and gothic arches. I could discover no tombs.

'This church had been conventual, belonging to a priory of Augustines dedicated to St Mary. There is reason to suppose they might have been of that class which was called Gilbertines and consisted of both men and women who lived under the same roof but strictly separated from each other by a wall as I discovered a piece of ground near the church called Doy Lleian or The Meadow of the Nun.

'Bedd Kelert had been the most ancient foundation in all the country except in Bardsey. Tanner ascribes it to our last prince but it must have been long before his days, there being a recital of a charter for certain lands bestowed on it by Llewelyn the Great who began his reign in 1194. It was favoured in the same manner by others of the succeeding princes.

'The prior had besides an allowance of fifty cows and

twenty-two sheep. The expenses of the house must have been large. It lay on the great road from England and West Wales into North Wales, and from Ireland and North Wales into England. In order to enable this place to keep its usual hospitality after it had suffered in 1283, by a casual fire, Edward I most munificently repaired all the damages and bishop Anian, about the year 1286, for the encouragement of other benefactors, remitted to all such who were truly repentant of their sins forty days of any penance inflicted on them.

'In order to complete the mountain ramble as far as was in my power, I made an excursion from this village up a narrow vale. Ascended a steep road amidst a thin hanging wood and saw from the road multitudes of black cattle coming down from all parts on their way from a neighbouring fair. The vale expands and is watered by the Colwyn which flows from a small lake we passed, called Llyn Cader. Left on the right another ascent to the Wyddfa where its base extends to a considerable breadth and is far less steep than that on the side of Nant-Beris. We soon reached the pretty lake of Cawellyn, noted for its char. Above the lake stood the house of Cae uwch Llyn or The Field above the Lake, from distant times the residence of the Quellyns (a family now extinct) who derived their name from the place. The mountains hereabouts approach near to each other. On the left, Mynydd Mawr forms a striking feature: its top is smooth but its front is formed into the most immense precipice, retiring inwards in a semicircular shape. Moel Eilio is another mountain of stupendous bulk, most regularly rounded and of a beautiful verdure. At Bettws Garmon, a village with a church dedicated to St Germanus, the scene changes into a range of beautiful meadows watered by a rapid stream.

'I here turn my back on the humble flats and resume my former road till I had passed Cawellyn. Not far beyond that lake, I turned to the right to visit Llyn y Dywarchen or the Lake of the Sod, long since celebrated by the hyperbolical pen of Giraldus for its insular erratica, its wandering island, as he calls it. That little lake is seated in the middle of a turbary and at this time actually exhibited the phenomenon recorded by a romantic historian. It had on it a floating island of an irregular shape and about nine yards long. It appeared to be only a piece of the turbary, undermined by the water, torn off, and kept together by the close entangling of the roots which form that species of ground. It frequently is set in motion by the wind, often joins its native banks and, as Giraldus says, cattle are frequently surprised on it, and by another gale carried a short voyage from the shore.

'Continue our journey to Drws y Coed or The Door of the Wood, a pass towards Clynnog. It is bounded by vast mountains: on one side by Tal Mignedd, on the other by a great cleft of Mynydd Mawr. Some years ago here were considerable adventures for copper of the pyritous kind, and in the rocks were sometimes found some very thin laminae of the native metal. I was tempted here to exceed a little the limits of my Alpine tour for now the mountains descend fast from their majestic heights, growing less and less as they approach the Irish sea. My motive was to obtain a sight of two fine lakes called Llynnieu Nanlle which form two handsome expanses with a very small distance between each. From hence is a noble view of the Wyddfa which terminates the view through the vista of Drws y Coed. It is from this spot that Mr Wilson has favoured us with a view as magnificent as it is faithful. Few are sensible of this for few visit the spot.

'Near these lakes Edward I, in the summer of 1284, resided from some days and from hence issued out more than one of his edicts. I find some dated July the 17th and the 20th. Others are dated in the same year from Bangor, Caernarvon, Mold and Hope. One from Caernarvon is dated as late as the 22nd of October which shows what attention he paid to the establishment of government in his new dominions. The place he resided at here was called Bala deu Lyn, or the place where a river discharges itself from two lakes; but at present all memory is lost of the situation of the town, the traces of which might perhaps be still discovered by diligent search.

'I returned by the same road and again reached Bedd Kelert where I made a coarse lodging. The evening was so fine that we were irresistibly tempted not to defer till morning our visit to Pont Aberglaslyn, a short walk from hence. The first part is along the narrow vale but in a very little time the mountains approach so close as to leave only room for the furious river to roll over its stony bed, above which is a narrow road, formed with incredible labour, impending over the water. The way seems to have been first cut out of the rock and then covered with great stones, as usual in several of our narrow passes. The scenery is the most magnificent that can be imagined. The mountains rise to a very uncommon height and oppose to us nothing but a broken series of precipices, one above the other, as high as the eye can reach. Here is very little appearance of vegetation yet in spots there is enough to tempt the poor goat to its destruction; for it will sometimes leap down to an alluring tuft of verdure where, without possibility of return, it must remain to perish after it has finished the dear-bought repast.

'The bridge terminates the pass and consists of a single arch flung over a deep chasm from rock to rock. Above is a considerable cataract where the traveller at times may have much amusement in observing the salmon, in great numbers, make their efforts to surmount the weir. Near the place is a salmon fishery. Here had been a royal weir in the reign of Henry IV which was then rented by Robert ap Meredydd.

'Opposite to Bedd Kelert is Moel Hedog [Hebog]. In a bog not far from that mountain was found a most curious brass shield which Mr Williams of Llanidan favoured me with a sight of. Its diameter was two feet two inches, the weight four pounds. In the centre was a plain umbo projecting above two inches. The surface of the shield was marked with twenty-seven smooth concentric elevated circles and between each a depressed space, of the same breadth with the elevated parts, marked by a single row of smooth studs. The whole shield was flat and very limber. I cannot attribute this to the Welsh, who seemed to despise every species of defensive armour.

'On my return to Bedd Kelert, a stone by the road side was pointed out to me, by the name of the chair of Rhys Goch O'ryri, the famous mountain bard, contemporary with Owen Glyndwr. He was of the house of Hafod Garregog at the entrance into Traeth Mawr from whence he used to walk and, sitting on this stone, compose his poems. Amongst others is a satire on a fox, for killing his favourite peacock. He died about the year 1420 and was interred in the holy ground of Bedd Kelert.

'From Bedd Kelert I returned to Pont Aberglaslyn and soon reached Traeth Mawr, a large expanse of sands between the counties of Caernarvon and Meirionedd, of most dangerous passage to strangers by reason of the tides which flow here with great rapidity. This forms the bottom of the vast bay of Cardigan. In the year 1625, Sir John Wynn of Gwedir [Gwydir] conceived the great design of gaining this tract, and a lesser called Traeth Bychan, from the sea, by an embankment. He implored the assistance of his illustrious countryman, Sir Hugh Middleton. Sir John's letter and Sir Hugh's reply will be the best account I can give of the affair; which was never carried into execution, as I imagine, for want of money:

"To the honoured Sir Hugh Myddleton, Knt, Bart.
' "Right worthy Sir, my good cousin, and one of the great honours of the nation, I understand of a great work that you have performed in the Isle of Wight, in gaining too thousand acres from the sea. I may say to you what the Jews said to Christ — We have heard of thy great works done abroad, doe somewhat in thine own country.

"There are two washes in Merionethshire, whereon some part of my being lieth, called Traeth Mawr and Traeth

Bychan, of a great extent of land, and entering into the sea by one issue, which is not a mile broad at full sea, and very shallow. The fresh currents that run into the sea are both vehement and great, and carry with them much sand; besides the southerly wind usually bloweth full to the haven's mouth, carrieth with it so much sand that it hath overwhelmed a great quantity of the ground adjacent. There, and also in the bordering countries, abundance of wood, brush and other materials to make mounds, to be had at a very cheap rate and easily brought to the place, which I hear they do in Lincolnshire to expel the sea. My skill is little and my experience none at all in such matters yet I ever had a desire to further my country in such actions as might be for their profit and leave a remembrance of my endeavours, but hindered with other matters I have only wished well and done nothing. Now being it pleased God to bring you into this country, I am to desire you to take a ride, the place not being above a day's journey from you; and if you do see the thing fit to be undertaken, I am content to adventure a brace of hundred pounds to join with you in the work.

"I have lead ore on my grounds great store, and other minerals near my house; if it please you to come hither, being not above two days' journey from you, you shall be most kindly welcome — it may be you shall find here that will tend to your commodity and mine. If I did know the day certain when you would come to view Traeth Mawr, my son Owen Wynn shall attend you there and conduct you thence to my house. Concluding me very kindly to you, do rest, your loving cousin and friend,

"J. Wynn. Gwydir. 1st September 1625."

"Honourable Sir, I have received your kind letter. Few are the things done by me for which I give God the glory. It may please you to understand my first undertaking of public works was amongst my own, within less than a mile of the place where I had my first being, 24 or 25 years since, in seeking of coals for the town of Denbigh.

"Touching the drowned lands near your living, there are many things considerable therein. If to be gained, which will hardly be performed without great stones, which was plentiful at the weight, as well as wood; and great sums of money to be spent, not hundreds but thousands — and first of all his Majesty's interest must be got. As for myself, I am grown into years and full of business here at the mines, the river at London, and other places — my weekly charge being above £200; which maketh me very unwilling to undertake any other work; and the least of these, whether the drowned lands or mines, requireth a whole man with a large purse. Noble Sir, my desire is great to see you, which should draw me a far longer way; yet such are my occasions at this time here, for the settling of this great work, that I can hardly be spared one hour in a day. My wife being also here, I cannot leave her in a strange place. Yet my love to public works and desire to see you (if God permit) may another time draw me into those parts. So with my hearty commendations I commit you and all your good desires to God.

"Your assured loving cousin to command, Hugh Myddelton, Lodge, September 2nd 1625."

Chapter Four

John Byng travelled very extensively in Britain during the late 18th century and kept very detailed journals. 150 years elapsed before the manuscripts were collected together and published as *The Torrington Diaries*. At the time of these journeys, Byng was a civil servant [Commissioner of Stamps]. His previous career had been that of a soldier, a lieutenant-colonel in the Foot Guards. For the final two weeks of his life he inherited the title Viscount Torrington. Byng had little thought of publishing his journals which came close to being lost and did not appear in print until 1934:

> 'Every rural wish within me tempts me to stain paper and attempt description. If I go on thus cramming tours and digesting travels, I shall become a minor Pennant; tho' without his arts or without his gain: my journals, wanting the decoration of embellish'd style and elegant drawings, never extend beyond the writer's glance; reader and writer united am I; so that it is not necessary to praise what I see as I am not to communicate what I write.'

The choice of transport open to long-distance travellers prior to the advent of railways lay almost inevitably between a horse and unaided human feet. Major road improvements in the 1700s opened Snowdonia to the relative luxury of horse-drawn carriages but the unimpeded horseman retained the advantage. Byng kept meticulous note of the distances he covered on horseback during his 1784 *Tour to North Wales*:

June	Places	Miles	July		
25	To Oxford	54	2	To Montgomery	25
26	To Cheltenham	40	3	To Llanvair	16
28	To Malvern Wells	21	4	To Dolgelle	26
29	To Hereford	22	5	To Bala	18
30	To Ludlow	23	6	To Dolgelle	18

8	To Barmouth &c.	26	20	To Bridgnorth	21
9	To Festiniog	20	21	To Worcester	27
10	To Cascade,	10	22	To Bengeworth	16
	Vale &c.		23	To Woodstock	32
11	To Caernarvon	25	24	To Caversham	36
12	To Anglesea		25	To Church	
13	To Bangor	9	26	A Short Ride	
14	To Conway	18	28	To White-Knights	
15	To Denbigh	26	29	Thanksgiving	
16	To Wrexham	24	30	Doing nothing	
17	To Llangollen	11	31	To London	40
18	To Salop	32	Miles	630	
19	A reposo				

'I left London on Friday morning, June 25, and in a post chaise overtook my horse at Uxbridge, that was sent forward under the care of Thomas Bush. Having a most particular dislike to the company of a servant on the road, I detached him forward to prepare for me, and my horses, proper accommodations at night. This is the true use of servants on the road, tho but seldom what their masters require of them, trusting to the waiter and chambermaid for dirty glasses and ill made beds, and confiding the care of their horses to drunken, roguish, hostlers; and while their own genteel followers are regaling themselves in a genteel early parlour, the horses are neither cleaned, nor fed. As for my sheets I always take them with me, knowing that next to a certainty, five sheets must be dirty, and three damp, out of number ten: these with a very few other necessaries, travel behind my servant; as for my night cap, great coat, and such other etceteras, they travel behind my own person, in and upon a small cloakbag.

'We came to Pont-Aberglasslyn, a bridge famous for its salmon leap, surprising situation and tremendous rocks. There are so many descriptions of this place that I must retire from weak relation, on my part; and only exclaim that the scene is most truly wonderful! A narrow-winding road looking down on a foaming stony river and overhung by the steepest mountains, much extravasated by old lead mines; threatening destruction to the astonished traveller.

'Below the bridge, we took a long stand to survey the gigantic products of nature, together with the salmon-leap, 6 yards high, up which these fish will fling themselves. Upon the most craggy precipices we could discover some venerable goats, who did us the honour of gazing down upon us and added lustre to the horror.

'After an half hour most profitably enjoyed in the luxury of observation, we pushed on to the little village of Begelhert [Beddgelert], a place as wretched as can be, where only eggs and bacon, with poor ale, could be procured, and that by the assistance and language of Mr Owen who told us that oatmeal, the provision of the poor, was within memory of man at the rate of 3s. 6d. for 40 quarts, and was now advanced to 8 shillings: horse corn and beer being as dear here as in any other country, the product not sufficing the consumption of the natives.

I plied busily at cookery whilst an old female spread our table with the liscious family fare, rancid cheese in a platter formed of an oaten cake, sour ale and slices of rusty bacon. My companions cocked their pipes at each other's noses and with difficulty did I at last destroy the duet by calling to pay and releasing the horses from their captive out-house. Mr Owen returned home, after many thanks given and compliments received, and we steered our course over a wild country and by the side of the Lake Llyn-trwenyn [Llyn Cwellyn], washing the base of a most fearful mountain called Drwsycood [Drws-y-coed], of awful and shagged front.

'After this, the country began to grow enclosed and pleasant and we soon came in sight of Caernarvon, the Streights of Menai and the Isle of Anglesea; all which only wanted a gay sun to render a most gaudy prospect. Within half a mile of the town we passed a well built bridge, and a good church with a steeple, which was to us a sight of magnificence, and at an ale house door at the little village of Bettus two miles distant from Nantes Mill there sat Mr Robin Edwards who was resolved to make further trial of his service, on our generosity.

'In the clean suburbs of Caernarvon we arrived at our inn (Boot Inn; a good house) where receiving abundance of letters and newspapers prevented any wish of rambling; and our evening was spent in reading and listening to the best harper we have yet met with (by name Erasmus, a sound bespeaking great learning, and antiquity). This is an instrument which I always admired but now, on its native ground (connected with the ideas of former hospitality and ancient minstrelsy) it becomes quite enthusiastic and I pity my grandchildren who will only hear its merits and fame in their grandfathers' and other pages, wishing in vain for that retrospective delight which I am now enjoying.

'Tuesday July 13. Although I went to bed last night at 11 o'clock yet, Mr Bush not calling me, I lay in bed till 10 o'clock this morning; a pretty touring hour! Not that it signified as Mr P. had gone some hours before to mount Snowden Hill; to which practices (for former reasons) I had declined accompanying. His old guide Robin Edwards went with him, being as equal to that business as any other man and doing it for a fourth part of what a Caernarvon guide demanded.

'Breakfast and writing finished, I took my walk along the Pulhelly [Pwllheli] road, by the river side, to the turnpike; and then crossed over the fields to the Festiniog road, and so home by the church. The eye is gratified in this walk with every thing it can desire, and the more the castle is viewed the more it must be admired.

'The people are all busily employed at hay harvest and none are lavish enough to wear feet to their stockings. I did not find this place so cheap as I imagined it would be; in some articles it is dear, for I paid 1s 4d for a pound of hair-powder, and Thos. B. expressed great anger at being obliged to give 3 pence to get himself shaved.

'Mr P. came back at 3 o'clock, after having scaled the summit of Snowden; and he will hereafter have the satisfaction of saying he was there, but not that he could see anything at the top but his guide, so rare it is to have a clear view at such amazing heights.'

The prospect of seeing a sunrise from the Snowdon summit encouraged many visitors to attempt a nocturnal ascent. Nicholas Owen, rector of Melltyrn, made just such an ascent from Llyn Cwellyn on the road between Caernarfon and Beddgelert. He describes it in *Caernarvonshire. A Sketch of its History, Antiquities, Mountains and Productions*, published in 1792:

'To ascend Snowdon is no easy exercise; it requires some resolution and activity to clamber rocks and skip over bogs yet persons on horseback have been known to reach the summit with a degree of safety. It is astonishing to behold with what agility the mountain horses move along the steep ridges or tread the stoney surface. Once, in ascending this king of hills, I found myself uncommonly weary at the end of the journey; having put on boots for warmth, they had not only retarded expedition, but rendered the footing less firm and secure.

'The night is usually chosen to begin the ascension, in order to be at the apex at sun rising, which is a prospect uncommonly magnificent, if the morning be clear. I left Caernarvon at 5 pm and arrived leisurely at the base of the mountain a little before eight, in the month of August. The azure now promised no fair weather, it being hazy and the wind high. However, from this hopeless circumstance I learnt some operations of nature which I should have missed had the sky appeared without a cloud. Quellyn Lake exhibited a surface boisterous to a degree that I had never observed before in fresh water: like a tempestuous sea, the billows foamed and roared. The wind rushing along the interstices of the mountains and being pent from expanding, exerted itself in an incredible degree of fury.

'Storms frequently prevail in the defiles of mountains, the wind rushing between them through a narrow channel at once increase in speed and density. I rested the beginning of the night at a small farm-house among the rocks: to begin to ascend it was too soon. At 12 pm I eagerly proceeded with a guide and arrived at the top, without any material occurrence of observation, about three in the morning. The dawn of the day now appeared and there was something very awful and impressing in the situation. Nature looked tremendous and frowning; and the atmosphere was every moment putting on a different aspect; at one instant the sky was clear, the next overcast with clouds: now a misty rain, then fair weather.

'Never shall I forget the horror and the pleasure I felt when the sun became visible. He appeared to come forth from the ocean in fiery redness and, like a giant, to run his course. A pure azure, for a few minutes, now displayed itself with refulgent beauty. The clouds were forming fast underneath and the wind, being brisk, soon carried them overhead. With such rapidity were they impelled from the great chasm of Llanberris that they seemed to rise like smoke out of a great furnace. Now and then the beams or rays of the sun darted from between the clouds like lightning, flashing upon the adverse rocks. The multitude of lakes in these mountains, and the humidity of the soil, bring on these phenomena. When the sun had ascended some degrees, the sky brightened but the exhaled vapours appeared visible and sometimes are so through the course of the day.

'About a third part of the way up the mountain is a remarkable spring, of great coldness in summer, and in winter it emits a steam. I observed no birds in the region, except the red kite, and a little brown bird, sparrow-like, and the cormorant. Goats are not unfrequent on some of the most inaccessible cliffs, and sheep on all easy acclivities. Though you are within an hour's ride of an hospitable and social people, yet the ideas of waste and solitude unavoidably prevail. The elevation of your footing is so unusual to the mind that, while you survey the amazing prospect with astonishment and admiration, you tremble at the contemplation of the slippery situation you are in.

'The sides of Snowdon, and almost all these mountains, were formerly deep fringed with wood; as is evident from the remains of oak trees, hazel, and the ash which are found in turbaries and bottoms. It was King Edward that ordered all the woods in Wales to be cut down as, without this precaution, the country could never have been conquered for these were their refuge and retreat in any warlike disasters.'

Joseph Hucks was 22 years old and newly graduated when he commenced his *Pedestrian Tour through North Wales* in June 1794. The poet Samuel Taylor Coleridge travelled with him. After a three-week stay in Oxford, they crossed the Severn at Gloucester and proceeded northwest through Leominster and Montgomery to Bala. Thence they took a circular route through Llangollen and Holywell and along the northern coast of Wales via Anglesey, Caernarfon, Beddgelert, Tan y Bwlch, Harlech and Barmouth. The final leg of their journey took them through Aberystwyth and Llandovery to Chepstow and Bristol.

The Menai Straits presented a formidable obstacle to travellers prior to the completion of Thomas Telford's suspension bridge in 1826 and Hucks provides a chilling account of a crossing made the more hazardous by poor visibility:

'The village of Abber Conway [Aberconwy], usually called Abber, from whence I dated my last letter, is situated upon the straits of the Menai, that at high tide is there about four miles across; but when the water is out, it appears perfectly dry; for the sea retires so far back that it only leaves a channel

78

of a quarter of a mile, or thereabouts, in breadth: all the rest is a complete flat and consequently the tide overflows it very rapidly. There are stated times to pass this ferry, which one should be very exact in observing.

'The clergyman of the place accompanied us to the boundaries of this wilderness of sand. He gave us the necessary directions for our passage, which were only to keep a white house in view that belonged to the ferryman on the Anglesea shore, and to make what haste we could since there was no time to lose, for we had four miles to walk over this frightful desert without shoes or stockings, having been advised to pull them off; for being regularly overflowed every twelve hours, a great part of the road is necessarily wet and dirty.

'We had scarcely got half way before it began to grow thick and foggy. The little village of Abber, which we had just quitted, was no longer perceptible and nothing behind us was to be seen but the steep and shaggy mountains of Paenman Mawr, and those known by the general name of Snowdonia, with the dark vapours floating upon their sides; and very soon even these became no longer distinguishable, but as one huge mass of clouds.

'Myself and another of the party had considerably outwalked the other two, who had lost sight of their landmark and were steering their course much too far to the right; when we discovered their mistake they were not so visible to us that we could tell what they were; all that we could discern was something very dark moving in a different direction to us; consequently we hailed them and waited till they came up to us, and we agreed to part company no more.

'Darkness had now overtaken us in good earnest and we could see nothing, nor hear any thing except the noise which the sea made in its approach, that alarmed us not a little; at length, to our infinite satisfaction, we distinguished the voices of the ferrymen, who were luckily waiting on this side of the passage. When they heard us, they were extremely impatient for our arrival, and continually called to us to make haste, which we wanted no monitor to urge us to do; we therefore made towards the spot whence the sounds came, which we conjectured to be about the distance of two hundred yards from us, but were unluckily intercepted by a small channel, already filling fast with the sea. We did not hesitate long, for in fact we had no alternative, and therefore boldly ventured through; it was fortunately only about two feet deep, and rather more than ten yards broad.

'We congratulated each other upon finding ourselves safe in the boat, though dripping wet, and shivering with cold. Like the Israelites, we had passed through the sea on dry land; but we had run a great risk of experiencing a similar treatment with Pharaoh and his host, from that unmannerly element.

'When we arrived at the inn at Beaumaris, we made a fire that would have roasted an ox, and ordered a supper sufficient for ten aldermen. Upon opening the window on the following morning, I observed the sea had covered all those immense flats we had so lately, I will not say with dry feet, walked over.

'Of all the ruins which Wales has yet presented to me, the castle of Caernarvon is the most noble and magnificent. "Vast as the pride of its founder", it evinces the warlike and invincible genius of the first Edward, of whose military prowess this country, as well as Scotland, furnish such numerous and melancholy proofs. Thank heaven, these fabricks of despotism are at length either levelled with the ground, or present a memorable lesson to mankind of the futility of human ambition.

'This castle was erected in order to secure the passage into the Isle of Anglesea, and to curb the people of the mountains, where the brave and hardy Britons had taken refuge from their insulting conquerors, resolved to prefer freedom and independence to ease and servitude. The eldest son of Edward was born here, and he was presented to the Welsh as their future prince. Such enormous buildings, abstractedly considered, excite only my abhorrence; because they have occasioned the exercise of a great deal of tyranny, and useless expense, and have been of no possible advantage to any nation; but have, on the contrary, afforded so many asylums wherein the sword of tyranny might take shelter; and were chiefly calculated to keep the surrounding districts in awe and subjection. Every castle that now remains is a monument of shame to our ancestors, and of the ignoble bondage under which they bent: and hence in part arises that satisfaction which the mind is conscious of feeling, in contemplating their ruins; for an association naturally takes place; and the recollection of the feudal vassalage and slavery of former days, is accompanied by the pleasing circumstances of the relative prosperity and freedom which we now enjoy. From this place we made a party of three, and crossed once more into Anglesea, where my ill stars seemed to have pre-ordained that I should meet with nothing but misfortunes.

'One of my companions was a very skilful botanist and his botanical furor induced him at all times to despise danger and difficulty, when in pursuit of a favourite plant, and this was the object of our present enterprise; but we had scarcely set foot on that inhospitable shore before it began to rain with great violence, and very soon growing dark, we were obliged to make the best of our way back again. This ferry is two miles across, and the water was much agitated, so that without the addition of the rain, which came down in torrents, the spray of the sea would have completely made us wet through; but, in the midst of our distress, we were agreeably interested by a sight as beautiful to us as it was novel; the surface of the water suddenly assumed a luminous appearance, now and then relapsing into an impenetrable gloom, and then again re-lumined, it conveyed to the mind some idea of what poets describe of Phlegethon in the shades below.

'By the time we reached our inn I had lost my voice, and gained a sore-throat; the following morning it was no better; but under some hope that exercise would cure the complaint, was induced to continue our tour to Bethkelert, which we reached that afternoon; the whole walk being more singularly romantic than any I had yet seen, and compelled us to make many a pause, in order to enjoy and contemplate its beauties.

'About half way, we passed over Llyngwennyn bridge, and immediately found ourselves in a fertile valley terminated by a wild and irregular cascade, one branch of which contributed to turn a mill that was almost concealed within the wood, which formed a kind of amphitheatre to this picturesque and interesting scene; a little further on a fine lake opened full upon the view; and not far from this another smaller one. The road winds along the banks of both.

'Bethkelert is a small village, or rather hamlet, situated at the foot of some prodigious high mountains which seem to encircle it on all sides, whilst the stream or torrent, that had accompanied us all the way from the first lake, here begins to be of more consequence, and forcing its way between these stupendous hills, with a continued and considerable descent, empties itself into an arm of the sea, called Traweth Mawr.

'As this is the usual place from which travellers make the ascent of Snowdon, we determined to do the same, and in pursuance of this resolution set off at eleven in the evening, though it was quite dark, and a very rainy and stormy night; however, there was a probability that it would be fine in the morning and the hope was sufficient to make us undergo a few inconveniences; but in attempting to find the guide's house, which was five miles from our inn and situated quite out of the road, at the foot of the mountain, we became completely bewildered; in this perplexity we were directed by the glimmering of a light to an habitation, which, with extreme difficulty and danger, we contrived to reach.

'It was a small hut and its inhabitants, if we might judge from the impenetrable silence that reigned within it, were all asleep. It was some time before we could prevail upon them to open the door, and answer to our entreaties for a proper direction; at length an elderly man appeared, to whom we endeavoured to make known our grievances; but alas! he only spoke his native language, and did not understand a word that we said. However, by frequently repeating the guide's name, 'Ellis Griffith', and pointing to Snowdon, at the same time giving him a glimpse of a shilling, we with much difficulty made him comprehend us; and putting himself at our head, he became our conductor.

'In about half an hour we found ourselves at the door of another small cottage: our guide vociferated Welsh for some minutes till we were admitted by a good-looking lad about 17 years of age, who was the person we had been searching for: he remonstrated against our ascending that night, with many weighty reasons, to which we easily assented; but to think of returning to our inn would be madness: we therefore called a council of war, and it was agreed that we should at all events stay where we were until morning; when, if it should be tolerably fair, we would ascend.

'Thus determined, we disposed of ourselves in the following manner; I barricaded myself in a chair, so that I could not fall out; two more reposed themselves on the benches on each side of the fire, and the fourth took up his "lodgings on the cold ground", with an earthen platter turned up-side down for his pillow. As for my part, I was not disposed to sleep, but took up the rush-light, which had been placed for security on the ground; and to pass away the leaden hours of time, pored over an old Welsh dictionary (which was the only thing like a book that I could find), till I was scarcely able to see. I could not help contemplating our singular situation and appearance in this strange place; on one side, around the dying embers of a peat fire, my good friends were enjoying as comfortable a repose as they had ever experienced in the most costly bed. At the other extremity of the room, separated only by a rug, the venerable owners of this humble cottage lay locked in each other's embraces whilst I, like Brutus in his tent at Philippi, sat reading by the mid-night lamp, till the light danced before my eyes, and the pale spectre of the night appeared to my imagination.

'Without doors nought but the 'pelting of the pityless storm' was heard, and the loud roar of the mountain torrents. Yet while I was contemplating the scene, under such peculiar circumstances, with a mixture of awe and surprise, these simple cottagers lay perfectly indifferent, and unconscious of any novelty in their situation. The noise of the cataract was by them scarcely ever remarked, or served to strengthen their repose; mountain floors, abrupt and broken precipices, were alike viewed by them with the utmost indifference; so soon does the human mind become familiar, and accommodate itself to any circumstances. Habit and custom are even so powerful as to change the very complexion of things, and render that finally pleasing which at first could not be viewed without fear or dislike.

'At four in the morning I thought it prudent to awaken the whole party, which I effected with some difficulty; we then sallied from our habitation, and made our observations upon the weather, which gave us no encouragement to proceed; however, they determined to venture upon their aerial excursion, more from the hope of finding the plants, for which this mountain is remarkable, than of seeing anything when at the top; at their persuasions, added to my own inclination, I declined the enterprise, as my cold had considerably increased during the night, and went back again to the inn, where I impatiently expected their return, which did not happen until four in the afternoon. It turned out, as might have been foreseen, a fruitless and fatiguing expedition; for when arrived at the top, they could see nothing but the impenetrable clouds that almost constantly envelope these huge mountains.'

Applying not so much a title, more a complete itinerary, John Ferrar compiled and published [in Dublin, 1796] *A Tour from Dublin to London in 1795 through the Isle of Anglesea, Bangor, Conway, Llangollen, Shrewsbury, Stratford-on-Avon, Blenheim, Oxford, Windsor, Hampton Court, Twickenham and Kensington.*

Passenger facilities at Holyhead for travellers from Ireland appear to have been remarkably limited in the years immediately preceding Telford's improvements. Ferrar's initial landing in Anglesey sounds decidedly crude:

'The tide being out when we landed at Holyhead, our boat was surrounded with men and boys chattering Welch, who soon brought us on shore on their backs and conducted us to the only inn — Jackson's — at Holyhead, where the hostess has resided many years and the people are very obliging.

'The wealth and population of this island have lately received a great increase, from the discovery of the famous copper mine on Pary's mountain, the largest bed of ore probably in the known world. It is wrought not in the common manner of subterraneous mines but like a stone quarry; and prodigious quantities of ore are raised, which is poor in quality but very abundant in sulphur. The purest part is exported raw to the smelting works at Swansea and other places; the more impure is first calcined and deprived of its sulphur on the spot. Quantities of nearly pure ore are obtained from the waters lodged beneath the bed of ore, by the intervention of iron. A lead ore mixed with silver is also found in the same mountain. All the copper coin in Wales is heavy, three times more valuable than the trash circulated in London.

'There are three ferries across the Straits; one to Caernarvon, one to Bangor, and another from Beaumaris, a port town in Anglesea. Bangor ferry is a safe one, and not so broad as the river Thames at London.'

One of the most picturesque guidebooks to North or South

Wales was Henry Wigstead's *Remarks on a Tour to North and South Wales in the Year 1797* with plates aquatinted by I. Hill. Published in 1800 by W. Wigstead of 40 Charing Cross Road, it includes a singularly unflattering description of Snowdonia's inhabitants:

'Llanberris Lake, at the base of Snowdon, ten miles from hence [Caernarfon], is worthy of notice. The road is particularly remarkable for being strewed with huge masses of stone, which appear to be the interior wreck of some vast mountain.

'At the verge of this water, we procured by signs (for English is not understood here) a flat-bottomed sort of dung barge, in which a couple of stout legitimate sons of Cumbria undertook to paddle us down to Snowdon's foot.

'The pinnacle of this sublime mountain, called in the vicinity The Cap, was fortunately free from the generally collected clouds and we had an uninterrupted prospect of all the beauties of the scenery. A very shattered remnant of a castle, called Dolbadern, is now standing and, in the distance, appears as a small knoll or lump scarcely to be discriminated in the vast expanse.

'The people here are really almost in a state of simple nature. The value of money is scarcely known: they pay the rent of their premises in cattle generally, which they breed on their land. Flesh is scarce ever tasted by them; and, except when visitors leave behind remnants of wine, ale, etcetera, milk is the principle beverage that passes their lips.

'They are remarkably observant of any decorations worn by the ladies, such as beads, laces, and feathers, which strengthened my opinion of their similitude with the Otaheiteans etcetera. These they admire, and handle with a sort of rudeness bordering on savage manners likely to raise alarm in the breast of the fair wearer.'

Chapter Five

The son of 'a respectable London tradesman', Richard Warner [1763-1857] was born in Marylebone. At the age of 13 he accompanied his parents to Lymington in Hampshire. His early thoughts were of a navy career but about 1790 he became curate of Wales [the smaller version, near Rotherham] where he remained a mere three months before returning to Lymington as curate of Boldre. In 1795 he settled in Bath and became active in the city's literary life during a stay of 22 years.

Warner's writings were varied and voluminous, including *Companion on a Tour Round Lymington*, histories of the Isle of Wight, of Bath and of Glastonbury, and a series of letters entitled *Thoughts on Duelling* signed by 'Gabriel Sticking Plaister'.

Both Warner's first and second journeys through Wales were recorded as a series of letters to one James Comrie and their lively style explains the popularity they enjoyed. Warner's claim that Snowdon is the highest mountain in 'the three kingdoms' is a curious error. Snowdon's 1,085 metre summit had long been acknowledged the highest peak in Wales but Ben Macdhui in Scotland was assumed to be Britain's highest mountain [1,310 metres] until 1847 when Ben Nevis was confirmed as being higher [1,343 metres]. Warner commenced the following Snowdon ascent in Beddgelert. His guide may have been in a playful frame of mind in telling Warner that the Afon Glaslyn was called Dŵr [water] which Warner seems to have misheard as 'Wu'. The route up Cwm Llan seems to have followed the path latterly named the Watkin or some variant of it:

'Caernarvon August 21st.

'Dear Sir, One great object of our expedition was, you know, to traverse Snowdon and its dependencies; to visit the summit of the highest mountain in the three kingdoms. We were therefore much disappointed on being informed this morning by the guide, who lives at the village inn during the summer in the capacity of waiter, that the day was unfavourable for our attempt, the head of the mountain being involved in impenetrable mist. It was vain to lament what could not be remedied; we therefore determined to make the best of a misfortune and spend the day in visiting some other magnificent scenery, which would have been incompatible with our expedition to the top of Snowdon. We accordingly agreed with the guide, William Lloyd, an intelligent man, to accompany us a few miles, and quitted our quarters about nine-o-clock.

'Our road conducted us along the bank of the little river Wu (the ancient Welsh name for water) which flowed on our right hand, to the beautiful pool of Llyn-y-dinas, stretching a mile and half in length; the dark brown mountains Arran and Lliweddy, rising to a stupendous height on the left. Here our guide directed us to turn round and observe an huge perpendicular rocky mountain, finely shaded with wood, which we left behind. He told us it was called Dinas-Emris [Dinas Emrys], and received its name from the famous old British magician Merlin or Merddin Emries, who, seated on its cloud-capped head, had formerly prophesied to the unfortunate Vortigern all the evils which afterwards befell himself, his kingdom, and his degenerate subjects.

'The summit of Snowdon, towering above us to the north, had hitherto been involved in a fleecy cloud which hung around it in the manner of a curtain, undulating with the wind. This now appeared to be drawn up higher than it had been; and to rest like a crown on the very point of the mountain. Our guide having attentively regarded it for some time, gave it as his opinion that we should have an opportunity of prosecuting our original plan, the misty mantle being unlikely to melt away altogether before the sun, which was now approaching towards his meridian. He observed, however, at the same time, that should we determine to visit the top of Snowdon, we should find the ascent from the point where we stood to be much more steep and disagreeable than the regular road would have been from the inn at which we had slept; that, notwithstanding it was a practicable way, and had been trodden by some travellers before us. We instantly resolved on attempting the ascent, and having by his advice, swallowed a draught of milk at a neighbouring cottage, and replenished our "leathern bottles" with some of the same beverage, we began the toilsome undertaking.

'The first stage of our journey was up a rugged steep, by the side of a mountain torrent, which, falling from ledge to ledge, stunned us with its unceasing noise. The principal branch of the Arran, little inferior to his mighty neighbour, heaved his unwieldy bulk into the clouds on the right hand under which a frightful hollow called Cwm-Llan, spread its hideous profundity, stretching a mile and a half in length, and nearly as much in breadth, a precipice of Snowdon forming one of its black perpendicular sides.

'While we contemplated this scene with marks of astonishment and dread, the guide related an anecdote to us, which was no bad satire upon the impressions of alarm that C and myself felt in the aerial situation. He told us, the farm we had passed in the bottom was called Llan farm and had been occupied till within these last few years by Mr William Griffiths, the father of the present tenant. That the old man attended constantly the market of Caernarvon, and in order to avoid a route rather circuitous by the turnpike road, he constantly crossed the mountain by the track which we had pursued, mounted on a little pony of that country, that crawled up with him through the crags, bogs and steeps of this side, and descended on the other by a road equally rude, abrupt and rocky. That, day or night, light or darkness, made no alteration to his system, which he pursued for many years without experiencing injury or accident. It may be properly observed, however, that in his perilous expedition he was more indebted to his horse than to himself for safety; and indeed, nothing but actual observation can give a just idea of that sure-footedness and caution which the little Welsh ponies possess.

'After two hours of very severe labour we gained the summit of Snowdon (a sharp narrow crag of rock not more than two yards over) and stood 3,568 feet above the level of Caernarvon quay. Our toil, however, seemed at first to be but ill repaid; a crown of clouds still covered the top and we remained involved in a mist that produced the most intense cold.

'We now had recourse to our bottles of milk which we found very grateful and refreshing but regretted at the same time that we had not some stronger cordial. Our guide, indeed, soon reconciled us to the absence of any powerful liquors by assuring us they were more productive of danger than comfort; as a very small quantity of them in these etherial regions was sufficient to intoxicate. He mentioned his having nearly fallen from one of the precipices himself, in consequence of drinking a glass of brandy; and that during the preceding summer, one of a party of London gentlemen had been so affected by the same quantity taken on the summit of Snowdon that he actually got a severe tumble which, though not fatal, produced some painful bruises. I mention this circumstance as a caution to you, should you visit these aerial heights. The guides, in general, make a point of recommending a quantity of spirits to be carried up as an antidote against the effects of a raw and chilling atmosphere but in reality not so much with a view to comfort the traveller as to indulge that propensity in themselves for strong liquors so common amongst the lower orders of people. A bottle of milk and water, however, with a small portion of brandy in it, will be found to be much more refreshing and agreeable than undiluted spirits and not likely to be attended with the unpleasant effects that an incautious use of them may produce.'

John Henry Manners, one in a line of dukes of Rutland so

named, commenced a tour into Wales on Monday July 23rd 1797 'in order to spend the summer months in as pleasant and improving a manner as possible'. He was accompanied by two churchmen, the Reverend Mr King and the Reverend Mr Hayes, travelling from London in relative comfort with a post-chaise, a curricle, and saddle horses:

'September 9th 1797. We rose early this morning, intending to be pretty soon on the march. We had been obliged to send for four horses from Carnarvon, a distance of 20 miles, no horses being kept at Tan y Bwlch. These did not arrive 'til 8-o-clock, and then baited 'til 10, a measure which we did not expect. Just after 10 we set off, and had first to ascend the mountains, which lift their heads over the inn.

'After travelling a mile on good road, we turned to the right at a place where it branches into two, the one to the left striking off to Penmorfa. From hence we had a most infamous road, as bad as, if not indeed worse than, any we had before encountered. We still kept winding up the mountains, 'til at length we found ourselves quite at the top of one ridge, and higher than we had ever yet been in carriages. Craggy rocks stared at us on all sides, and in wild confusion covered the mountain's summit. For seven miles, we could proceed only a gentle foot's pace, one moment going down so steep a pitch that the horses were forced to depend solely on the reins for support, and immediately having an almost perpendicular ascent to surmount. Add to this the road was so completely covered with large stones and rocks that it was impossible to proceed above a foot's pace.

'We had the whole time a view of the sea, to which we sometimes approached very near, and also of Harleck Castle. I certainly never yet saw such an impassible road for carriages in my life, and for a long time I thought we could not possibly be right. The gateways were also so narrow that we could scarcely drive the curricle through them. The post-boys, through inattention or bad skill, drove the carriage against a rock close by one of the gateways, nor was it for some time that they could extricate it. In order to mend the matter, they knocked down one of the largest stones on the wall at the next gateway. I got out of the curricle and walked five miles, travelling in this way fully as fast as the carriages could go.

'After journeying in this manner, amongst the lofty and barren mountains, through seven rocky and tedious miles, we suddenly turned round an angle of a projecting hill and burst upon the famous Pont Aberglasslyn. This is one of the finest scenes in North Wales, the rocky and craggy mountains, seven or eight hundred feet in height, approach so near to each other as only to admit the furious torrent and a road wide enough for carriages. The two ridges of hills are connected by a bridge, which is the whole width of the pass. The river makes a precipitate descent just above the bridge, where is an old-established salmon fishery.

'We stood some time admiring this wonderful and tremendous pass, and then journeyed on to Beddkelert where resides the man who generally acts as a guide to those passengers who wish to ascend the steep precipices of the lofty Snowdon. On consulting him of the possibility of our performing this scheme, he informed us that he believed the mountain was perfectly clear but that the wind was so high as to render it dangerous to attempt ascending it, on account of the precipices which it would be necessary to pass. Besides this, he informed us that we should find it very uncomfortable upon the extreme coldness of the atmosphere in those lofty regions, and also that the weather was so very stormy that, although one moment its summit might be clear, yet in another it would perhaps be so thick that nothing would be visible. On this candid information from the guide we deliberated, and at last determined to proceed without attempting an ascent.'

Manners proceeded direct to Caernarfon 'where we stopped at a noble hotel lately built by Lord Uxbridge. Towards the close of the evening, we sauntered out for an hour and were much delighted on viewing the majestic and grey walls of the castle, illuminated by the placid light of the moon, while the waters of the Menai Straits, immediately upon which it stands, dashed gently at its base.'

'1797 September 11th. At half-past-one I reached the ferry house at Bangor, which is a good inn, and immediately passed over the ferry with two horses, intending to ride to Lord Bulkeley's. The ferry is here about half a mile broad and on the otherwise are two or three rocky islands. From the middle of it, you have a fine view down towards the sea, which at high water covers the Lavan sands, about four miles broad, reaching from Penmaenmaur to Beaumaris, whose harbour and shipping opened very beautifully upon me as I crossed the ferry.

'It was in contemplation some time ago to build a bridge over the ferry, which would have been of infinite convenience to travellers and for the mail-coach which is forced to cross it every day, or at least the bags of letters. It was judged practicable but, the people of the country objecting to the expense, the plan was laid aside.'

Manners and his companions continued their travels thence to Holyhead, by boat to Douglas and onward from the Isle of Man to explore Scotland.

In 1798, an undergraduate law student at St Peter's College Cambridge commenced a tour of North Wales which led to one of the most perceptive studies of the region ever published. Born in Doncaster, William Bingley [1774 to 1823] saw his *Tour Round North Wales* published as two volumes in 1800. A second visit to Snowdonia in 1801 resulted in *North Wales Delineated from Two Exdcursions* which appeared in 1804:

'My mode of travelling was principally as a pedestrian, but sometimes I took horses and at other times proceeded in carriages as I found it convenient. A traveller on foot, if he has health and spirits, has in my opinion many advantages over all others: of these, the most essential is that complete independence on everything but his own exertions which will enable him without difficulty to visit and examine various places that are altogether inaccessible to persons either in carriages or on horse-back.'

Bingley's enthusiasm for botany is evident in the following description of a climb on the cliff face of Clogwyn du'r Arddu. It was written when climbing was considered as little more than a dangerously vertical form of pedestrian progress to be employed only as a final resort. Bingley was accompanied on the climb by the rector of Llanrug and Llanberis who is credited with conceiving this quick route to heaven. His initial route appears to be that described earlier by Thomas Pennant:

'In my first journey I went from the castle [Dolbadarn] to Cwm Brwynog, but, instead of following the above route, I wandered to Clogwyn du'r Arddu, to search that rock for some plants which Lhwyd and Ray [the naturalist, John Ray, 1627-1705] have described as growing there. The Reverend Peter Williams accompanied me, and he started the wild idea of attempting to climb up the precipice. I was too eager in my pursuit to object to the adventure, and we began our laborious task without once reflecting on the dangers that might attend it. For a little while we got on without much difficulty, but we were soon obliged to have recourse both to our hands and knees, in clambering from one crag to another. Every step now required the utmost caution, and it was necessary to try that every stone was firm in its place before the weight of the body was trusted upon it. I had once lain hold of a piece of rock, and was in the act of raising myself upon it, when it loosened from its bed, and I should have been precipitated headlong, had I not in a moment snatched hold of a tuft of rushes, and saved myself.

'When we had ascended somewhat more than halfway,

there seemed no chance of our being able to proceed much farther, on account of the increasing size of the masses of rock above us. We rested a moment from our labour to consider what was to be done. The danger of again descending was much too great for us to think of attempting it, unless we found it absolutely impossible to proceed. On looking down, the precipice, for at least three hundred feet, seemed almost perpendicular.

'We were eager in our botanical pursuit, and extremely desirous to be at the top, but I believe it was the prospect downwards that determined us to brave every difficulty. It happened fortunately that the steep immediately above us was the only one that presented any material danger. Mr Williams having on a pair of strong shoes with nails in them, which would hold their footing better than mine, requested to make the first attempt, and after some difficulty he succeeded.

'We had along with us a small basket to contain our provisions, and hold the roots of such plants as we wished to transfer to his garden; this he carried behind him by means of a leathern belt fastened round his waist. When, therefore, he had fixed himself securely to a part of the rock, he took off his belt, and holding firmly by one end, gave the other to me: I laid hold, and, with a little aid from the stones, fairly pulled myself up by it. After this we got on pretty well, and in about an hour and a quarter from the commencement of our labour, found ourselves on the brow of this dreadful precipice, and in possession of all the plants we expected to find.'

Bingley's second Snowdon ascent was up the valley from Llanberis to Gorphwysfa and thence along the Miners' Track to Llyn Llydaw and Glaslyn. The miners in question sought copper and remnants of their efforts can be clearly seen on the approach to the lakes and near the lake edges. This industrial legacy becomes a particularly undesirable one where the ascending path from Glaslyn joins the Pyg Track . . . a small group of very deep shafts forming a dangerous hazard to the unwary walker:

'A considerable vein of copper ore was discovered a few years ago in Cwm Glas Llyn, The Hollow of the Blue Pool, near the foot of Clogwyn y Garnedd. Some of the gentlemen of the county associated themselves for the purpose of getting this ore and the work now goes on with considerable spirit. It is, however, by no means so rich or valuable as that from the Llanberis mine and this circumstance, together with the expense of conveying it nearly over the summit of the mountain to Caernarvon, may possibly prevent its ever being worked to any extent. The proprietors have made a tolerably good sledge-path from the Beddgelert road, near Llyn Cwellyn, to Bwlch Glas, a hollow just below the highest point of Snowdon, and from thence a winding footpath down to the mine. To Bwlch Glas the men carry the ore in bags on their shoulders; here it is loaded on small one-horse sledges in which it is dragged to the road. A house has lately been erected near the mine for the accommodation of the workmen during bad weather: some of them live here altogether.

'Much difficulty and many hardships are to be overcome by the workmen in the variable climate of these alpine vales: in winter, heavy snows which frequently drift many yards in thickness; in spring and autumn, the most violent hurricanes; and, in the height of summer, thunder-storms uncommonly tremendous are to be withstood by the labourers in this copper mine.

'In the winter of 1801 the snow drifted so deep before the mouth of the mine that the men were under the necessity of cutting a level through it and of thus going to their work under a long arch of snow. Sometimes the mouth of the new level they were forming in the rock was so closed round with snow that they were not able to tell exactly where it was; and when with difficulty they had found it, it cost some labour to clear an entrance. This snow-drift was in many places near 20 yards deep and some of it was to be seen in the recesses of the rocks till even the middle of May.

Thomas Pennant by Moses Griffiths

A view of Penmaenmawr by J. Boydell, 1750

A View of Snowdon by J. Boydell, 1750

Ceunant Mawr by J. Boydell, 1750

Pont-y-pair Bridge, Betws-y-coed by S. Middiman, 1830

WILLIAM   WILLIAMS,

Pallace

At the GOLDEN LION, or PLASE ISA,

in DOLEGELLEY.

To Eating	—	0 .. 13 .. 0
Wine	—	
Rum	—	0 .. 2 .. 6
Brandy	—	0 . 6 .. 2
Punch	—	
Negus	—	
Coffee	—	
Tea	—	
Cider	—	
Porter	—	0 .. 2 .. 0
Ale	—	0 .. 1 .. 8
Beer	—	
Tobacco	—	0 .. 0 .. 6
Poftage	—	
Wafhing	—	
Servants Eating. and Ale		0 . 2 . 10
Horfes Hay and Corn		0 . 15 . 9

Jea — £ 2 . 5 . 2

John Byng's receipt from the Golden Lion, Dolgellau

100

Dolbadarn Castle by W. Radclyffe, 1872

Penrhyn Castle by W. Radclyffe, 1872

Pont Cyfyng, Capel Curig by W. Radclyffe, 1872

Llyn Gwynant by W. Radclyffe, 1872

*Snowdon's summit late in the 19th century. The sign over the 'hotel' doorway
reads 'Bazzar & Refreshment   Well Aired Beds
Ham and Eggs &c   Choice Beverages   Roberts & Owens Proprietors'
(by kind permisson of Gwynedd Archives Service)*

*Victorian tourists on the shore of Llyn Llydaw
looking towards the summit of Snowdon
(by kind permission of Gwynedd Archives Service)*

"Gladstone addressing a crowd on Snowdon, 1892"
(Gwynedd Archives/Lloyd George Trustees)

'Accidents may also happen in winter from the ice on the rocks; of this an instance has already occurred. A workman was going to the mine from his cottage in Cwm Brwynog early one frosty morning when, in descending the steep above the mine, he slipped on some frozen snow and was thrown along the rocks for near 100 yards. He was there providentially stopped by a hovel that had been built to contain the workmen's tools. Almost every part of his body was bruised by the violence of the fall and one of his eyes was so much injured that, at the time, it was doubtful whether he would ever recover his sight.

'I was informed that the wind had often been so furious among the rocks that the workmen had found the utmost difficulty in preventing themselves from being blown over the edge of the precipices. Sometimes when they heard its approach by the roaring along the vales, they were compelled to fall down on their hands and knees and, laying fast hold on each other, to wait in this position till the violence of the gust was passed; or, when it was likely to continue, they had to creep along till, under shelter of the side of the mountain, they could proceed in safety. A party of the men were one morning going to the mine when the wind was heard to roar loudly along one of the hollows. They all, except one man, laid down till the gust had passed by: he ridiculed their cowardice and, holding out his jacket on each side, observed that as a fine breeze was springing up, he should spread his sails and make the best of his way by scudding before the gale to his work. The wind in a moment bore him from the ground to the distance of 10 or 12 yards where he was thrown down with the utmost violence. He repented his folly and, though he was not much hurt, the accident had a good effect in teaching the men to act with the utmost prudence in similar perilous situations.

'Two Denbighshire gentlemen who are also partners in this concern had caused a pretty good mountain horse-path to be made from Gorphwysfa, beyond Llanberis, to the copper mine. This will now render the ascent to the summit of Snowdon from Capel Curig and the village of Llanberis perfectly easy.'

Bingley adds in a helpful spirit:

'Welsh tourists have been much in the habit of over-rating the difficulties that are to be encountered in the journey to the summit of this mountain. To provide against these, one of them recommends a strong stick with a spike in the end as a thing absolutely necessary; another advises that the soles of the shoes be set round with large nails; and a third inveighs against attempting so arduous and so difficult an undertaking in boots. I can only say that to have nails in the shoes and to take a stick in one's hand may both be useful in their way but, if a person is in good health and spirits, he will find that he can do very well without either.

'I should recommend to the traveller to allow himself sufficient time; to be upon the journey by five or six-o-clock in the morning when the sun has not yet attained much power and when the air is cool and refreshing. The chief thing required is a little labour and this, by going gently along, will be rendered very easy. There is also another advantage in having plenty of time; by stopping frequently to rest himself he will be enabled to enjoy the different distance prospects as they rise above the mountains and to observe how the objects around him gradually change their appearance as he rises higher and higher. It will always be necessary to take a guide for otherwise a sudden change in the weather might render the attempt extremely perilous to a stranger. But these changes are of no consequence to the men who are in the habits of ascending the mountain very frequently, for they have marks by which they would know the path in the most cloudy weather. A sufficient supply of eatables is also absolutely necessary: the traveller will find the utility of these long before he returns.'

Snowdonia began catering in earnest around 1800 for tourists with the opening of Beddgelert's Goat Hotel. Bingley considered the Goat to be a considerable improvement on the accommodation he had been obliged to tolerate:

'The inn, or rather public house, that I found at Beddgelert in both my journeys, was one of the worst and most uncomfortable houses in which necessity ever compelled me to take up my abode. In my first journey I found only one bed in the place that was not wretchedly bad. The room in which I slept for three nights (for the other two bedrooms were occupied) was at the back of the house, and partly over the kitchen. The floor, the ceiling and the boarded partition were all so full of large holes as to seem only an apology for separation from the rest of the house. I was so intolerably pestered by myriads of fleas, bred and harboured among the filth accumulated in every part, that had I not every night been fairly wearied out with my rambles during the day, it would have been altogether impossible for me to have taken any rest.

'After I had been here one night, I complained to the servant of the inexcusable negligence that had suffered these animals to become so numerous as now to defy all attempts at their destruction: "Lord, sir" (said she), "if we were to kill one of them, ten would come to its burying". Nothing in this state of the house could possibly have induced a traveller to remain here through the night but the exquisite scenery around the place. In my second journey, I found several very material improvements in consequence of Mr Jones of Bryntyrion having begun to build a comfortable house for the reception of travellers, on the other side of the river at a few hundred yards distance. This is now opened and, I am told, affords excellent accommodations. It is called the Beddgelert Hotel. The sign over the door is of a goat clambering among the mountains of Snowdon and underneath it is the motto "Patria mea petra". The guide from Beddgelert to the mountains is William Lloyd, the village schoolmaster, whose boys, during the summer, are always engaged in rustic employments. He thus explains his summer occupations in a bill wafered on the inn door: "William Lloyd, conductor to Snowdon, Moel Hebog, Dinas Emrys, Llanberis pass, the lakes, waterfalls etcetera. Collector of crystals and fossils and all natural curiosities in these regions. Dealer in superfine woollen hose, socks, gloves etcetera." '

Born at Usk, Monmouthshire, John Evans took up the family calling as preacher to a London baptist congregation. Two years later he opened a school, initially in Hoxton Square, North London, and subsequently at Islington, which he sustained for 30 years. His *Tour Through North Wales* [1798] provides an exceptionally detailed description of copper mining under and around Snowdon:

'At a small distance from the village [Llanberis], on the western side of the lake, are mines of copper, the property of Asheton Smith, Esq. of Vae nol; and by him are leased to Messrs. Roe, Hudson, Smith, and Mills, under the firm of the Macclesfield company; who are also concerned in the Cronebane copper works in Ireland.

'There are seven levels driven into Snowdon. The rock consists of hard whin, and schistose hornblende. The ore is chiefly formed in a matrix of quartz. It is a rich yellow ore, containing copper in union with iron and sulphur.

'Though there are seven levels, two only are worked. The one called the new level is a hundred and eighty yards in length. The shafts are numerous, as they are the communications from the one level to the other. A person therefore may enter at the first level, and by the different shafts pass through the intermediate ones, and emerge into day-light again at the seventh level.

'The mode of draining the work does not reflect great credit upon the spirit or ingenuity of the undertaking. A shaft is sunk, about forty-five yards below the depth of the new level. Into this the superfluous water runs from the work; and as it collects, is raised into the level by means of a winch and barrels; and hence it is carried down into the lake. These mines were discovered about fifty years ago, by John Jones Roberts, who, by a simple process, obtained ore enough in six months, to sell for £300. After this they lay neglected, till they were taken up by the company, who at present work them.

'The number of miners are about eighty, who work by the square yard in blasting the rock; their earnings consequently are very uncertain, depending upon the nature of the matrix that contains the ore. They work by candle-light, clad only in a shirt and small clothes; and they observe, that it is warmer under ground in winter than in summer: which corroborates the doctrine of the mean temperature of the earth being about forty-eight degrees. This compared with the height at which the thermometer stands in winter and summer, in the open air, will account for this paradoxical sensation, without having recourse to subterraneous fires. The ore contains a quantity of sand, or superfluous earth, from which it is cleared by means of breaking, stamping, decanting, etcetera.

'Women and children are employed with hammers, to break the large pieces of ore and then to wash and sort it into three different kinds of diverse qualities; some containing one-tenth, and some one-fifth copper. It is then taken to the stamping mill, where it undergoes the further process of pulverisation. The stamping mill is formed of six large oaken beams, shod at the end with steel, placed vertically over a large trough: by means of a crook, these are alternately raised by the power of a water wheel, and let fall upon the ore in the trough. When pounded sufficiently small, it is carried into a reservoir by a stream of water, where it is again purified by decantation, etcetera. It is then removed in boats down the lakes, whence it is conveyed by carts to Caernarvon Quay, and shipped for the company's smelting works near Swansea.'

Chapter Six

Itinerant barristers followed a close second to churchmen in publishing their memoirs of Snowdonia. Henry Skrine (1755 to 1803) was born at Warleigh Manor in Somerset and entered Christ Church, Oxford, at the age of 19. He later became a member of Lincoln's Inn before being called to the bar at 27. Skrine's *Three Tours in the North of England and Scotland* was published in 1795, to be followed in 1798 by *Two Tours of Wales* and in 1801 by *Rivers of Note in Great Britain*. The village of Tan-y-bwlch caught his attention, as it did that of many other travellers approaching or leaving North Wales:

'Agriculture seemed entirely banished from these tremendous wastes, and a few goats and sheep, the only denizens of this savage country, were observed browsing on precipices to which few human steps could venture to follow them. In the midst of such a desert, extending far around it on either side, the beautiful valley of Festiniog disclosed suddenly the strong contrast of its charms, and the pleasant inn of Tan-y-bwlch afforded us a welcome refuge from the storms with which we had been persecuted.

'Elevated on a high terrace, beneath a profusion of spreading groves fronting the south, the handsome mansion of the Griffith family at Tan-y-bwlch [Plas Tan-y-bwlch], enjoys at one view all the placid beauties of the valley, while the rugged and misshapen mountains that encompass it form an awful close to the scene of delight and forbid the eye to wander farther in search of pleasure. This delightful spot has been greatly improved by the spirit and taste of Mr Oakley, who married its heiress; nor has its attention been confined merely to his own territory, the whole neighbour-hood having profited by his exertions.

'On my second visit to this country, after an interval of six years, I found two noble bridges with a causeway, built across the valley, and the rugged track which led through the wilds of Merionethshire from Dolgelly, converted into one of the finest roads the art of man could devise, and so ingeniously drawn as to avoid all the laborious steeps, except one abrupt descent into the valley. Neither was the Caernarvonshire side without its progressive amendment under the same auspices, and in consequence of this example, the hovel at Bethkelert was converted into a decent inn, and even the pass over the mountains from Tan-y-bwlch to the Pont-Aberglaslyn was rendered more easy, though the heights to be surmounted in that quarter were far too arduous to be conquered with perfect success. Thus is a traveller now conducted, not only without fear but with an incredible degree of ease and pleasure, through the centre of the most mountainous part of our island and over eminences till of late impervious to a carriage, and with difficulty surmountable by a horse.'

Skrine saw little of Snowdon itself, having 'at two different seasons . . . been baffled by the severity of the climate, which pursued me with unremitting adversity'. His one attempted ascent was made from the Beddgelert to Caernarfon road in the vicinity of Rhyd-ddu:

'It was in vain that we tried on this quarter to climb the side of this British atlas; a misty sky and tempestuous day continued to resist our efforts; and obliged us, after a fruitless wandering about its rocky base, to take shelter in a miserable hovel at Bethkelert. From thence the wild aspect of the country frowned on us with the utmost asperity, and the rigour of an inclement season added fresh horror and majesty to the grand pass of Pont-Aberglaslyn.'

Observations on the Snowdon Mountains by William Williams was published in 1802 with an introductory dedication to one of the great local landowners. Williams was the Anglesey-born son of a stonemason, William ap Huw ap Sion, and after a very brief formal schooling served a seven year saddlery apprenticeship at Llannerch-y-medd. Private study and the influence of the Welsh poet and author, Hugh Hughes, aroused a passion for collecting antiquarian information which would later be drawn upon by, among others, Richard Fenton. Williams moved to Llandegai, becoming a clerk on the Penrhyn estate. In 1782, he encouraged Lord Penrhyn to take control of the slate quarries at Cae Braich y Cafn which became the vast Penrhyn quarry with Williams as its supervisor. The book begins with a very modest dedication:

'The following little work was originally intended for the private use of the Right Hon Lord Penrhyn. On its being suggested that the printing of it might excite a spirit of enquiry among the learned and ingenious, the author has at length ventured to submit the perusal of it to the public. He humbly hopes that considerable allowance will be made for the rusticity of his style for he had never the good fortune to reap the advantages of even a regular school-education.'

The mountain's name and ownership are tackled thus:

'The chain of mountains which extends from one end of the country of Caernarvon to the other, nearly in the direction from north-east to south-west, has been called from time immemorial by the general name of Eryri and Creigiau 'r Eryri. The most distinguished for sublimity is that which in the English language is called Snowdon, doubtless from the circumstance of its being so commonly covered with snow. The Welsh appellative, Eryri, seems derived from a different source, viz from Eryr, an eagle, which word in the plural number is Eryri, Eryron or Eryrod; so that Creigiau 'r will literally signify The Crags, as they are called in Scotland, or The Rocks of Eagles. There is moreover some tradition amongst the inhabitants of these mountains that eagles have heretofore bred in the lofty clefts of these rocks and some wandering eagles are now and then in these times seen skulking in the precipices. Had the Welsh name been derived, as the English one is, from Snow, it must have been Creigiau'r Eiry or Eira; and none but a sciolist in the British language can suppose that Eryri and Snowdon have any corresponding signification.

'Gwyddfa, or Yr Wyddfa, signifies literally Gwydd-fan; Gwydd means presence and fan, or man, place; so that Gwyddfa may be rendered The Conspicuous Place or Object. Gwyddfa means also a monument, I suppose from its elevation and prominence above the common level of the ground. This eminence is by the English called Snowdon. Its vast base touches upon three different parishes, namely Llanberis, Bettws Garmon and Bethcelert.

'A neck of land on the north-east side of it called Cwm y Moch, the Hog's Coom or valley, which belongs to Sir W. W. Wynne, extends itself from Llanberis valley quite up to the summit.

'All that part from the north-east to the west point and quite up to the highest peak belongs to Sir Thomas Asheton Smith Esq of Vaenol in this country and is mostly called Cwm Brwynog i.e. the Rushy Vale.

'The south-west side which is in the parish of Bettws Garmon and up to the top belongs to the same gentleman and is called Bron y Fedw, the Birch Slope.'

The hills and mountains of North Wales are plentifully endowed with the remains of former habitations in such primitive condition that they can scarcely be recognised from randomly scattered rocks. By far the best example is the earlier-mentioned Iron Age hill fortress of Tre'r Ceiri overlooking the west coast of the Llŷn Peninsular south of Trefor. This is located on one of the slopes of Yr Eifl which is covered by a vast number of rocks that formed the raw materials of the fortress walls and inner structures. Williams provides useful light on these structures:

'Many of the highest hills have on their tops great heaps of loose stones which testify their having been when Wales was a seat of war gwylfau, i.e. watchplaces; and consequently are no doubt the remains or ruins of temporary buildings for sheltering men when upon the watch in war-time. The walls were made without any mortar but probably stuffed with moss to keep out the wind and rain, which is the substitute for mortar used at present in all the mountain buildings, dwelling-houses excepted, which are now mostly plastered with lime-mortar.

'But Snowdon, though always allowed to be the highest of all the hills, has no heap on its top: and it is something remarkable that a mountain so eminently overtopping all others in its vicinity should not have been made choice of for a watch-place; but it may be conjectured that its peaked top gave no sufficient space for marshall-exercise which the other hills afforded.'

Williams contributes the following notes on diet and economy:

'The inhabitants of the British mountains are so humane and hospitable that a stranger may travel amongst them without incurring any expense for diet or lodging. Their fare an Englishman may call coarse; however they commonly in farm-houses have three sorts of bread, namely wheat, barley and oatmeal; but the oatmeal they chiefly use: this with milk, butter and potatoes is their common summer food. They have also plenty of excellent trout which they eat in its season. And for the winter they have dry salted beef, mutton and smoked rock venison, which they call Coch ar Wyden i.e. the Red upon the Withy, being hung by a withy made of willow or hazel twig.

'They very seldom brew ale except in some of the principal farm-houses: having no corn of their own growing, they think it a superfluous expense to throw away money for malt and hops when milk or butter-milk mixed with water quenches the thirst as well.

'From the extensiveness of their meadows and wastelands, many Gentlemen have supposed that the lands are let much under value and consequently have raised the rents in some places considerably. But they may raise and raise for ever; the farmer has no method whereby he can swell his purse to twenty shillings more in a twelve month unless he can sell his cattle at a higher price; and indeed a wonderful advance in the price of cattle has taken place of late years. I remember the time when a fat mountain sheep might have been bought for five shillings; but now such a sheep cannot be purchased under fifteen shillings, and other cattle in proportion. Butter, which I have seen at so low a rate as three-pence per pound, is not now sold under eight-pence and sometimes as high as nine pence or ten pence or even twelve pence.'

The Snowdon summit attracts visitors of all ages. One of the eldest to write of his ascent was William Hutton who climbed the Ranger's Path, or a route very close to it, in 1799 at the age of 76. Born and schooled in Derby, Hutton taught himself the trade of bookbinding and in 1749, at 26, walked to London and back to purchase the necessary tools. He opened a small bookshop in Southwell, Nottinghamshire, the same year before moving in 1750 to Birmingham. After a varied career in papermaking and land speculation, he became an author specialising in local history. If a vegetarian diet and a voracious appetite for long-distance walking keep a man healthy, Hutton was a good example of it. He survived to 92; his *Remarks Upon North Wales* was published in 1803:

'Although the beauties of Caernarvon and its environs delight the gentry who visit for pleasure, health, air or sea bathing, yet it is unfashionable not to visit the Lakes of Llanberris but chiefly Snowdon. Though they lie together, they cannot be examined together, each demands a day.

'This, the principal mountain in Wales, is nine miles from

Caernarvon and said to have been covered with timber which I rather doubt because the rocky soil and exposed situation are unfavourable to growth. It is guarded by two passes which are easily made inaccessible, Mynedd Vawr and Pont Aber Glaslyn, about eight miles asunder. Here Owen Glendwr retreated from the vengeance of Henry IV in 1401 after he had sacked the English marches, burnt the towns and destroyed the people.

'Long interested in this sovereign mountain, I consulted many authors but they were too defective to form a judgement; I also conversed with many persons who had climbed it but found them unintelligible, sometimes contradictory and much given to the wonderful. I wished for an impartial judge who would describe fairly and cause me to see as he saw.

'At Aberistwith in 1787, they pretended to point it out but I believe they knew no more of it than myself.

'At Barmouth in 1796, I was assured it was visible at a few miles. I walked fourteen, enquiring for Snowdon. No soul understood me, I had forgotten the word y Wyddfa.

'In 1797, I rode twice over its foot in hopes of a sight. It was covered to the root. Returning through Bangor, I had for a few moments a glance of its summit at about twelve miles distance. It appeared amazingly grand. This quickened desire.

'Residing a month at Caernarvon in 1799, I thought a sight could not escape me but as Pennant justly observes "The days proper for seeing are very rare". A fortnight elapsed with weather too dreadful to visit anywhere. Disappointment still urged me.

'Walking along the shore two miles from Caernarvon, I gained a glimpse of this emperor of the rocks. August the 30th, I packed up some provisions, for I thought a hungry journey was before me, hung my great coat over my arm, and set out at daybreak solus, and on foot, to ascend Snowdon, and return, if able, at night. I was a total stranger to the task assigned; I might as well have attempted a miracle. Fortunately, it began to rain as soon as I entered the street, and crushed my quixotism.

'September 1, I set off with an intention of walking to the Lakes of Llanberris, five miles; boating over them five more; walking round the foot of Snowdon, keeping the mountain on the right, sleeping at Beddkelart, and mounting up if the next morning was suitable. Upon enquiry, when I passed the great Lake, I found but one man who could speak English, and he would have five shillings to conduct me to Beddkelart, which he said was fifteen miles. But considered that I had set out late in the day, had lost two hours in waiting for a boat, that fifteen miles was a long stretch, it drawing apace towards the evening, and that night prospects were of little avail, I altered my plan and agreed a man, who could not speak English, half a crown to conduct me over the mountains into the road at the great Lake Quethlin, from whence I knew the way home.

'As my honest guide did not understand the word 'half' crown, I showed him one, which he offering to take, I withdrew my hand lest I should be treated as I was treated in Herefordshire. Being lost, in the evening, I agreed with a person to conduct me to Laisters Church; but, when possessed of the money, he quitted his charge and left me to find my way in the dark.

'I now had Snowdon on the left all the way but hid like an eastern prince while all the surrounding mountains were clear.

'The next day, September 2, walking in the Isle of Anglesea, I had a view of its summit most of the way; and on the third, strolling over another part of the Island, had the same view, with the addition of a cloud of beautiful white foam pent in the interstices of the mountains, while all above was bare.

'Being led on the fourth to the Kilgwyn Mountain, the Slate Quarries, and Lakes of Nant Nanlle [Nantlle], I for the first time gained a sight of this prince of mountains from bottom to top, distant five or six miles.

'September the 6th, I ordered my horses at seven and reached the guide's house by the cascade at the foot of Snowdon by nine. He, my servant, and I, immediately began to ascend. The sun was not hid one moment during the day. I asked, "What distance to the top?" "Nearly four miles." I thought if I could divide the road into distinct parts, I should be the better able to guess at the distance.

'I ascended about a mile, rather boggy, but easy to rise. Some of the land would make good pasture ground, at a small expense. I then crossed a fence and was led half a mile, rising less, but more boggy. Next, a swamp about 400 yards, which is the only level spot in the whole walk. I had now gone about a mile and three quarters in a straight line, at the expense of one hour. A prodigious chasm in the mountain was on the right all the way, and the summit in view, which seemed at so small a distance that a man might almost reach it with the cast of a stone. At the bottom of this chasm were three pools of considerable magnitude.

'I now suddenly turn to the right and keep a line in the form of a bow, with a quick rise for two miles, equal on the average to the rise of a moderate flight of stairs. The whole of this road is rough but not equally so, with loose slates, large stones and pointed rocks. No path, neither did the guide seem to wish one lest the road be found by others.

'Walking required that attention to the feet which prevented me from viewing an object without standing still. Though there was a gentle wind, yet the heat of the sun reflecting from a vast inclined plain, elevated perhaps forty degrees, overcame me, the blood was in a ferment, a sickness and giddiness ensued and I was obliged to recline perhaps twenty times. Neither did I find much relief, for I might be said to lie upon a burning mountain. I deposited myself under a small rock, the shade of which, with drawing up the limbs, covered me, and I found refreshment.

'The mountain is replete with beautiful stones of various colours and fine texture which I think would take a polish perhaps equal to those of the Peak; others resemble spar with incrustations. I believe, too, there are singular herbs but I am not skilled in botany. Had my friend Dr Withering been there, he would have entertained me as he did July 2, 1786, upon Sutton Coldfield, with their names and virtues.

'Travelling a little more than a mile in this fourth or last division, I came to the Green Well, so called from the verdure of its borders caused by the stream, which my guide said "ran the same round the whole year". The passage must be rapid in so steep a descent; the flow of water would fill a tube about the size of a man's arm. The water is exceedingly clear, cold and well tasted. Here we opened our provisions and tapped our brandy.

'Within half a mile of the top, the way became extremely steep and rugged. Here another chasm opens on the left or opposite side of the mountain, perhaps three times as large as that mentioned above, horrid in the extreme, and here the traveller complains of the narrow and dangerous road in which, if he misses a step, destruction follows. But he is not bound to venture upon the precipice; the road is safe and he may every where make choice of his step for a space of half a mile in width, except within a few yards of the summit and even there it cannot be less than twelve or fourteen feet wide.

'I now reached the summit, which is level, a circle of eight feet diameter surrounded by a wall two feet high and one thick, composed of loose slate stones, the produce of the mountain; one of them, near falling, I adjusted. Here I put on my great coat, which the guide had carried, and I had carried his stick, which proved a useful stay.

'We sat down in this elevated ring to consume the remainder of our store, for the guide had brought water from the well. My design was to stay at least one hour but I found it too cold to be borne, therefore did not stay more than a quarter. The guide I thought inadequate to his office. He made no observations nor spoke but when spoken to and then I could barely understand his English. He ought to have been master of the prospect and, like a showman, pointed out the various objects.

'Such a day, though clear, is not the best for a comprehensive view because the air, replete with sun beams, hinders vision; the best is when the light clouds are high and the sun is hid. My situation was wonderful and indescribable. Here a man may fairly say "He is got above the world". The mountain is said to be 1,189 yards high.

'Objects seemed diminished to the sight, four parts in five. The adjacent mountains seemed reduced to hills, except Crib y Dystyl, which attempted to raise its proud, beautiful and rival head.

'The noble Lake Quethlyn, at the foot of Snowdon, a mile and a quarter long, and three quarters broad, appeared but little larger than a duck pool. The two Traeths, Mawr and Bach, where two years before I was lost, appeared under my eye and excited surprise that I could be lost in so diminutive a place.

'I saw the whole of the road between the lakes of Llanberris and that of Quethlyn, which I had walked five days before, and knew was five miles, but now did not appear to be half an hour's stretch. As Snowdon extends to both, the diameter of its base must be about the above measure.

'The distance between the Lakes of Nant Nanlle and Snowdon, viewed two days before, appeared twice as far as now, viewed from Snowdon to the Lakes. Thus elevation reduces space.

'A stone I had passed in climbing the mountain, perhaps twenty feet high and ten thick, was reduced to the size of a block that a man might seemingly lift. Not an habitation, tree or bush of any kind appeared in these desolate regions. All was wild and rude nature.

'Below, the heads of four rivers appeared to issue from the mountain. On the north, the fountain which feeds the Lakes of Llanberris, five miles long, becomes the river Seiont and ends in the sea at Caernarvon. On the south, another, which supplies the lake Quethlyn, becomes the river Gwyrfai, and meets the sea three miles south of Caernarvon. A third, on the south-east side of the mountain, becomes the Colwyn; and north-east, the Glaslyn, which uniting with the last at Beddkelart, terminate at Traeth Mawr.

'My situation was a compound of wonder, grandeur and terror. A stationary white cloud on the north horizon prevented me from seeing Cumberland, Westmoreland, Scotland and the Isle of Man. A line of sea appeared from the north, stretching behind Anglesea, and far to the south, to the extent of perhaps two or three hundred miles; and on the back ground, I saw four of the Irish mountains. The most beautiful part of the prospect was Anglesea. It appeared almost under my feet, though twelve miles off, yet so plain that a man might be induced to think he saw every inclosure and so minute that if one person owned the whole it would not be a vast estate.

'Four mountains, Crib y Dystyl, Crib Coch, Llwddy yr Arran and Clewdd Coch, which Pennant calls the Sons of Snowdon, and I confess they are sons of a monstrous size though much inferior to their father, stand as buttresses and seem to aid their ancient parent. We should almost think, at a glance, he stands in need of their support, from the decay of his strength by the two amazing chasms in his sides. He and his sons unite in a friendly style as every family ought and are abstracted from others for round them appears a foss and round that foss a circular range of mountains as if, like faithful subjects, to guard the royal family. The diameter of this foss, I apprehend, is about eight miles; it is bounded by the Cader Mynyth Vawr, the two Llyders, the two Glyders, etc, forming a circumference of more than thirty miles.

'I was seriously told, and it was believed by the teller, "That a man standing in this elevated circle might drop a stone out of each hand which in one minute would be seven miles asunder". The truth is one would fall down the great chasm but the other would be impeded by the stones before it could arrive at the lesser; or, if it was possible to arrive at the bottom, the distance does not seem more than a mile.

'The guide told me he had led his horse up to the circle. This I believe possible for a Welsh keffel will climb almost as well as his master.

'A clergyman remarked that a man rode his horse to the top and round the wall on the outside. I took particular notice of this journey, which must have been nine yards, six of which a madman might ride, but on the other three I could not conceive there was room for the foot.

'Two gentlemen and a lady in September, 1797, began to climb this famous mountain. The sun shone, the day was windy and the clouds low. In rising, they were obliged to hold each other for fear of being blown away and were as wet with the rain as if dipped in the sea. In this dreadful state they reached the top. The lady, elated with success though she could see nothing, pulled off her hat and cap and huzzaed for joy. Returning, the wind took them both away. The guide told me he found the hat a year after by a pool in the great chasm and wore it himself. The amazonian lady no doubt was the leader of the party and designed, like some others of her own sex, to govern ours. The lofty Snowdon, however, reduced the more lofty spirit of the female adventurer. She fell into fits, her life was despaired of, and she was brought in a chaise the next morning to Caernarvon at four, in a state of distress which excited pity.

'The extreme cold, after the intense heat, being more than I could sustain, induced me to quit this elevated station in the time mentioned, which was done with regret, having as from Pisgah been indulged with only one short sight, long wished-for but to be seen no more.

'Making no doubt but I should descend with greater facility, I again entered the burning heat of the reflecting sun which often obliged me to recline, nor was I much relieved, being deprived of shade.

'I soon perceived that going down was more dangerous than going up, for the short dry herbage glazed the soles of my shoes into a polish which, from the extreme steep, made it difficult to command my feet. Neither did the smooth soles suit the stones and a man had better meet ten falls in rising that one in descending. In ascending, if a man falls, it must be upon his hands, which I did several times; if, in descending, upon his back, or rather his right side, which I did once.

'Arriving at the well, we relished the plain water, our bottle being empty. Time and hard labour brought me down the great steep of two miles when, entering the swamp, and the powerful heat of the sun ceasing, I reached the hut of the guide with more energy.

'I had been from nine to twelve in ascending this grand eminence; and from twelve to three in returning — six hours of the severest labour in my whole life; and, perhaps, I am the only man that ever took a wanton trip to the summit of Snowdon at the age of seventy-six.'

'A stranger to the country, to the language, and almost to a man, I returned from Nant Gwynan, slept at Capel Cerig, and was wandering over Lord Penrhyn's new road, towards Caernarvon, my present home. The cascades on my left were rolling down with violence, after heavy rain, when a sheet of water a mile long and three quarters wide presented itself to view, which I knew must be Ogwen Pool. At the extremity of the pool, I found myself upon a most beautiful valley, nearly one mile wide and four long.

'When I had travelled about three miles along this sequestered valley, I saw four people contriving how to mend a gate. I singled out one, whom I had no doubt understood English, nay I could almost have told it from the very cut of his coat. I asked several questions regarding the road and the objects before me, all of which he readily answered; for being dressed in black I might be taken for a clergyman which is an excellent passport for a stranger. "My way, I am informed Sir, lies through Nant Frankon [Nant Ffrancon]. Pray how shall I know when I am in it?" "You are in it now".

'Lord Penrhyn is constructing excellent roads in the most barren part of the island and will no doubt accommodate the traveller with one of the greatest benefits, which comes at least expense, mile stones. The stranger is always glad to see one because he sees a friend who will not deceive him. They enliven a tedious journey and are peaceable company in solitude. If he travels from necessity, we ought to soften his hardship. If from pleasure, to heighten it. Neither should the stranger be at any trouble to discover them. They ought, as far as circumstances will allow, to stand conspicuous on the same side of the road and be painted white.

'Lord Penrhyn has recently taken a farm of 3,000 acres into his own hands and his next step will be to drain it, which will teach the farmers what they never knew: to improve their own lands. This is adding real wealth to a country, a benefit incalculable. It is a conquest without blood. It will convey to his mind more pleasure than killing twenty men in the field of honour, and I shall enjoy the thought of being the last historian who shall record the rent of land was two-pence an acre!

'Observing a male goat in a field near Caernarvon, I was so struck with his dignified appearance that I could not pass on. I attempted at an intimacy with this venerable sovereign of the place but he resolved that distance should lie between us. Before a week passed, I saw, with a melancholy eye, his skin hang at a shop window, for sale. I remarked to the master that he had destroyed a friend and made a widow. I am told the landlords discourage goats because they are injurious to the growth of timber by nibbling the bark.

'During my repeated visits to Caernarvon, I frequently set my foot in Anglesea and was always pleased with the excursion though I lost much by my ignorance of the language. Five ferries in the compass of twelve or fourteen miles communicate with the island:

'The most southern is Abermenai.

'Three miles north of this is that of Caernarvon (Tal y Foel).

'Four miles still north is Moel y Don (The Hill in the Waves).

'Three miles beyond this is Bangor (Porthathwy) [Porthaethwy], the narrowest part of the Menai, not half a mile wide.

'The fifth, at Beaumaris, four miles over. I have passed at the three central.

'I determined to spend two whole days in one line of research and set out, with my servant, September 3, 1799. I entered the common ferry boat with about forty passengers; not one could speak English. Surprised to see every person carry a luggage for family use: bread, cloth, shoes, brushes, flour, etcetera. I was given to understand they were obliged to cross the water for a supply, nor could they eat a breakfast till they had fetched it from Caernarvon, though some of them resided at the distance of six or seven miles. That it was the practice of the Anglesea farmer to sell his wheat in autumn to the Liverpool merchant and, prior to another crop, often purchase it again at an advanced price.

'This ferry (Tal y Foel) I was assured was three miles over. I believe it much less but we are sure to meet with the wonderful in Wales. The boat, as near as I could guess, went at the rate of three miles an hour. The voyage was exactly thirty minutes.'

Chapter Seven

William Fordyce Mavor was born near Aberdeen and became an Oxfordshire schoolteacher in 1775, initially in Burford and later at Woodstock where his pupils included the children of the duke of Marlborough. The duke evidently developed a good opinion of Mavor and helped establish him as vicar of Hurley in Berkshire. Mavor exchanged this living for the rectory of Bladon-with-Woodstock and eventually returned to teaching, as headmaster of Woodstock grammar school. He was ten times elected as mayor of Woodstock. He also found time for a very large output of books, sustaining an enthusiasm for topography as well as education, and invented a system of shorthand. It was during his church career that Mavor left Woodstock, on Monday July 8th 1805, travelling into Wales along a route that would become popular with many 20th century motorists. This took him through Cheltenham, Ross-on-Wye, Bicknor, Abergavenny, Crickhowell and Brecon to the west-coast harbour of Aberaeron. Thence he journeyed north through Aberystwyth, Llanrhystud and Llanidloes to Dolgellau and on into Snowdonia. The result was *A Tour through Wales in the Summer of 1805*:

> 'At this season of the year, it would have been a prudent precaution to have forwarded a messenger to secure lodgings at Beddgelert, which is 28 miles from Dolgellau, as there is only one house of accommodation here and no other nearer than Caernarvon, though this is the grand route of travellers. Once more, however, fortune befriended us and we found excellent lodgings at The Goat, an elegant new-built house with the appropriate motto under its sign: Patria mea petra — My country is a rock.
>
> 'From hence an excursion is often made to the summit of Snowdon, distant about seven miles, three of which may be taken on horseback. On enquiring, however, we found that the easiest and most advisable point of ascent would be from The Saracen's Head [subsequently the Snowdon Ranger

126

Hotel, now a youth hostel], a small public house about five miles off the road to Caernarvon, where a guide resides and the distance to the top of the mountain does not exceed four miles, three of which a horse can travel with safety. This determined our party to adopt that route in preference to the other and, though only one of us had the resolution of attempting to behold the sun rising from this prince of Welsh mountains, and who politely yielded to the general wish, all were anxious to devote the morning to the arduous task and to prepare ourselves for it by rest and refreshments in the morning before we left the hotel.

'The gentlemen who we had met more than once were again arrived here before us and occupied an adjoining parlour. While supper was getting ready, one of them who was an excellent performer on the German flute, which formed part of his viaticum, went out into the area before the house and produced some of the sweetest notes that were ever heard in the vale of Beddgelert. The evening was calm and the surrounding echoes from the hills reverberated the notes so as to form a concert from a single instrument.

'At supper we had the company of a gentleman just arrived from Ireland who was proceeding to Tenby, the place of his residence, and who favoured us with comparative statements of the advantages which south Wales enjoyed over the northern division of the principality. He confirmed, from his own knowledge and observation, several extraordinary customs which exists among the Wallians, recorded by tourists, and strengthened my conviction of the truth of the opinion I had already formed that few persons reach longevity in this country but, on the contrary, that great numbers are carried off in early youth by pulmonary consumption.

'The landlord here, who has the merit of paying every possible attention to his guests, informed us that Sir Robert Williams, MP for the county, a man respected and loved by all who know him, and with whom I have had the happiness to spend some agreeable hours, as captain of a score of volunteers called the "Snowdon Ranger", lately had them reviewed on the top of that mountain when, to the astonishment of strangers, they performed their manoeuvres and evolutions with as much precision and indifference as if they had been on level ground.

'Hitherto we had been favoured with such fine weather that in the course of 12 days, and travelling early and late, we had never once had occasion to unfurl our umbrellas on account of the rain though we had sometimes done so to shield us from the sun. The next morning, when we got up at an early hour as had been agreed on, we had the mortification to find that a deep mist hung on the hills and that there was every indication of a wet day. The night had been excessively hot and sultry and, whether from this cause or the confined situation of this romantic place, all of us complained of languor and depression of spirits.

'Finding it impossible to ascend Snowdon with any chance of enjoying its landscapes, we resolved to wait here till we saw how the day would turn out and, while my friends revisited Pont Aberglaslyn in order to fish for salmon, I walked round the narrow limits of the vale of Beddgelert and picked up what incidental information my opportunities would allow. In this little plain is an almost exhausted turbary but still some peat and turf are dug here. The best land lets at 20 shillings an acre but the average of the neighbourhood is from half-a-crown to five shillings with unlimited right of common on the mountains which produce little to the nominal proprietor except where mines have been discovered and worked to advantage.

'Several attempts have been made to procure copper near Pont Aberglaslyn but the ore is not reckoned very rich. Similar trials have been made near the very summit of Snowdon as well as among the other mountains, and not wholly without success, but Anglesey for the richness and value of its copper is still unrivalled. It can scarcely be doubted, however, that several valuable metals are concealed in the bowels of these sterile regions. Nothing is made in vain and where nature has been most unpropitious externally she often contains hidden treasures which compensate for her other defects.

'Examined the neat little church of Beddgelert with a single bell in its steeple as is usual in Wales except in towns. Tradition says it was erected on the spot where Llewelyn raised a tomb to the memory of his favourite greyhound which still gives name to the village. The story of this dog savours of the marvelous and I will not detain my readers to repeat it.

'In this perambulation I had to regret that many of the rocks which surround Beddgelert which had once been covered with oaks from the effects of dissipation of want of taste are now consigned to the axe. One proprietor, however, is raising new plantations on his estate and it is to be wished that others may imitate such a laudable example. We have undoubted evidence that Snowdonia was once a forest; at present, except in the vales, scarcely a tree is to be seen.

'The goats, which are less numerous than we expected to find them, and which generally keep in the most inaccessible parts of the mountains, are said to be very destructive to young trees by barking them in winter and browsing them in summer. They sometimes descend during the night into the vales and commit their depredations; hence, though private property, they are proscribed in many places and killed without mercy. I saw several men, with each a goat on his back, coming down from the mountains but could not learn for what purpose they had been caught. Wherever they abound, they increase the beauty of the landscape and I would restrain but not extirpate them.

'Purchased a few crystals etcetera which are found pretty plentiful in Snowdonia of the widow of the late guide from Beddgelert. She had a tolerable collection of crystals, spars and minerals picked up by her husband in his various rambles among the mountains but none of them arranged or particularly curious. They serve, however, to amuse loiterers at the solitary place and a few shillings are not ill expended in purchasing some of them as a memorial of the spot and as an encouragement in civility and honest industry. A widow with a young family has always claims to attention and it seems her husband in some measure fell a martyr to his too frequent journeys up Snowdon which threw him into a decline.

'From the Saracen's Head the ascent to the summit of Snowdon is only four miles and a road from thence has lately been made to bring down the copper ore on sledges which is found at a great height in the mountains. These sledges, drawn by two horses, will carry six hundredweight and we saw an old man of 70 who is daily employed with a couple of poor animals in this toilsome occupation. The old man seemed asthmatic and well he might for, had not his lungs been uncommonly strong, he could not have stood so much climbing for half the time that he appears to have done. The guide, who was not quite disinterested in his opinion after being repeatedly appealed to, declared that he thought the summit of Snowdon or Yr Wyddfa would be free from clouds before we reached it, and accordingly, having laid in such a stock of refreshments as the little inn afforded, we set out in a grand cavalcade full of the wonders we were to behold though not without a mixture of fear of disappointment. We had scarcely, however, gained the first ascent when Mrs . . . began to grow faint and giddy and, as I was less enthusiastic than either of the other gentlemen, I requested they would proceed and give me an accurate account of their expedition while I engaged to take care of the lady till their return. In a short time I had the satisfaction to see her perfectly recovered and, as we observed a number of persons pouring from the hills in every direction, and taking their course along the brow of the eminence on which we stood, by way of filling up our time we resolved to join the train in hopes that we might see a congregation of Jumpers. A civil old man from Caernarvon, whom we had seen playing the fiddle at a little inn and who spoke English, now joined us and informed us that a meeting was to be held at a near house which he pointed out where the persons assembling were of that fanatical class of methodists who occasionally betray the utmost extravagance during their devotions.'

While collision with other traffic may have been less dangerous before the age of the motor car than it is now, road surfaces in pre-19th century Snowdonia were very far from ideal. The Welsh highlands lagged behind the lowlands in road improvement as such work was left almost entirely to the local inhabitants. The one convincing persuader of a predominantly granite terrain, gunpowder, was expensive. In 1806, a refugee from the French revolution, Antoinne Philippe d'Orleans, broke contemporary speed records when his groom fell from their four-wheeled carriage into a ditch while steering round a deep hole. The groom ran after the carriage and caught the horses by the bridle but, far from stopping them, only succeeded in frightening them into a gallop. Seeing the reins dragging uselessly out of reach, D'Orleans' servant promptly jumped out of the carriage, escaping with a bruised knee. Remembering an acquaintance who had broken both legs jumping out of a curricle, D'Orleans himself stayed put. Before long he observed a traveller coming in the opposite direction on a donkey and shouted a warning at her just in time to prevent disaster. Moments later, a cart drawn by two horses approached from the opposite side of a narrow bridge which would shortly also have to accommodate D'Orleans and his runaway vehicle. Once again, the approaching traveller managed to take evasive action. Carriage and passenger proceeded at the will of two horses 'completely mad galloping at their greatest rate, down some of the steepest hills, through many very short turnings, over those narrow bridges, for the space of about four miles and a half, in about a quarter of an hour'. The horses eventually began to tire and were brought to a stop by a groom who had shown to presence of mind to give chase after himself nearly being bowled over. The road in question, from Beddgelert to Caernarfon, offers scenery today very little changed since 1806.

Edward Pugh's *Cambria Depicta* is a large book exceptionally well illustrated in colour by 'a native artist'. It is based on a tour claimed to be of several months' duration made about 1807. Pugh draws heavily from Pennant and a few contemporary travel writers but the following brief sketch appears for the most part original:

> 'These mountaineers are a hardy race and accustomed to fare which an Englishman would think meanly coarse. Their bread, made of barley or oats (rarely of wheat), is generally eaten with buttermilk, salt, butter, cheese and potatoes. In winter, they live much upon dry salted mutton and smoked rock-venison or goat which is called Coch ar Dden, or the Red upon the Withe, being hung upon a withe constructed on the twigs of a willow.
>
> 'They are very sober, ale not being in their bill of fare, and milk and water allaying their thirst just as well. The luxury of ale brewing is confined to the more wealthy farmer. Thus the hardy inhabitant of the mountain runs his race through life; and, though his meals are coarse and short, his employments are warranted, his sleep certain and refreshing, neither interrupted with the lashes of the guilty mind, nor the aches of a crazy body.
>
> 'From their childhood accustomed to ramble upon the mountains, to look after their cattle, these people are by habit inured to the utmost inclemency of the weather; their employment, however, though requiring hardiness, cannot be said to be very laborious. As they are great economists, they go bare-footed in the summer to save the article of shoes, the wear of which would be rendered more expensive upon their rocky territories.'

Fear of Napoleonic invasion was high throughout Britain in the early 1800s and added to the innate suspicion with which the inhabitants of North Wales continued to view the slowly rising tide of tourists. Pugh experienced this in high measure:

> 'Feeling a want of refreshment, I inquired for the public-house but was informed that the village enjoyed no such luxury. A farmer's wife, however, kindly invited me to partake of what her table afforded. The fare, though coarse, was very grateful to an appetite rendered voracious by the keen air of the mountains.
>
> 'This good women, in the course of a conversation, with a modest apology, inquired what could induce me to travel through a trackless country where it was difficult even for the natives to find their way. She observed that sometimes strange people were seen at Bethgelert with large books (portfolios) making maps of the country. They would often ascend Snowdon for the purpose, it was supposed, of ascertaining places of landing on the sea-shores, and it became necessary for the natives to be a little watchful over them. She however intimated that I was exempted in her mind from any suspicions of this nature.
>
> 'I replied that those who were seen with books etcetera were probably gentlemen professing an art admired by all the world, and were, I might venture to say, all of them loyal subjects to the king; but that it was nevertheless proper to have an eye upon all strangers lest any foreigners, with some treacherous intent, should make their ingress amongst them and, under the pretence of drawing the views, might the more easily accomplish their designs.'

The years between 1795 and 1810 saw the construction of the road from Tremadoc to Beddgelert, which even today can be seen to have been hard-won from the granite slopes on the west bank of the Glaslyn. This road was continued in the same period through Nant Gwynant to Penygwryd and on to Capel Curig. The road from Shrewsbury through North Wales to Anglesey had long been used by travellers to and from Ireland. Such road as existed, however, fell far below the standards even of the early 19th century. William Akers, representing the Post Office, declared to a House of Commons committee as late as 1815:

'Many parts of the road are extremely dangerous for a coach to travel upon. At several places between Bangor and Capel Curig there are a number of dangerous precipices without fences, exclusive of various hills that want taking down.

'At Ogwen Pool there is a very dangerous place where the water runs over the road, extremely difficult to pass at flooded times. Then there is Dinas Hill, that needs a side fence against a deep precipice. The width of the road is not above twelve feet in the steepest part of the hill and two carriages cannot pass without the greatest danger.

'Between this hill and Rhyddlanfair there are a number of dangerous precipices, steep hills and difficult narrow turnings. From Corwen to Llangollen the road is very narrow, long and steep; has no side fence except about a foot and a half of mould or dirt which is thrown up to prevent carriages falling down three or four hundred feet into the River Dee.

'Stage coaches have frequently been overturned and broken down from the badness of the road, and the mails have been overturned; but I wonder that more and worse accidents have not happened, the roads are so bad.'

Richard Fenton served for several years as a barrister on the Welsh legal circuit. These travels aroused in him an intense interest in the principality and its history. The eye for detail demonstrated in his *Tours in Wales* compares at times with the best of Thomas Pennant whose writings were much in his mind during an attempted Snowdon ascent via Cwm Dyli on Thursday August 2nd 1810. Fenton's journey began in Beddgelert:

'Rose early intending to have followed Mr Pennant's steps to Cwm Dily, but found before I came to Llyn Gwynen that I had mistaken the place of his ascent, which I thought was by the fall which spreads itself in a white sheet over the rock which forms the shelf for the cataract almost opposite the new house called Plas Gwynnen. Leaving my horse at the farmhouse at the foot of the mountain, with a shepherd boy for my guide, and induced by the very romantic appearance of the opening the water of the cascade issued from, I began my ascent, and after winding backwards and forwards for two miles, came to a moory plain of very small extent producing a kind of short hay, which had been harvested. An amphitheatre of broken crags of great heights surrounded this little spot, and the river which issues from some lakes behind these crags murmured through in a very narrow stream. I found, without a guide, there was no doing anything effectually and that, to see what I wished, Cwm Dily, I ought to have gone farther up the vale, for 3 or 4 miles, to get a proper ascending place. I enquired if they resided in the havodty which I saw on the heights for any length of time in summer. I was informed that, during the hay season, they brought food with them, and were there all day, but always descended to sleep.'

Fenton returned to Beddgelert ('not having profited much by my toilsome excursion') where he visited the church and 'the old public house'. He travelled thence to Pontaberglaslyn and noted mining activity, signs of which are still visible on the eastern bank of the river just north of the bridge. The horizontal remains of a copper mine on the east bank can still be seen and visited in the National Trust grounds just upstream of Pont Aberglaslyn. It goes in for 100 paces, curving slightly to the right, with an interior parking space for a couple of mountain bicycles on the left at 50 paces. The roof is decently high and the floor firm but wet even in the dry season; wellington boots and a reliable torch are essential. One inch drill holes are visible in the walls along the tunnel and at the flat far end:

'Stop at Aberglaslyn and saw one fish without success attempting to surmount the fall above the bridge, consisting of one arch, and thrown over a deep part of the river.

'Opposite to the bridge is an adit of a copper mine now working by some Cornish adventurers who are laying out a great deal of money there, as if there was a great prospect of advantage. The ride to Tremadock, the estuary being full, was very fine, but much inferior to that from Dolgelly to Barmouth. The mountains of that tract between Pont Aberglaslyn and Tanybwlch, with the Knicht at their head, the most pointed of all our mountains, were clear, of a fine colour, and appeared to great advantage.

'The town since I saw it last was somewhat enlarged and opposite the principal inn and town hall was a large opening, a kind of square, in the centre of which was a cross and a town pump which hereafter may be improved into a public conduit.

'After dinner walked down to see the new embankment, a gigantic undertaking, and which would have appalled any other genius than that of the gentleman to whose enterprising spirit we owe it.'

On another visit in early August 1813, Fenton ascended Snowdon from Rhyd-ddu and his opinion of the 'rocky and narrow' ridge will be shared by all who have carried a sense of vertigo across the final stage of Bwlch Main. His return journey was via the less precipitous slopes of the Miners' Track.

'Ascended half past one, riding for some little way with much difficulty. Then, leaving our horses, we walked up a pretty narrow steep mountain till we came to a rocky summit, having a narrow path on one side hanging over the hollow of Cwm Clogwyn yawning beneath. To me the path was terrible to pass, which passed, I came to a very narrow isthmus, which separated Cwm Clogwyn from another still deeper cwm on the other side. I had then for a considerable ascent a more terrible path to encounter taking several sharp turnings through a rocky and narrow ridge, with this Cwm exactly under me. Thank God, I got to the end of it but with a determined resolution not to return that way. Saw Llynnie Nanlle to great advantage. After another sharp but not terrible ascending stage, I reached the summit. But it is of so tame a character on that side that there is nothing of the grand to attract notice and it derives all its consequence from the surrounding peaks, whose blasted features betray their conflict for ages with the elements. And as to the peak of Snowdon itself, it only acquires importance from its known height, and from your being conscious that you are on its summit. The rifted side of the Peak of Snowdon, as seen from Llanberis, from this point does not appear.

'Descended a very practicable way through a road made and taken by the carriers of mine from a work under Snowdon in the vale where Llyn Llydaw is, and got home safe, thank God, by eight o'clock.'

Edmund Hyde Hall's *A Description of Caernarvonshire (1809-1811)* remained unpublished during its author's lifetime, probably due to the large size of the manuscript. It was acquired in 1932 by the library of the University College of North Wales from a Bangor bookseller who had apparently purchased it from a retired postmaster, J. D. Jones. The document was edited by Emyr Gwynne Jones M.A. and published by University College of North Wales in 1952. Little is known of the author though his family lived for a time in Jamaica. Hall himself appears to have attended Harrow School in 1785 and later studied law. He provides a contemporary account of William Madocks' efforts to construct the embankment which now protects Traeth Mawr from the sea immediately south of Porthmadog:

'The last work entered upon by the enterprising proprietor of the place [Madocks' home, Plas Tan yr Allt] must be praised as useful, while it is admired as spirited. The success of the first embankment already mentioned has induced an attempt to subject to productive purposes that vast expanse of sand at low water known by the name of the Traeth Mawr.

'Along this tract downwards from Pont Aberglasslyn, the river (which drains with continual accessions of volume a vast mountainous range of Caernarvonshire and Merionethshire) descends in a course worn by its action on the eastern side of the estuary. The sea, on the other hand, advanced with every flood tide to the occupation of the sands, and frequently driven upwards by the violence of a southerly wind, rushed on with a force and weight that seemed uncontrollable by the exertions of man. The attempt has, however, been made. Near the western bank (opposite to the tongue of land by which the two estuaries are divided) a few rocky islands offered themselves as abutments upon which the commencing work might rest, and between which the sluices for the passage of the mountain waters might be fixed.

'Upon an average, between the neap and spring tides, the gates are calculated to remain closed against the sea for about three hours each tide. The piers are of excellent masonry and solid construction, and the width of the summit of the embankment itself was taken at six yards upon a calculation that its work progressively expand towards the base of the work in proportion to the depth of the stream.

'It is now agreed, I believe, that in attempting the construction of the work, a fundamental error has been committed, as by beginning the embankment from the two ends at once, and progressively advancing towards the middle of the frith, the greatest struggle was exactly reserved for the period of completion. But the difficulty was not only reserved but greatly aggravated by this mistake, for the water gradually compressed on both sides became furious in its course, almost doubled its depth by the violence of its action, and bore away in its rapid recess ere they could reach the bottom a mass of materials which could only be replaced by a most consuming expenditure. But the work was still pushed forwards until it was found that the bases of sand themselves were swept away from beneath the embankment. To meet this evil, mats of rushes made of prodigious extent were floated to the appointed spots, over which they were spread, sunk, and fixed to the bottom by the incumbent weight of the stones thrown upon them. Upon these were laid platforms of a width still greater than that of the base of the work itself, beyond which at low water they may be seen spreading.

'Five hundred thousand cubical yards were calculated to be sufficient for the completion of the embankment, which was to be about sixteen hundred yards in length. The continual loss of materials, however, must have tended to increase this quantity, a loss doubtless rendered greater by the shaly nature of the stone employed, which, by the exposure of its large flat surfaces to the action of the water, must in many instances have been borne away to a considerable distance. The gunpowder alone used in the separation of the rock must amount to a serious sum, and in its effects the frequent explosions going off recall the recollection of a siege upon a small scale. The work has at the same time been facilitated by laying down upon it a railway as it advanced, and thus making it contribute to its own construction. Boats are also used for the purpose of conveying the materials where they are to be thrown.

'The quantity of ground taken in by the enclosure is supposed to amount to many thousand acres, and of its quality a favourable opinion is entertained on account of the shells and other marine exuviae contained in it. A great increase of soil is also anticipated from the alluvion of sand below the embankment, which, by breaking the advance of the tide reduces it to a partial state of stagnation, and thus obliges it to deposit the sand and earth suspended while in motion in it. The noble granite mole in Dublin Bay has already produced this effect, as behind it a tract has thus been accumulated of a height sufficient in many places to overtop itself, and of an extent so great as to occasion a legal contest for its possession between the Corporation of Dublin and the holders of the adjacent property, in whose favour, I understand, the decision of the law was given.

'An incidental advantage to both Caernarvonshire and Merionethshire may probably be produced by this work, as along it the traveller may pass at any time of the tide, nor be exposed to the inconveniences of the fords, at all times unpleasant and sometimes dangerous. The tedious curve also, by the carriage-way over Pont Aberglasslyn, will be avoided and time and distance thus be both saved. The markets, as also the extent of Tre-Madoc, may reasonably be expected to increase when access to it from the neighbouring parishes of Merionethshire shall be opened.'

Chapter Eight

Dr Samuel H. Spiker, Librarian to His Majesty the King of Prussia, arrived in Britain in September 1815 for an extended study of England, Wales and Scotland. His exploration lasted 14 months and formed the basis of an excellent yet little-known book entitled *Travels through England, Wales and Scotland in the Year 1816*. He summarised his motivation for the visit thus:

> 'Having been engaged for several years in the study of the history, constitution and literature of Great Britain, I felt an eager desire to become acquainted with a country the internal perfection and improvement of which I had, from everything produced in it, conceived the most favourable opinion.'

Thomas Telford's road from London to Holyhead had the incidental effect of opening North Wales to coach traffic from the English Midlands. Work was in progress at the time of Spiker's journey:

> 'The construction of this road must have been attended with vast trouble, from the number of projecting rocks that obstruct the way. Marks of the gunpowder are everywhere visible in the rocks which bound the left side of the road. I asked the labourers employed in spreading stones and levelling the surface how long they had been employed on it; and they answered me 10 months, which is comparitively speaking a very short period when we consider that the length of the road is at least from 12 to 15 miles and that besides the main road 10 or 12 well-built stone bridges, some of one and others of two arches, have also been erected. We must allow that it will be difficult to match the undertaking in the same space of time in any other country.'

The challenge of bridging the Menai Straits had attracted the attention of earlier engineers than Telford, notably John Golborne in 1783, William Jessop in 1784 and John Rennie in 1801. Their various schemes had all been rejected by the admiralty as obstructing the passage of shipping. It was also feared that the Menai would be completely blocked by the temporary supports erected during construction. Faced with the same constraints, Telford suggested bridging the Menai with a rigid iron arch 500 feet in length. This would be supported during construction not from below but from above. The admiralty remained unimpressed. Although the centre of Telford's proposed arch was high enough for the tallest masts, the curving iron sides presented a risk of damaging any vessel which strayed from the middle of the Straits. In 1818, Telford proposed a long-span suspension bridge. This too would be supported from above, not as a temporary contrivance but as a permanent part of the structure. The underside of the bridge would be flat, not arched, and high enough above the water to present no threat whatever to passing vessels. The only disturbance to Menai shipping during construction would be the few hours needed to raise each suspension chain.

Work on the Menai suspension bridge commenced in 1819 using limestone building blocks quarried from Penmon on Anglesey's north-east coast. These were transported by boat and along a temporary railway to build two massive towers, Telford called them 'pyramids', which would take the weight of the supporting chains. On April 26th 1825, the pyramids and their approach roads having been completed, Telford directed the raising of the first chain. The engineer in charge of construction, William Alexander Provis, described the proceedings:

> 'Though one of the party, it is not vanity that induces me, but an act of justice to all concerned, to say that no operation could be conducted in a more regular and satisfactory manner. Every man was at his post and anxious to do all he could to ensure success. Not the slightest accident, nor even a single blunder occurred, from the time of casting off the raft till the chain was secured in its places.
>
> 'Mr Telford now ascended the pyramid to satisfy himself

that all was right, and there, surrounded by his assistant, the contractors and as many as could find a place to stand on, received the congratulations of many a friend to the bridge. The hats on the pyramids were soon off, the signal was understood by all round, and three cheers loud and long closed the labours of the day.

'This ceremony was scarcely over when one of the workmen got astride the chain and passed himself over it to the opposite side of the Strait. Another followed soon after and actually had the temerity to raise himself up and walk over 30 or 40 feet of the middle of the chain, though the slightest slip must have sent him to destruction, the chain being only nine inches wide and its height at that time above the surface of the water not less than 120 feet.

'That nothing should damp the ardour of the men, nor check those feelings which gave a willing impulse to their exertions, plenty of ale with substantial accompaniments were provided for them, in the disposal of which they showed the same active zeal which had marked their previous conduct.'

John Smith, distinguished from other John Smiths as 'Lecturer on Education', saw the Menai Bridge before its official opening and wrote a brief account of an unofficial crossing in *A Guide to Bangor, Beaumaris, Snowdonia and Other Parts of North Wales*:

'Although the planks were not properly fastened and the least carelessness might have been fatal, we proceeded fearlessly along the vast curvature, 590 feet in length, to the pier on the Anglesey side. Over the centre of the straits we sat down on a small stage, which had been placed there for the band of musicians on the day when the last chain was suspended.

'Admiration of the stupendous and almost superhuman work, and of Mr Telford's consummate skill, breathed in every observation we could make, and I thought that when death should deprive the country of the further services of

that able engineer his epitaph, simple as that upon Sir
Christopher Wren in St. Paul's Cathedral, "Si monumentum
quaeris, circumspice!" will be abundantly sufficient, if it
state that his monument is suspended over the Straits of
Menai.'

The Menai suspension bridge was opened for traffic the
following January. Telford himself wrote of the occasion:

'Upon my report of the state of the works, the
Commissioners determined that the passage over the bridge
should be opened on the 30th of January 1826. The weather
about that time proved very stormy and, previously to the
opening day, Sir Henry Parnell and myself examined the
entire structure and found all necessary arrangements made.
On Monday morning, at half past one o'clock, the London
mail-coach, occupied by W. A. Provis, W. Hazledine, the
two junior Wilsons, Thomas Rhodes and the mailcoach
superintendant, was the first that passed across the estuary,
at the level of 100 feet above that tideway which heretofore
had presented a decisive obstruction to travellers.

'The Chester mail passed at half-past three o'clock and Sir
Henry Parnell, with myself, drove repeatedly over; about
nine o'clock, and during the whole of the day, was an
uninterrupted succession of passing carriages, horsemen and
pedestrians who had assembled to witness and enjoy the
novelty, and in the evening all the workmen were regaled
with a joyous festival.'

The Reverend Peter Bayley Williams' *Tourist's Guide through the
County of Carnarvon* (1828) gives the original tolls for crossing the'
Menai Bridge, adding that "Although the tolls are exceedingly
low, yet the amount collected the first day exceeded £18":

2s 6d	Stage or mail coach.
3s 0d	Post chaise, coach, landau, berlin, barouche or

	other carriage with four wheels and four horses.
2s 0d	Ditto with four wheels and two horses.
6d	Chase, chair or gig with two wheels.
1s 0d	Wagon, wain or such other carriage with five wheels.
6d	Cart or other carriage with two wheels.
2d	A horse, mule or ass not drawing any carriage.
1s 0d	A drove of oxen, cows or neat cattle per score.
6d	A drove of hogs, calves, sheep or lambs per score.
1d	A foot passenger.

The son of a surgeon, Robert Hasell Newell (1778-1852) was educated at Colchester School and at St John's College, Cambridge. He entered the church but later studied art under William Payne. The decline of the wild goat is noted in his *Letters on the Scenery of Wales*, published in 1821. Where the 20th century traveller finds sheep, his predecessors up to the early 19th century tended to find goats. These were in still earlier times a source of raw material for the wig-making industry:

'Some profitable excursions may be made round Beddgelert, for almost every step presents a new picture. The mountain which faces the inn is often drawn, and not, perhaps, from a better station. The outline is good, and there are some handsome ash trees under it; the ash grows remarkably gracefully in this neighbourhood.

'A stroll towards Pontaberglassllyn will furnish some useful studies of water and rock. Of the latter it has been justly remarked that "there is nothing landscape painters in general have studied more negligently. The modes of stratification, and the peculiar characters of the different kinds, are seldom sufficiently distinguished, even where they are most strongly marked".

'As you descend toward the bridge, the mountains at one particular part of the valley appear all but to meet. This view may be worth taking for its singularity and as a characteristic scene of barren grandeur. The winding road, river and mountainous perspective give variety to the picture and relieve its heaviness.

'Goats are sometimes seen here. I surprised two on the rocks near the water, and the only place where I ever met with any except in a wood near Bualt. It is a ludicrous fancy, which some take up, that in Wales goats, harps and ponies are to be found at every turn. Goats are all private property now; none, as formerly, running entirely wild. But they rather seem superseded by sheep which almost rival them in adventurous spirit, so unlike their English timidity.

'Goats are useful animals in a landscape, marking its character and affording considerable variety of colour and attitude. Claude introduces them freely: I have seen a whole herd in some of his pictures. He sometimes puts them, with good effect, in shade, upon the edge of a precipice, to break the outline.'

Contemporary with Newell's Tour, *The Cambrian Tourist or Post-Chaise Companion through Wales* was published anonymously and, despite at least as cavalier an attitude to place-name spelling as any earlier visitor, has enough originality to merit quotation. The author's guide is credited in a footnote as: 'Evan Thomas, works in the copper-works at Aber-Glaslin, and lives at a place called Dous Coreb, about a mile and a half beyond Beddgelert':

'An intelligent man offered himself as our guide to the rich copper mines in the vicinity of Pont Aber-Glaslyn. This miner, having worked both here and at the Paris Mountain, confidently asserted that one pound of this ore was now esteemed equivalent to twice the quantity produced in Anglesey. Stupendous cliffs, by the road side, literally rise 860 feet perpendicularly and hang in the most capricious forms over the torrent which, straggling amongst the recesses of stone, is hastening forward to disembogue itself into the estuary of Traeth Mawr. The pass is not more than 70 feet; after much rain, it is entirely inundated by the overflowings of the Glaslyn which reflected, as in a mirror, the blackness of the impending cliffs. On the Caernarvonshire side are several lead mines but they have not proved sufficiently rich to reward the labour of working.

'The situation of our inn at Beddgelert is very romantic and would form an interesting drawing by taking in a small bridge of two arches below the house. It is completely encircled by lofty mountains which may be considered as subject to the "cloud-capt Snowdon".

'We engaged the miner as our conductor over the mountain, who entertained us much with displaying in strong colours the tricks and impositions of his brother guides, and more particularly of the methodistical landlord of our inn who is generally employed on these occasions. His pride, too, is not a little elevated by having conducted the Great Doctor to its highest summit; this seeming ridiculous phrase for some time puzzled us but we have since found out that our guide was talking of no less a man than the present respectable and learned Dean of Christchurch who ascended this mountain last year. Though our guide was pompous and rather too partial to the marvelous, yet I strenuously recommended him to all tourists.

'At half past twelve we started from our inn, determined to see the sun rise from its highest summit. The night was now very dark and we could just discover that the top of Snowdon was entirely enveloped in a thick impenetrable mist: this unpropitious omen staggered our resolutions and we for some time hesitated respecting our farther progress; but, our guide assuring us that his comfortable cottage was not far distant, we again plucked up resolution and, quitting the high way about two miles on the Caernarvon road, we turned to the right, through a boggy unpleasant land and in danger of losing our shoes every step we took. This soon brought us to the comfortable cot, the filth and dirtiness of which can better be imagined than described: a worm-eaten bed, two small stools, and a table fixed to the wall, composed the whole of his furniture; two fighting cocks were perched on a beam, which Thomas seemed to pride himself in the possession of; the smoke of the fire ascended through a small hole in the roof of this comfortable mansion, the door of which did not appear proof against the "churlish chiding of the winter blast".

'Such indeed was the situation of this Cambrian mountaineer and, though, in our own opinion, misery, poverty and dirt personified seemed to be the real inhabitants of this cottage, yet there was something prepossessing in his character; for frequently, with the greatest vehemence imaginable, and in the true style of an Anchorite, he declared that "though he boasted not riches, yet he boasted of independence and, though he possessed not wealth, yet he possessed the home of happiness, an honest breast".

'The morning appearing to wear a more favourable aspect, we again sallied forth; the bogs, however, still rendered it extremely unpleasant. But this inconvenience was only temporary: we soon came to a part of the mountain entirely composed of loose stones and fragments of rock which, by affording a very treacherous footing, render you liable to perpetual falls. The mountain now became much steeper, the path less rocky and our mountaineer, the higher we proceeded, more induced to exhibit his agility by occasionally running down a short precipice and then, by a loud shout of vociferation, showing us the obedience of the sheep who instantaneously flocked round him at the sound of his voice. It is singular, the caution implanted in this animal by instinct for the mutual protection of each other; from the liberty they enjoy, they seldom congregate in one flock but are generally discovered grazing in parties from six to a dozen, one of which is regularly appointed sentinel to watch the motions of their inveterate enemies (foxes and birds of prey) which infest this mountain.

'A wider expanse of the hemisphere disclosed itself and every object below us gradually diminished as we ascended. The freshness of the mountain whetted our appetites and our conductor, with very little persuasion, soon influenced us to open our little basket of provisions. The sun, the "rich hair'd youth of morn", was just peeping from its bed and, having refreshed ourselves, with eager impatience we again climbed the rugged precipice for we had still a considerable height to ascend.

'We now passed several steep declivities by a narrow path not more than three yards wide with a dreadful perpendicular on each side, the sight of which almost turned us giddy. As we were passing this hazardous path, a thick mist enveloped us and an impenetrable abyss appeared on both sides; the effect, indeed, can scarcely be conceived; our footing seemed very insecure and a total destruction would have been the consequence of one false step. The air grew intensely cold and, by our guide's recommendation, we a second time produced our pistol of rum, diluted with milk, but this cordial must be used with caution as a very small quantity of strong liquor affects the head, owing to the rarefaction of the air.

'On our reaching the summit, all our difficulties were forgotten and our imaginary complaints overborne with exclamations of wonder, surprise and admiration. The light thin misty cloud, which had for some time enveloped us, as if by enchantment, suddenly dispersed; the whole ocean appears illuminated by a fiery substance and all the subject hills below us, for they resembled mole-hills, were gradually tinged by the rich glow of the sun whose orb, becoming at length distinctly visible, displayed the whole island of Anglesey so distinctly that we described, as in a map, its flat and uncultivated plains, bounded by the rich and inexhaustible Paris Mountain, in the vicinity of Holyhead. The point on which we were standing did not exceed a square of five yards and we sickened almost at the sight of the steep precipices which environed us; round it is a small parapet formed by the customary tribute of all strangers who visit this summit and to which we likewise contributed by placing a large stone on its top; this parapet, indeed, sheltered us from the chilly cold and protected us from the piercing wind which this height must naturally be exposed to.

'We remained in this situation for a considerable time and endeavoured, without success, to enumerate the several lakes, forests, woods and counties which were exposed to us in one view; but, lost and confounded with the innumerable objects worthy of admiration, and regardless of the chilling cold, we took a distinct survey of the Isle of Man, together with a faint prospect of the Highlands in Ireland, which appeared just visibly skirting the distant horizon; but another object soon engrossed all our attention. For we unexpectedly observed long billows of vapour tossing about half way down the mountain, totally excluding the country below and occasionally dispersing, and partially revealing its features; while above, the azure expanse of the heavens remained obscured by the thinnest mist. This, however, was of no long continuance: a thick cloud presently wet us through and the point on which we were standing could alone be distinguished. As there appeared little or no chance of the clouds dispersing, we soon commenced our descent.

'The first two miles of our descent we by no means found difficult but, wishing to take a minute survey of the picturesque Pass of Llanberris, we changed the route generally prescribed to strangers and descended a rugged and almost perpendicular path in opposition to the proposals of our guide who strenuously endeavoured to dissuade us from the attempt, alleging the difficulty of the steep and relating a melancholy story of a gentleman who, many years back, had broken his leg. This had no effect. We determined to proceed and the Vale of Llanberris amply rewarded us for the trouble.'

G. J. Freeman's account of a Snowdon ascent from Beddgelert is so laboured and expansive that one feels, reading it, almost as though one is ascending with him. It is evident from his *Sketches in Wales* (1823) that he knew the mountain well, except for 'the ascent from Capel Curig' which was the starting point for Pyg Track and Llyn Llydaw explorations before the opening of the Penygwryd hotel. Though aware of one route from Beddgelert, he either did not know that which came to be called the Watkin Path or considered it insufficiently popular to merit description:

'There are four common ascents to Snowdon, namely, from Dolbadarn, from Llyn Cwellyn, from Capel Curig, and from Beddgelert. There is another direct from Llanberis, which is very toilsome, from the prodigious walls of rocks that lie in the way. But they who chance to be at the Llanberis Inn are always conducted along the lake-side to the neighbourhood of Dolbadarn before they commence the ascent, which lies on an inclined plane and is conducted by zig-zag paths along the ridges that impend over Llanberis vale.

'That from Llyn Cwellyn [Snowdon Ranger Path] is possibly the easiest of all the ascents; at least, I remember a good deal of grass, and plain walking. In the higher part it attains a direction pretty nearly the same as that from Dolbadarn. The guide's house stands near the lake, by the road side.

'The ascent from Capel Curig I do not know but there is a great deal of ground to be gone over before it is commenced, at least four miles. A similar objection may be made against the ascent from Beddgelert, for you are taken two miles or more on the Caernarvon road before the business of ascending begins. Of this ascent it is now, however, for me to speak. I certainly prefer it myself and, having recommended it to my friends, was very glad to find in the sequel that they highly approved of my choice.

'The early aspect of the morning had been anything but favourable but, before the business of breakfast was over, the sun looked forth in his loveliness and lit up all our countenances with pleasure. Our guide, whom I found at Mrs Prichard's kitchen fire with his canteen and wallet already slung and his staff beside him, a willing fellow ready to brush gaiters or toast bread, to chatter of his vocation and to tell stories of craven or of adventurous climbers, told me he had good hopes of the day on the whole, though he feared the hill tops would not be free from clouds; and informed me also that we were not the only candidates for the excursion but were to be joined by another party, consisting of a gentleman and three ladies.

'In fact a busy note of preparation now ran through the house and every one was on the alert. Mr B.'s car, and five horses, were brought up to the door. One of the steeds was for my son, on whose superfluous activity it was necessary to put a veto for his health and strength's sake; Mr B. had procured two others to be used by the ladies of our party as their occasion needed and, reflecting that we were to retrace our route of the preceding evening for some distance, he ordered the car to take all who were willing along the road till it became necessary to diverge. This proved a comfortable plan for the car was able to proceed more than a quarter of a mile out of the high road up to a farm-house which became a place of rendezvous for all of us. Here, indeed, we collected first into one body and proceeded under our guide's direction.

'Our party altogether, with the guide and his man, consisted of fourteen. Community of interests soon drew us all into conversation and we found that our companions had landed not long before at Beaumaris from Liverpool, had visited Bangor and Caernarvon, and were bound for Aberystwith and Tenby. In fact they were set in for a regular Welch tour and I afterwards gave them a few memoranda for their journey, which I hope proved useful. It was singular enough that they were perfectly well acquainted with the name of my friend B. though not with his person, and that B.

himself was equally struck by their telling him they resided in Somersetshire where he had a brother. It was at length discovered that B.'s brother and our Snowdon friends were intimately acquainted. The chain of union was no sooner developed than it was relinquished.

'We began to mount near to a rapid torrent which I understood to be called Afon-twyn [Afon Colwyn] and which descends from under the Aran. The peak of Snowdon bore at this time N.E. The Aran was on the right, a huge precipice on an elevated bank, and presently on the left hand we opened Llyn Cwellyn between Moel Eilio and Mynnydd Mawr. We made a tolerable straight line among rough masses of rock rising out of swamps and moory vegetable earth till we came to a spot called Lethog [Llethog] when, having got over the broad uninteresting base that the mountain throws out on this side, we found the ground suddenly break and conduct the eye into one of those profound and desolate hollows which seem intended to discover the very bowels of the earth! Deeply seated in its obscure bottom, with their lines as distinctly marked as if on a map, we observed four pools. The farthest from us, under the mural steeps of Snowdon, they told me, was called Ffynnon glas, the blue pool, and near it Llyn Coch, the red pool. The two others were called Llyn-y-nadroedd, the adder's pool, and Llyn fynnon gwas, the servant's pool. They were inclosed by a semicircular range of sublime precipices, the most distant of which, being those of the Red Ridge, rose point above point into the clouds.

'Continuing our way along the edge of these cliffs, called Clogwyn or the precipice, we arrived at a spot where the guide informed us we must leave our horses. They who were on horseback accordingly dismounted and we all betook ourselves to our feet, moving very slowly up a steep and very stony hill whose angle of inclination was much the same as that of a house roof, till we arrived at the commencement of Y Clawdd Coch, or the red ridge, a spot that astonished us by its grandeur. My friend Mr B., who arrived there first, cried out to me with uplifted hands and in a fit of enthusiasm, that he had never seen Snowdon till now though he had been on the mountain twice before! I was delighted with this expression of his feelings. But we were beside ourselves with the view we here enjoyed which was in truth the most extraordinary I ever had the fortune to look on.

'Let the reader picture to himself, in the first place, the earth failing on each side of him, and descending in precipices, leaving him only a narrow portion to support his footsteps, and that to such a place he comes suddenly after a long ascent which has shook his nerves and distended every muscle of his limbs! These precipices are of no moderate depth but reach into the very heart of the mountain. Stones dropped from either hand of a man standing on the centre of the ridge would find their headlong way into valleys of a thousand feet in depth and will be, when they stopped, as Mr Bingley conjectures, more than half a mile apart! The length of this ridge is upwards of two hundred yards and, at one or two places, it is not above four feet across! It is in no place equal and level but encumbered by stone and overhung by spiral rock, presenting the most fantastic features. Such was our station; what were the views we had from it!

'Looking before us, the cliffs of Y-Wyddfa were seen in perspective, forming the segment of a circle whose concave was towards us, and connecting themselves by means of a ridge less lofty than that where we were, with Lliwedd, a great mountain towards Nant Gwynan. The tops of both were veiled by a uniform cloud that cast a very deep shade over their sides. Just between them, and beyond the ridge, there was an opening or vista (to which fleecy festoons of thin mist formed the framework) wherein we saw the stony face of the great Glyder, many miles off, strongly illuminated by sunshine, every rock reflecting the solar ray with such dazzling brilliancy that the whole looked like a paradise of diamonds. I never shall forget the magical effect of this scene!

In three or four minutes it had vanished. The clouds broke asunder and exposed the rude summit of Lliwedd, on one side of which we saw the lakes of Capel Curig and, on the other, parts of the beautiful Nant Gwynan where a few verdant fields and rich plantations looked smiling in the midst of desolation. The sun poured a flood of light over all this side of the country and, with our eyes turned on such a delightful prospect, we sat down to take refreshment, resting our backs against the rocks.

I chanced presently to climb to a pinnacle above the heads of the party, when I had the luck to witness one of those fearful and striking contrasts which can only occur in such a region as this. The ladies, on my calling to them, joined me immediately, and stood on the very top of these tremendous rocks without the slightest indication of fear. On one side of the ridge was sunshine; perfect obscurity on the other. On the right hand every vale and hollow, every peak and cliff, every falling torrent, pool and mountain, was displayed in bright light and our view was unbounded. On the left, volumes of dense clouds seemed to rise up en masse from beneath our feet, out of a profound and fathomless abyss, utterly concealing all remote things and so partially revealing nearer objects as to inspire those sublime emotions that come of extreme privation. Mrs B., who stood beside me, shuddered at the sight of this chasm, whose depth and terrors were thus left wholly to her imagination and, turning the contrary way, declared she thought she saw another and better world. We walked leisurely along the ridge, seeing on one side and deprived of all view on the other, vigilant to observe a change.

'We were shortly gratified in an unexpected manner. The clouds on the left opened at two points in telescopic vistas and discovered two lakes. These looked ghastly; the dun livid hue of the clouds gave them the appearance of cauldrons of molten lead. The light that was spread over them was not to be taken for that of heaven but was rather the dull infernal glare of witchery and incantation. This singular vision continued some time, keeping us stationary; at length the wind dispersed the vapours and we found we had been looking on the lakes in Nant-beris.

'Leaving Y Clawydd Coch, not without the most grateful recollections of the succession of prospects it had afforded us during every stage of our progress, we began to mount again. My son and Mr Brettell, both exceedingly anxious to reach the top, pushed on before and were there first. But, between the ridge and that summit, there is a good deal of climbing and some of our party were much fatigued.

'We reached the apex of Snowdon in four hours and three quarters after we had left Beddgelert. We did not remain here so long as we did at the red-ridge. The view was not clear and the attractions less than those we had left behind. The mountain was sometimes enveloped in thick clouds so that we could scarcely see anything and in a moment afterwards a ray of sunshine seemed to penetrate and dispel them; but for the most part a quantity of light fleecy misty vapours, half opaque, half transparent, kept continually sailing over and about the mountain, acting as a veil upon a beautiful woman, which we were so much the more anxious to see through. But our anxiety was fruitless. The view to the north was hindered by a gloomy atmosphere; southward we could not see beyond Harlech; the western prospect was the clearest, the line of the Irish sea over the rock of Holyhead being very plain; but that unobstructed view, which everyone seems to desire who goes on a mountain, we had not.

'As we sat in different groups on this rounded and ruined summit, I could not help thinking on the various feelings and employments of the different persons who have resorted to the same spot. Man, destined for immortality, seems much more mutable than matter. The mountain remains. They who visit it come and depart, live and die, and are forgotten! And how unlike are they to each other and to themselves! What merriment has there been here! What alarm! What joy!

What devotion! What folly! What enthusiasm! What pride! What poetry! What terror! I have heard of a man who crept down on his hands and knees; of another who, spreading his garments, leaped upward on the buoyant wind! What strange variety of feeling!

'We added another variety to the heap; a new one I would say, for I suppose there hardly was a letter written here before. Yes; a letter was actually begun and completed on the summit of Snowdon! And it was regularly Snowdonian for, though it contained the sentiments of five persons, who took the pen in their turn, yet all those five spoke only of one subject and her magnificence. This letter was sent to my mother.

'In our descent from the mountain, we rested again at the red-ridge, where we were again favoured with a view of great beauty. The sun's descending orb burnished the waters of the bay of Cardigan with a bright yellow light while above, and over all the mountains of the coast, the clouds hung dark and heavily. The peaks of the Peninsular of Lleyn were illumined, as well as the sands of Traeth Bach and Traeth Mawr, which were the colour of gold. The extreme distances were of a light purple. In the lower part of the descent, for we did not vary from our morning's route, I selected a spot for the accompanying view, in which the black precipices of Mynydd Mawr are seen impending over Llyn Cwellyn. In the middle distance I observed the towers of Caernarvon castle beautifully thrown against the pale waters of the Menai. Yet further is Anglesea while the rock of Holyhead terminated the land view, having the line of the Irish sea over it.

'On our return to Beddgelert at six o'clock, Mrs Prichard set before us some broiled salmon and chickens, which met with a most cordial reception on our parts. I must not forget to mention that, previous to our departure in the morning our hostess brought out several sticks to assist us in climbing, and among others a tall, stout but light, fir staff which I selected for myself and was so well pleased with that I begged it of her on my return. She gave it to me readily, though not without enhancing the value of the gift by telling me it was her own constant companion and support whenever she went out to visit her neighbours. This stick became a regular pet of mine and, like that of pets in general, its end was unfortunate. After having carried it about an hundred miles, I was just setting out from Tan-y-bwlch for the purpose of ascending Moelwyn when I saw a snake in my path, in dispatching which my poor stick broke in two!'

Chapter Nine

An apology for the low productivity of North Welsh agriculture, and for the deplorable behaviour of the local goats, is contained in William Cathrall's *History of North Wales*, published in 1828:

'This county, in general, being rocky and mountainous, is more adapted for the purposes of pasturage than the culture of grain; and the inhabitants of the upland districts in particular, having been accustomed to purchase the principal part of the quantity of corn necessary for their sustenance to the Caernarvon market, from the Anglesey farmers, pay more attention to their flocks and herds than to the cultivation of their lands; and even in the lowlands, where the soil is good, and might be cleared and improved to great advantage, it is too generally suffered to lie nearly in a state of nature, over-run with small stunted gorse and heath, briars and thorns, and covered with large stones: the fences are also low and crooked, and badly made with small loose stones, so that the cattle are constantly trespassing, and frequently destroying the small quantity of corn which the unskillful or indolent farmer has sown in his fields.

'This is the general appearance of a great part of this county, particularly where the farmers are employed for many months in the year in the carriage of slate, copper and lead ore, etcetera to the different harbours and sea-ports: and many of them having no capital, and no other means of paying their rents, are thus tempted to neglect their lands; and when seed-time is approaching they remain at home for a few weeks, and plough and harrow their lands in a very imperfect and injudicious manner and sow their seed without any, or with very little, manure; they likewise frequently take three, four and five successive crops off the same land and then suffer it (according to their idea) to recover itself from this exhaustion, instead of laying it down in good tilth with clover and hay seed.

159

'There are, no doubt, many laudable and excellent exceptions to this culpable negligence and inattention to agriculture, and the Agricultural Society established in this county has been of considerable utility in this respect, as it holds out rewards to tenants who keep their farms in the neatest order, and who raise the best crops of turnips etcetera.

'Before the late Lord Penrhyn's rail-road was completed, most of his tenants were engaged in the carriage of his slate from the quarry to Aber Cegin [Port Penrhyn], and many of them were of opinion that, when they should be deprived of this mode of employment for their teams, they would be unable to pay their rents. When, however, this precarious resource, which scarcely remunerated them, was cut off, they betook themselves sedulously and earnestly to the cultivation of their farms, and they soon found that they paid their rents more regularly, and that the most frugal of them had a small sum at the end of the year in reserve for the day of adversity.

'Many allowances, however, ought to be made for the backward state of agriculture in this county, for the farmers labour under great disadvantages and have many difficulties to contend with: in general, they hold their lands under rack-rent; in the next place they have no capital and consequently their stock is small and the implements of husbandry very simple and ill adapted for the purposes intended. The lands adjoining the mountains and along the sides of the valleys are also covered with large stones and fragments of rocks, and on that account are expensive to clear, and there is nothing to excite their emulation as they see but few examples of improved cultivation except amongst gentlemen of considerable property whom they consider it would be presumption in them to follow. In addition to the above circumstances, the badness of the roads may be mentioned as another great obstacle: they are in general exceedingly steep, rocky and stony, and very narrow, in many places not admitting of two carts to pass; besides lime is expensive as the stones are for the most part brought from Anglesey and the coals to burn them from South Wales.

'The Welsh princes were greatly attached to the amusements of the field: hunting, fishing, hawking and fowling constituted their chief pleasure, exercise and amusement, and the Welsh court was for a great part of the year migratory or ambulatory, that is the prince with his attendants took his rounds or made regular circuits through the most mountainous parts of Gwynedd and provision was made by law for the maintenance of his hounds, horses and attendants in the neighbourhood of the llys (or palace). In these excursions, Creigiau'r Eiry or Snowdon Forest claimed his chief attention and seemed to have been the principal scene of attraction as appears from a number of places still bearing the name of Llys, and the different castles and manors in the intermediate neighbourhood of Snowdon which originally belonged to the Welsh princes. One of these (Llys yn Dinorwig, in the parish of Llanddeiniolen) was first conferred on Sir Grufydd Lloyd, of Tregarnedd in Anglesey, by Edward 1st, then at Rhuddlan castle, when he brought him the news of the birth of the first Prince of Wales of the English line. The king's weir of Aberglaslyn, his mills of Dwyvor in Eivionydd, and the lands at Dolbenmaen and the constableship of Cricketh [Criccieth] castle were bestowed on Sir Howel y Fwyall (or the battle axe) who is reported to have taken John, the French king, prisoner and was knighted by the Black Prince at the battle of Poictiers [Poitiers]. 'The Welsh princes has also a seat and castle at Aber where they frequently resided, another near Llyniau Nantlli [Nantlle] in the parish of Llanllyvni, called Bala Deulyn, where Edward 1st spent several days after his conquest of Wales.

'Besides these conveniences of hunting, this part of North Wales was very strong in a military point of view for here were beheld a range of lofty mountains extending from one sea to the other, i.e. from the great Ormshead and

Penmaenmawr near Conwy to the Rivals near Clynnog on one side and Gest near Penmorva on the other, and having in addition to these the river Conwy as a barrier on the north, and Traethmawr on the south, over which the Welsh usually retreated when they were pressed by the English arms.

'The principal defiles likewise which opened through that range of vast mountains were secured by strong fortifications. The castle of Diganwy was placed on the banks of the Conwy nearly opposite to the present town of that name; that of Caer Rhun was situated at the foot of Bwlch y Ddan Faen on the east side with a fort at Aber on the west; Dolwyddelen nearly central as a place of safety between the mountains; a watch-tower at Nant Frangcon; Dolbadarn castle in Nant Peris and Castell Cidwm in Nant y Bettws, with a fort at Dinas Emrys in Nantgwynant, and the passes of Traethmawr and Traethbach guarded by the strong castles of Harlech on one side and Cricketh on the other, with a watch-tower at Penrhyn Daudreath, another at Cesail Gyfarch and a fort at Dolbenmaen. All these various fortifications, placed in the most advantageous situations, marked for a rude age great military sagacity.'

In the valleys between the mountains the land is generally divided into four separate allotments. The meadows and lower enclosures are appropriated to hay and corn; next above these are the cow's pastures; still higher are the friths or large kind of parks, where young cattle and horses usually graze; and above all, and occupying the sides and summits of the highest mountains, are the sheep pastures; and when some of the wethers, from three to five years old, become fat (as they often do) in these situations, they are considered to be the most delicious mutton.

'The walls between the cattle-pastures and sheep-walks are generally made five feet three or four inches high; but not withstanding this precaution, some of the rams and wethers are so light and active that they frequently contrive to leap over them and make incursions upon the vale below. Some of the most sagacious of these marauders will frequently go along the whole line of wall, followed by their weaker companions, like soldiers examining the strength of an enemy's citadel, and wherever they deem a breach practicable, they retreat a few yards and then run with violence, and attempt either to get over or to knock down one of the coping-stones; and if one of these can be dislodged, a breach can be effected, which becomes wider as the others follow.

'The number of goats in this county is of late years greatly diminished, as gentlemen of landed property discourage their tenants from keeping them, on account of their being so destructive to young plantations; and as they are great climbers, and fond of browsing on the young sprouts and tender shoots, it is found to be very difficult, if not impossible, to make the fences sufficiently high to guard against their depredations: when they are pursued by dogs they retreat to the fastnesses of the rocks and there have been instances of their having descended from one ledge or cliff to another until at last they have got into such a situation that they could not be extricated without lowering a lad down with one rope round his body and another in his hand to fasten about the goat, and thus both have been drawn up again by strong active men standing near the summit of the rock.'

Turning his attention from goats to linguistics, Cathrall offers a few English/Welsh equivalent expressions, avoiding the pitfall which traps many phrasebook compilers who forget that their questions should permit a very simple response:

'The English tourist may find the following directions and queries useful in travelling through the less frequented parts of Wales.

Good morning to you.	Bore da i chwi.
How do you do?	Sut yr ydych chwy?

How are they at home?	Sut i mae nhw gartref?
Put up my horse.	Rhowch fy ngheffyl yn y'stabl.
Give my horse some water.	Rhowch ddŵr i'm ceffyl.
Feed my horse.	Ffidiwch fy ngheffyl.
Clean my horse.	Glanhewch fy ngheffyl.
Bring me a candle.	Dowch a chanwyll i mi.
A bedroom candle.	Canwyll ystafell wely.
Show me my room.	Dangoswch i mi fy ystafell.
I want to be shaved.	Mae arnaf eisio fy shavio.'

The London to Holyhead road was completed in 1827 and contributed to a growing output of published tours of North Wales. Tourist trade increased still more dramatically in the mid 19th century with the arrival of the railways, George Stephenson accomplishing for the steam locomotive what Telford had achieved for the horse-drawn coach. Narrow-gauge railways followed later, constructed to serve local slate quarries and copper mines. These roles were cut short by a rapid expansion of maritime trade made possible by steam-powered shipping which allowed slate, copper and another local product, granite, to be landed from overseas at lower cost than the Welsh-won materials. Several of these lines now carry human traffic through some of the wildest and most beautiful scenery to be found anywhere in Britain, notably the Festiniog Railway which descends on a gradual incline from Blaenau Ffestiniog to Porthmadog. The original slate wagons also carried horses which pulled the empty trucks back up to Blaenau after using gravity alone for the long downward trundle.

Most of the hotels in Snowdonia date from the age of railway construction and retain, in one guise or another, the stables from which horse-drawn vehicles ferried guests to and from the nearby stations. Though in real terms more expensive than today, railway travel was substantially cheaper than horse-back or horse-drawn travel over long distances. Not until the 20th century did motor vehicles bring road travel back into ascendancy, a circumstance which Telford foresaw in his encouragement of steam-powered road transport.

Travellers willing to explore as pedestrians did not necessarily make their journey to Snowdonia on foot. By the 19th century, horse-drawn coaches on well-made roads were reducing long-distance journey times to an extent that would have been a credit to early motor vehicles. In 1837, Joseph Onwhyn published his *Hints to Pedestrians, or How to Enjoy a Three-Weeks Ramble through North and South Wales*:

> 'On Saturday evening the 10th September 1836 I left London by the Monarch coach, passing through Maidenhead, Reading, Newbury and Marlborough on my way to Bath, where I arrived about half-past seven Sunday morning. There are no fees to coachmen or guard by this coach, a plan, bye the bye, I wish most heartily all coach proprietors would adopt; that of fixing it on the fare is a much more satisfactory way.'

For the return journey, from North Wales to London, Onwhyn advises:

> 'The best coach from Shrewsbury is the Wonder, which leaves the Lion Inn, morning, quarter before six, through Shiffnal, Wolverhampton, Birmingham, Coventry and St Alban's, and arrives in London about nine in the evening.'

In 1840, Thomas Turner of Gloucester issued, for private distribution, his *Narrative of a journey associated with a fly from Gloucester to Aberystwyth and from Aberystwyth to North Wales July 31st to September 8th 1837*:

> 'An ascent to the summit of Snowdon becomes the primary object of the tourist on his visit to Llanberis. After breakfast, therefore, the anxious enquiry was raised, as the morning was bleak and somewhat stormy, whether or not the task would be practicable. Chances appeared much against the attempt but hope revived towards 10-o-clock. Still there was a

manifold disposition to with-hold the needful help of a guide with his ponies. Drops of rain yet occasionally fell and a strong breeze continued to agitate the brown bosom of the lake. My mind was, however, bent on the expedition and at length, after another half hour's controversy, the man and the animals were forthcoming and we entered on the base of this stupendous mountain at a very short distance from the hotel.

'Promising myself a visit to the fall of Ceynant Mawr which to the right, on our return, we gradually ascended a stony but sufficiently wide and safe path for about a mile. Here we entered upon a defile, first, however, halting and turning round a charming view of the lakes below, over which the Glydir and Llydir mountains rose with grand effect, displaying a variety of beautiful tints as the sun now happily shone out upon their craggy sides. About a mile further to the right is the frightful perpendicular rock aptly entitled The Black Precipice and it certainly forms a stupendous and striking feature in the ascent. At the base of this enormous mass of rock is a small lake and a copper mine which is worked, but not, I understand, to much advantage,

'A winding and very steep portion of the mountain now succeeds which patience and a little toil overcame and we arrived at a spring somewhat more than a mile from the crown of our ambition, Yr Wyddfa, the highest peak of Snowdon. My dismay can easily be conceived when at this spot thick mists, not only enveloping the entire summit of the mountain but gradually rolling around us and below us, encountered our career. Again the day became uncongenial and the guide, with a woeful aspect, declared that a farther advance was futile. Having, however, accomplished more than three fourths of the ascent, my determination was to proceed though the residue of our task required some perseverance and caution, chiefly caused by the dense state of the atmosphere which prevented our distinguishing any object even at three paces distant. Large fragments of loose rocks were scattered in the way and the prospect, as the wind sometimes partially scattered the mist, exhibited for an instant over perpendicular ridges of the mountain the appalling abyss beneath our path. Three or four times it seemed to me that the summit of our mountain was attained when a declivity occurred and again we halted on a flat surface, a still higher point appearing and rendering farther exertion needful.

'At length the guide announced that the top of the next acclivity would in reality terminate our labours and we had scarcely attained our object when a trio of pedestrians, whose escort it appeared was the brother of my guide and who had effected their ascent from the opposite side of the mountain near Beddgelert, greeted us. Here then we were assembled having toiled for upwards of two hours and condemned, as we believed, to suffer a cruel disappointment. The dense fog, together with the cutting wind, rendered the cold excessive, and we were glad to shelter ourselves under a dwarf wall which has been erected for the comfort of tourists, and to discuss some brandy and biscuits. We now stood on the highest pinnacle of the mountain upon a space not more than 20 feet in diameter. The scene as the wind partially scattered the mists, opening perhaps through a fearful chasm a fine lake to our view, was awfully grand. Again and almost in an instant clouds and, as it were, "thick darkness" entirely closed the scene. Scarcely, however, had we finished our repast when hope again began to revive and never perhaps on a similar occasion did this smiling cherub awaken a more grateful feeling. One could almost have been sentimental.

'Soon afterwards the consummation of our wishes was fully attained. The horizon gradually cleared, the curtain was raised and in bright sunshine the most magnificent and unbounded prospect emerged to our view which the imagination can conceive.

'The formation of the new road to Caernarvon, together with the establishment of two hotels and a considerable increase in trade produced by an extension of the slate quarries, all tend to diminish the solitude for which it was a very few years since so noted. In the afternoon we pursued our course along the former to our present destination. The distance is nine miles, the first three of which run by the side of the lake, Padern [Padarn], which is separated from the Llanberis lake by the river Seiont.'

Few visitors to Snowdon came to much harm during their stay, those at least who survived to record their experiences. One exception was G. J. Bennett 'of the Theatre Royal, Covent Garden'. Bennett's *Guide to North Wales* was published in 1838 and recounts a fall which, though minor, is noteworthy for having occurred while he was asleep in bed:

'About a mile from [Llyn Gwynant] is a place called Gwrydd where there is a small public house with a sign signifying nothing. Here I resolved to "rough it" for a day, intending to fish the lakes situated immediately above this spot as nature's cisterns to water the pleasant valleys. The public house possesses a small parlour, carpeted, with half a dozen hair-bottomed chairs and a mahogany table. A silent but most importunate monitor urged me to discover what food this mountain chalet could produce. Eggs and bacon was the expected reply to my question and I soon had the pleasure of seeing this humble but most grateful fare being placed before me and, in spite of the indifferent style of the cooking, I partook of it eagerly having that incomparable sauce "a good appetite".

'After I had repaired my broken rod, I ascended the mountain at the back of the house and arrived at a large oval lake in which the black and sterile rocks that form inaccessible ramparts on one side are reflected in its generally unruffled surface. The scene is wild and desolate, such as Despair herself would select for her abode. There are plenty of fish in this lake but they are all small and extremely shy. I remained upon its margin until the shadows of night gave me warning to attend to my safety and make the best of my way to my lodging where I speedily ascended by a ladder-like staircase to a kind of cock-loft which was divided into two compartments, one for the accommodation of the family, man, wife, children and servants, the other fitted up for travellers.

'Sleep soon overtook me and I should have continued to sleep, I have no doubt, until breakfast time had I not been awakened by a trifling accident which is that I was visited by a dream, in which the ghost of a lobster popped his head out of a salad bowl and demanded upon what authority I had presumed to make mincemeat of his body, when a loud crash roused me from my slumber and I found myself with my knees doubled up to my chin upon the floor, the bedstead having broken in the middle and deposited my in this unenviable position. I need not say that, for the remaining part of the night, I was wholly left to waking reveries and uncontrollable desires for the blessings of daylight which at last greeted my longing eyes and, hurrying on my clothes, I descended and walked forth to scent the morning air in the direction of Llanberis.'

Just as 20th century motorists are advised to check the condition of their vehicles, so 19th century tourists were advised to consider their stomachs, their clothing and their feet. Such is the recommendation emerging from the Reverend Emilius Nicholson in the preface to the 1840 edition of the *Cambrian Travellers Guide*:

'Walking can only be pleasing to those who have been accustomed to that exercise, and when not limited to time. He who takes a horse and saddle-bags has certainly much the advantage of a pedestrian in most situations; he passes over uninteresting tracts with celerity and surveys at ease the attractions of both near and distant objects. The latter, though he be at liberty to scramble up a mountain or a rock, has to suffer more from that addition to his common fatigue. It is true that he can step aside to botanise and examine the beauties of nature and art, in situations where a horse would be an incumbrance; walking can also be engaged in whenever a person is ready to start, and is the most independent mode of passing on; but when he arrives wet and weary at an inn, at ten at night, he has sometimes to suffer the mortification of being received with coldness, treated with subordinate accommodations, if not refused admittance; obliged, perhaps, to accept the necessaries of a mere public-house, or proceed further.'

'I have hitherto travelled on foot, a mode possessing many advantages. The principal objection which I can make is that of conveying luggage. When a guide is employed, he will relieve you from such incumbrance. I never dine in my excursions but, generally rising at six, walk a few miles and make a substantial breakfast of coffee with a boiled egg. After the toil of the day, a good supper is a welcome repast. Intermediately, I take tea, and often a crust and a draught of water, than which, in the heat of summer, nothing can be more refreshing.

'A cloak made of oiled silk is preferable to an umbrella as you can fold it up and put it in your pocket. The stuff called jean is proper for a walking dress, being light and strong, and a straw hat is desirable. A case made of calf-skin by a saddler is the most convenient deposit for your change of linen and other necessaries, all of which may be limited in weight to 4 or 5 lbs. I once met in Cwm-glas a party of four gentlemen on foot, whom a little boy followed upon a small pony, with the joint conveniences of each in a large wallet; but then how rarely can two persons be found, whose pursuits are similar, and whose desires are alike! The chance of four being so agreed is proportionately more uncertain.

'Walking becomes exceedingly painful when blisters upon the feet result from this exercise. But this inconvenience may be prevented by wearing strong, pliant and easy shoes, or those which are made from two lasts to the shape of the feet; by wearing fine soft flannel or woollen socks next to the skin, and by washing the feet with water before going to bed. If, for want of such precautions, blisters should arise, let out the serum with a needle without breaking the skin, bathe the part with equal quantities of vinegar and luke-warm water, and apply a thin liniment of wax and oil, with a little sugar of lead, and anoint with oil. Mr Hawker, in his *Instructions to Sportsmen* says, "If your heel should become galled, apply a piece of goldbeater's skin, and over that a little court plaster, in order to defend the part doubly. But there is a right and a wrong way of going to work. Instead of cutting with scissors and merely wetting the plaster, let it be slightly heated by the fire as well as wetted, being previously stamped with a wadding punch, by which means, from having no angles or corners, it will stick as fast as your skin provided that, when on and dry, you put over it a little cold cream, to repel the damp in hot weather. A little fuller's earth, mixed with water to the consistence of an ointment and applied to the feet on going to bed, is also recommended, from experience, to such persons as by walking are liable to have their feet painfully blistered.

'To make shoes water-proof: Take drying linseed oil half a pint, bees'-wax 1 ounce, turpentine 1 ounce, burgundy pitch half ounce. Melt these over a slow fire, and add a few drachms of essential oil of lavender or thyme. With this rub your boots or shoes with a brush, either in the sun or at some distance from the fire. The application must be repeated till the leather be fully saturated.

'Consider in the morning where you are to sleep at night, and dispose of your time accordingly.

'Avoid bathing in mountain lakes, unless you be a good swimmer. They are generally inverted cones.

'Wash your pencil sketches with thin starch; it does not shine.'

Having explained the practicalities of pedestrianism, Nicholson warns his readers about the cost of hiring guides and horses:

'Upon the banks of Llyn-Cwellyn, the largest of the lakes on the road from Beddgelart to Caernarvon, is a small public-house kept by Mrs Morton who engages to supply Guides to Snowdon. Her expectations runs as high as 7 shillings for attending a single person, and from a party 5 shillings each. Her customary complement is half a guinea more, besides the expense of a person to hold the ponies when the steepness renders it impossible to ride any farther, which is within half a mile of the top of the mountain. Having never ascended Snowdon from this point, I have not had occasion to put Mrs Morton's disposition to the test; but I have derived some information from my worthy friend Mr Benjamin Stokes of Worcester who, in the year 1812, in company with Mrs Stokes and three gentlemen, took ponies at Caernarvon and, on arriving here, engaged the guide. No corn for the ponies was to be had nor hay. A few handfuls of grass were, however, cut for them. The travellers were accommodated with a few rashers of bacon, bread, and some milk and water, for which, besides 10 shillings to the guide, 15 shillings were rigorously demanded.'

The dramatic reduction in travelling times resulting from road improvements and railways during the early 1800s is noted by Nicholson:

'In 1803 there was only one public carriage in Radnorshire, a post-chaise at Rhaiadyr, and one or two at Aberystwyth; but none at Cardigan, though the county town where the assizes were held. Now good roads and steam have almost annihilated time and space, and London can be reached from Aberystwyth in twenty-four hours when formerly it required that time to accomplish the distance from Aberystwith to Shrewsbury.'

Chapter Ten

Carl Gustav Carus accompanied the king of Saxony on an eleven-week tour of Britain in the summer of 1844. Leaving Dresden on May 21st, they crossed the channel from Ostend to Dover and stayed as guests of Lord de la Warr at Buckhurst, Kent. Their meandering route embraced in turn Brighton, Chichester, Portsmouth dockyards, the Isle of Wight, London, Windsor, the Peak District, Birmingham, Oxford, Stonehenge, Weymouth, Plymouth, Liskeard, Penzance, Land's End, Bristol, Chepstow, Newport, Merthyr Tydfil, Brecon, Devil's Bridge, Aberystwyth, Dolgellau, Beddgelert, Snowdon, Caernarfon, Menai, Anglesey, Bangor, Penrhyn Castle, Aberconwy and Chester. Thence north to the Lake District and Scotland, leaving by the steamer *Lightning* on August 5th to land at Hamburg.

The route taken by Carus up Snowdon appears to have been from Rhyd-ddu and his descent probably via what was later to be named the Watkin Path. Carus titled his tour *The King of Saxony's journey through England and Scotland in the year 1844*:

'Great poverty seems to prevail in the mountains. On our way hither, we saw many most miserable stone huts, and in many a lonely dell, thin lines of smoke arose from such huts, behind some vast mass of scattered rocks. A few poor cattle appeared here and there to pick up a scanty pasture, and numbers of children, begging, ran along the roads, endeavouring by their troublesome importunity to win a trifling alms from the passing stranger. Occasionally, too, they offer rock crystals, or other mountain productions, and woollen knitted caps, for sale.

'In the midst of all this poverty and wild scenery, there is, however, a large and elegant hotel, which makes up forty-five beds.

'Bangor, July 12th — Evening.

'Early this morning, according to our previous design, we

made the ascent of Snowdon; the appearance of the weather was by no means encouraging, the sky was lowering and the clouds hung deep around the mountain top. Still there was no rain — many signs of a favourable change — and we took our chance of the advantages in our favour and set out. We made early preparation for our journey and, at seven o'clock, mounted a light carriage, accompanied by a skilful guide. We followed the road towards the foot of the mountain, as far up its flank as was accessible to any description of carriage. We commenced the ascent. Our path lay for some distance over wet pasture and spongy meadows — after which the path became steeper and occasional masses of bold projecting rocks occurred.

'We were not the only travellers, whom the day tempted to try their good fortune on the summit of the highest mountain in England. Some ladies, mounted on ponies, rode sometimes before and sometimes behind us, and several parties followed them on foot. The summit of the mountain lay concealed in clouds — the rocks stood forth bold and black from the green of the Alpine meadows, on which the beautiful anthericum ossifragum grows in great profusion, and a cold wind blew from the ravines which skirted our path. A young Alpine lark, only imperfectly fledged, fluttered along the ground before our feet; our guide easily caught it with his hands but the old ones flew around uttering such painful screams that I induced him again to put the poor panting little creature upon the grass behind a large block of stone.

'When we ascended a little further, the view to the westward became partially free — and we saw the sea, the isle of Anglesey and Caernarvon Castle. As we ascended, however, the clouds again closed around us, and finally we found ourselves completely enveloped in the penetrating fog of these moist goddesses. The ascent also in many places now became difficult; the wind blew cold along the side of some rocky walls, or from the depths of the neighbouring ravine —

the thick fogs continued to roll more densely along the mountain sides — but fortunately, so far, they did not thoroughly penetrate our clothes with their moisture.

'Still onward, from height to height! — deep ravines lay at our side, the bottom of which, filled with thick fog, yawned horribly below. Vegetation now almost wholly disappeared, except merely a few rare Alpine plants — and on every side of us rose lofty crags of black chlorite slate. Having taken some repose after the efforts of the ascent, behind a projecting rock which sheltered us from the wind, we again set forth, and in about a quarter of an hour (two hours in all) we reached the pinnacle of the mountain — 4348 feet above the level of the sea. View there was none! We found refuge in a small wooden shed, erected for the protection of travellers from the rain and wind, in which the host kept up a welcome fire. The man presently prepared a singular brown mixture, which he sold for coffee, and furnished some grayish oatmeal cake as an accompaniment. There were no spirituous liquors of any description to be had, because the occupier, with no small degree of self-satisfaction, gave us to understand that his wooden hut was to be regarded as a Temperance Inn. Not far from the mountain hotel, which I must state to be the first imperfect house of accommodation we had yet met in England, was a small stone hut in which the rest of the travellers, together with their ponies, had found a harbour not much better than our own.

'Having spent some time upon the summit, dried ourselves, and ranged about among the craggy rocks and through the fog, we found our visit was in vain — no hopes of the weather clearing were being entertained, and we prepared to proceed on our descent. Before we had descended far from the summit, the clouds presented occasional breaks, and we were able to snatch partial views into the beautiful deep valleys which lie between the converging ridges of the mountain; and on one occasion the clouds rose like a curtain and revealed to us a splendid prospect of the sea. In these occasional glimpses, we perceived for a moment that the declivities of the mountain were enjoying the full beams of the sun, and immediately we were again closely enveloped in our foggy mantle of clouds.

'There was a continual play of currents of air and waves of fog with the earth. Such phenomena furnish highly interesting subjects of contemplation to those who have greater leisure for their contemplation than we ourselves had. Of such extraordinary atmospheric phenomena, however, it may be said — they show the life of the clouds, but cloud the image of life! If, however, the observation of such phenomena be made the chief object of a whole excursion, they will be found to have something in them unsatisfying. The unconscious life of nature always falls in value in the eyes of him who has thought upon and experienced the mighty movements and impulses of the mind and feelings. What signify earth, and suns, and planets, if there were no eye to see, no intelligence to give them life?

'Having proceeded somewhat further on the descent, our guide prepared to follow a different route in our return, through a deep precipitous valley, in which the king immediately acquiesced. The task, however, was by no means easy — it involved the necessity of going straight down a sharp declivity of the mountain, at least 1000 feet high, and very sparingly covered with moist earth and tufts of grass. We were obliged to aid ourselves as well as we could by the firmness of our tread, taking a zigzag course, and by the appliances of our hands and sticks, and at length reached the bottom in safety. The path, however formidable to us, would undoubtedly not have presented many difficulties to a well-trained Alpine hunter; to those, however, who are not accustomed to such clambering, it must be regarded as making a severe demand upon the exercise of their muscular power, and as a species of training which, when successfully completed, must always result in good. Even on reaching the valley, there was no path, and we were obliged to make our way over stock and stone, through bog and brook, till we came to a lower and smoother region.

'During our descent, we were also obliged to endure the alternative of heat and cold, of sunshine and rain; at length, however, we reached some mines, at which rude paths began to appear, and presently after found ourselves at our carriages, and drove by another road again back to Bethgellert. On this road, too, we enjoyed the sight of some splendid mountain scenery. The weather had now become clear and sunny, whilst the top of Snowdon still lay thickly enveloped in masses of dark clouds. A small lake lay stretched out before us in the vale, full of picturesque beauty, and noble mountains beside and beyond, rose and towered one above the another. I heartily envied an artist, who had established his studio on the edge of a mountain brook and appeared to be diligently engaged in his work. What a pleasure it must be, to be engaged in an attempt to give a faithful delineation of such noble forms!

'About half-past two we reached the hotel at Bethgellert, and our mountain excursion was at an end. After spending a short time in refreshing ourselves, and at luncheon, we took our departure, and drove westward· through the valleys towards the sea-shore. The country here became much less interesting; but we had ample compensation in the ancient castle of Caernarvon, at which we arrived in about two hours.'

Carus also visited the Penrhyn slate quarry when it was at its most productive:

'It was raining hard when we arrived at the remarkable and extensive Penrhyn slate quarries, which are of great importance to the whole of Wales. They are situated about six miles to the N.E. of Bangor, on the slope of the hill, and have been particularly rich and productive for the last fifty years. When one arrives at this quarry from below, it presents the appearance almost of a crater open towards the front, along the lips of which twelve or fourteen terraces run, one above another, each of which is from forty-five to fifty feet high, and upon which the works of blasting and digging are carried on by about 2000 workmen. The stone is of a reddish brown; sometimes, also grayish slate of fine grain which splits well into plates and takes a fine polish. The mass never contains organic remains but is frequently traversed by a strata of quarry or limestone in which crystals of some metals, principally copper and iron, occur.

'The manner in which these quarries are worked is the following: On the galleries, or terraces, large masses of slate are first detached by means of powder and then roughly hewn into shape. There are laid along each of these terraces tram-roads formed of rails loosely laid down, upon which the masses of slate, in waggons with suitable wheels, are thrust along by men to the little houses situated on the declivity of the mountain, at the extremities of the galleries. Here they are split into smaller plates; and it is curious to observe how regularly the slate splits into finer and still finer plates, down to the thickness of three or four lines. Several pieces are allowed to retain a thickness of an inch or an inch and a half, and are used for tables and flagstones, the thinner ones covering roofs etcetera. The manner, too, in which they are squared, being cut out at once by a sort of hatchet according to a line made by means of a ruler, is very curious. The plates thus formed are distinguished by very amusing names. Thus the largest are called queens, the next princesses, then duchesses, ladies, and so on.

'The enormous quantity of slate produced may be estimated from the facts that a railway has been constructed specially from these quarries to Penrhyn harbour, at an expense of £170,000, which every week takes down between 500 and 600 tons, or about 12,000 hundredweight of slate; and that the yearly net produce has sometimes brought in as much as £60,000 to the owner of the quarry, Sir Douglas Pennant.

'The quarrying itself is attended with considerable danger. The workmen, when a portion of the rock is to be blasted from the upper part of a gallery, are obliged to bore the hole, suspended in mid-air by ropes, to load the hole so bored, to set fire to the match, and then to place themselves beyond the reach of the explosion. They are also exposed to the chance of accidents from the falling of portions of the sharp slate; and it was curious, even yesterday — on which, being pay-day, the work was not regularly going on — to hear now and then the explosion of the blasting of some part of the rock, at the same time that it was almost difficult to pass along the galleries without falling over the little railways or some of the sharp pieces of stone.

'The manner in which Queen Victoria was received here, on her visit two years ago, must have produced a curious effect. As soon as she arrived, 1300 explosions were heard from all parts of the quarry, having been all previously prepared for this purpose.'

Another German traveller, Georg Johann Kohl, observed work in progress on the first Ordnance Survey of North Wales during his ascent of Snowdon in 1845. Kohl's *Travels in England and Wales* was translated into English by Thomas Roscoe whose own *Wanderings and Excursions in North Wales* appeared in 1853:

'Snowdon narrows as you approach the summit, into a complete cone on the top of which a surveying party found only room sufficient to spread a small tent and arrange their mathematical instruments. The soldiers on duty at this tent, erected for the purpose of a new survey of the country, had constructed a pathway of stones around their frail canvas dwelling, which added considerably to the facility of commanding a prospect of the scenery on every side. The officer of the post, for the better accommodation of himself and his men, had raised several other tents on the little levels lower down. We were told by the officer of the engineers that the old breed of eagles had long been banished from their eyries on the peaks, the last of the race having been seen, some years ago, taking his flight forever from his patriarchal hills.

'We visited, on our return, the huts of some mountaineers who, declaring themselves to be "Cymraeg", affected perfect ignorance of the English language. Though despised by the English, these huts are superior to the Irish cabins or those of the Scotch highlanders. They reminded me of the Russian houses in the Ukraine, being whitewashed all over; a practice, I was told, derived from the Silures — their forefathers. The operation, being repeated every year, gives them an air of great neatness, and so great is the zeal of the people in the performance of this process that they often whitewash walls, roof, window-frames and door, and sometimes extend the same care to fence, pig-sty and every other apertenance.'

The fifth son of historian and financier William Roscoe, Thomas Roscoe (1791 to 1871) was born at Toxteth Park near Liverpool. He worked in his father's bank until 1816 when it ran into difficulties and was suspended. Thomas Roscoe turned to journalism, his varied output including a biography of William the Conqueror and a guide to the London & Birmingham Railway. His *Wanderings and Excursions in North Wales* appeared in 1853 and includes a vivid outline of the slate quarrying which still scars the Nantlle valley facing the west flank of Snowdon:

'I turned off from the road to the distance of about 100 yards to examine the immense slate quarries of Nantlle, and to witness the process of blasting the rock. The face of the chasm was quite perpendicular, and cut into stages of different heights, and the workmen were ascending and descending with incredible activity by means of ropes fastened to strong iron bolts at the head of the rock. A party was at work on one of these ledges about 30 feet from the ground, drilling a hole to receive the gunpowder. All being now in readiness, the train was fired and immense masses of slate were instantly dislodged and precipitated to the lower stage, the noise of the explosion echoing on all sides and reverberating for a considerable time amongst the mountains and hollows. The depth of the quarry was probably about 200 feet, and at the bottom a drift was at that time being formed to relieve the upper part from the water that by this means is directed into a well from which it is pumped by a steam engine.

'The next process which I observed was that of splitting the blocks of slate into their proper thicknesses, which was accomplished with astonishing ease and rapidity, the workmen dividing them into flat slabs for household and mortuary purposes, or into thin plates for architectural operations. The surrounding scene was full of activity and interest — water-wheels, pumping engineers, inclined planes, railways, steam engines, bridges and aqueducts meeting the eye at all points.

'Near this place, Wilson made his celebrated view of Snowdon which from this point is seen through the long vista of the pass, rising with extraordinary grandeur, having the bare ridges of Crib y Ddysgl and Y Wyddfa on the right and left. I now retraced my steps to Beddgelert along the high ground by Llyn y Gader where it is said Edward, the ruthless conqueror of Wales, charmed by beauty of the place, used to linger day after day, and from thence by a walk of continued descent reached the comfortable hospitium of mine host of the Goat.'

A few months after Roscoe's visit, the causeway which carries the Miners' Track across Llyn Llydaw was completed. A slate panel commemorates the work:

'This causeway was built by the Cwm Dyli Rock and Green Lake Copper Mining Company under the directions of the mining captain, Thomas Colliver. During its construction the level of the lake was lowered 12 feet and 6,000 cubic yards of waste rock from the mine were used to build the embankment. The causeway was first crossed on October 13th 1853.'

George Borrow's 1854 visit to North Wales included sojourns at many inns and hotels which in structural terms have changed only superficially in the intervening years. Here he arrives at Capel Curig:

'Turning round the northern side of the mighty Siabod I soon reached the village of Capel Curig, standing in a valley between two hills, the easternmost of which is the aforesaid Moel Siabod. Having walked now twenty miles in a broiling day I thought it high time to take some refreshment, and inquired the way to the inn. The inn, or rather the hotel, for it was a very magnificent edifice, stood at the entrance of a pass leading to Snowdon, on the southern side of the valley in a totally different direction from the road leading to Bangor, to which place I was bound. There I dined in a grand saloon amidst a great deal of fashionable company, who probably conceiving from my heated and dusty appearance, that I was some poor fellow travelling on foot from motives of economy, surveyed me with looks of the most supercilious disdain, which, however, neither deprived me of my appetite nor operated uncomfortably on my feelings.

My dinner finished, I paid my bill and having sauntered a little about the hotel garden, which is situated on the border of a small lake, and from which, through the vista of the pass, Snowdon may been seen towering in majesty at the distance of about six miles, I started for Bangor, which is fourteen miles from Capel Curig.'

Most of Borrow's journeying through Wales was on foot,

frequently rejoining his wife and stepdaughter (Henrietta) who travelled by horsedrawn coach. In the same year, 1854, Borrow ascended Snowdon with Henrietta. Their route was via the Llanberis path and the description says as much about Borrow as about the mountain:

'The Wyddfa is about thirty feet in diameter and is surrounded on three sides by a low wall. In the middle of it is a rude cabin, in which refreshments are sold, and in which a person resides throughout the year, though there are few or no visitors to the hill's top, except during the months of summer. Below on all sides are frightful precipices except on the side of the west. Towards the east it looks perpendicularly into the dyffrin or vale nearly a mile below, from which to the gazer it is at all times an object of admiration, of wonder and almost of fear.

'There we stood on the Wyddfa, though the day was almost stiflingly hot in the regions from which we had ascended. There we stood enjoying a scene inexpressibly grand, comprehending a considerable part of the main land of Wales, the whole of Anglesey, a faint glimpse of part of Cumberland, the Irish Channel, and what might be either a misty creation or the shadowy outline of the hills of Ireland. Peaks and pinnacles and huge moels stood up here and there, about us and below us, partly in glorious light, partly in deep shade. Manifold were the objects which we saw from the brow of Snowdon, but of all the objects which we saw, those which filled us with most delight and admiration were numerous lakes and lagoons which, like sheets of ice or polished silver, lay reflecting the rays of the sun in the deep valleys at his feet.

' "Here," said I to Henrietta, "you are on the top crag of Snowdon, which the Welsh consider, and perhaps with justice, to be the most remarkable crag in the world; which is mentioned in many of their old wild romantic tales, and some of the noblest of their poems, amongst others in the *Day of*

Judgment, by the illustrious Goronwy Owen where it is brought forward in the following manner:

'Ail i'r ar ael Eryri,
Cyfartal hoewal a hi.

'The brow of Snowdon shall be levelled with the ground,
And the eddying waters shall murmur round it.

' "You are now on the top crag of Snowdon, generally termed Y Wyddfa, which means a conspicuous place or tumulus, and which is generally in winter covered with snow; about which snow there are in the Welsh language two curious englynion or stanzas consisting entirely of vowels with the exception of one consonant, namely the letter R.

' "Oer yw'r Eira ar Eryri, — o'ryw
    Ar awyr i rewi;
  Oer yw'r ia ar riw 'r ri,
  A'r Eira oer yw 'Ryri.

' "O Ri y'Ryri yw'r oera, — o'r âr,
    Ar oror wir arwa;
  O'r awyr a yr Eira,
  O'i ryw i roi rew a'r ia.

' "Cold is the snow on Snowdon's brow,
    It makes the air so chill;
  For cold, I trow, there is no snow
  Like that of Snowdon's hill.

' "A hill most chill is Snowdon's hill,
    And wintry is his brow;
  From Snowdon's hill the breezes' chill
  Can freeze the very snow."

'Such was the harangue which I uttered on the top of Snowdon; to which Henrietta listened with attention; three or four English, who stood nigh, with grinning scorn, and a Welsh gentleman with considerable interest. The latter coming forward shook me by the hand exclaiming:

' "Wyt ti Lydaueg?"

' "I am not a Llydauan," said I; "I wish I was, or anything but what I am, one of a nation amongst whom any knowledge save what relates to money-making and over-reaching is looked upon as a disgrace. I am ashamed to say that I am an Englishman."

'I then returned his shake of the hand; and bidding Henrietta and the guide follow me, went into the cabin, where Henrietta had some excellent coffee, and myself and the guide a bottle of tolerable ale; very much refreshed we set out on our return.'

Off the beaten tourist track, the inhabitants of North Wales were inclined to greet wandering strangers with suspicion even as late as the 19th century. Borrow was aware of this and frequently made play of it, to the notable embarrassment of the occupants of a public house near Dinas Mawddwy:

'Seeing a kind of inn, I entered it and was shown by a lad-waiter into a large kitchen in which were several people. I had told him in Welsh that I wanted some ale, and as he opened the door he cried with a loud voice "Cumro!" as much as to say, Mind what you say before this chap, for he understands Cumraeg — that word was enough. The people, who were talking fast and eagerly as I made my appearance, instantly became silent and stared at me with most suspicious looks. I sat down and when my ale was brought I took a hearty draught, and observing that the company were still watching me suspiciously and maintaining the same suspicious silence, I determined to comport myself in a manner which should to a certain extent afford them ground for suspicion. I therefore slowly and deliberately drew my notebook out of my waistcoat pocket, unclasped it, took my pencil from the loops at the side of the book, and forthwith began to dot down observations upon the room and company, now looking to the left, now to the right, now aloft, now alow, now skewing at an object, now leering at an individual, my eyes half closed and my mouth drawn considerably aside. Here follow some of my dottings:

"A very comfortable kitchen with a chimney corner on the south side — immense grate and brilliant fire — large kettle hanging over it by a chain attached to a transverse iron bar — a settle on the left-hand side of the fire — seven fine large men near the fire — two upon the settle, two upon chairs, one in the chimney-corner smoking a pipe, and two standing up — table near the settle with glasses, amongst which is that of myself, who sit nearly in the middle of the room a little way on the right-hand side of the fire.

"The floor is of slate; a fine brindled greyhound lies before it on the hearth, and a shepherd's dog wanders about, occasionally going to the door and scratching as if anxious to get out. The company are dressed mostly in the same fashion, brown coats, broad-brimmed hats and yellowish corduroy breeches with gaiters. One who looks like a labouring man has a white smock and a white hat, patched trowsers, and highlows covered with gravel — one has a blue coat.

"There is a clock on the right-hand side of the kitchen; a warming-pan hangs close by it on the projecting side of the chimney-corner. On the same side is a large rack containing many plates and dishes of Staffordshire ware. Let me not forget a pair of fire-irons which hang on the right-hand side of the chimney-corner!"

'I made a great many more dottings, which I shall not insert here. During the whole time I was dotting the most marvellous silence prevailed in the room, broken only by the occasional scratching of the dog against the inside of the door, the ticking of the clock, and the ruttling of the smoker's pipe in the chimney corner. After I had dotted to my heart's content I closed my book, put the pencil into the loops, then the book into my pocket, drank what remained of my ale, got up, and, after another look at the apartment and its furniture and a leer at the company, departed from the house without ceremony, having paid for the ale when I received it. After

walking some fifty yards down the street I turned half round
and beheld, as I knew I should, the whole company at the
door staring after me. I leered sideways at them for about half
a minute, but they stood my leer stoutly. Suddenly I was
inspired by a thought. Turning round I confronted them,
and pulling my note-book out of my pocket, and seizing my
pencil, I fell to dotting vigorously. That was too much for
them. As if struck by a panic, my quondam friends turned
round and bolted into the house; the rustic-looking man with
the smock-frock and gravelled highlows nearly falling down
in his eagerness to get in.

The name of the place where this adventure occurred was
Cemmaes.'

Born in Ireland in 1820, John Tyndall worked initially on the
ordnance survey of that country before transferring in 1842 to the
English survey. He then pursued a career in mathematics and
chemistry and in 1853 became professor of natural philosophy at
the Royal Institution, succeeding Michael Faraday in 1867 as its
superintendent. It was by the upper Penygwryd route, the Pyg
Track, that Professors Tyndall and Huxley ascended Snowdon,
with a guide, on December 28th, 1860. Tyndall describes the
ascent in a chapter added to his book, *Hours of Exercise on the Alps*:

'The scene was grand in the extreme. Before us were the
buttresses of Snowdon, crowned by the conical peak; while
below us were the three llyns, black as ink, and contracting
additional gloom from the shadow of the mountain. The lines
of weathering had caused the frozen rime to deposit itself
upon the rocks as on the tendrils of a vine, the crags being
fantastically wreathed with runners of ice.

'The summit, when we looked at it, damped our ardour a
little; it seemed very distant, and the day was sinking fast.
From the summit the mountain sloped downward to a col
which linked it with a bold eminence to our right. At the col
we aimed, and half an hour before reaching it we passed the

steepest portion of the track. This I quitted, seeking to cut off the zig-zags, but gained nothing but trouble by the attempt. This difficulty conquered, the col was clearly within reach; on its curve we met a fine snow cornice, through which we broke at a plunge, and gained safe footing on the mountain rim. The health and gladness of that moment were a full recompense for the entire journey into Wales.

'We went upward along the edge of the cone with the noble sweep of the snow cornice at our left. The huts at the top were all encased in ice, and from their chimneys and projections the snow was drawn into a kind of plumage by the wind. The crystals had set themselves so as to present the exact appearance of feathers, and in some cases these were stuck against a common axis, so as accurately to resemble the plumes in soldiers' caps.

'It was three-o-clock when we gained the summit. Above and behind us the heavens were of the densest grey; towards the western horizon this was broken by belts of fiery red, which, nearer the sun, brightened to orange and yellow. The mountains of Flintshire were flooded with glory, and later on, through the gaps in the ranges, the sunlight was poured in coloured beams, which could be tracked through the air to the places on which their radiance fell. The scene would bear comparison with the splendours of the Alps themselves.'

One of the few women to publish their observations of North Wales was the Scottish novelist Catherine Sinclair. She was born in 1800 and was secretary to her father (Sir John Sinclair, first president of the board of agriculture) until his death in 1835. She then began writing children's titles, initially for a nephew, followed by a mixture of adult fact and fiction including *Hours in England and Wales*:

'I never observed a single instance of intoxication during our progress through Wales, where the national beverage is butter-milk kept until almost putrid — a luxury in which there seems little temptation to exceed. The whole country must be united in one vast temperance society, or else such associations are quite superfluous here. We may hope the people act on principles similar to that of a clergyman who replied, on being asked to take the oath of abstinence, that he belonged to the oldest temperance society in the world, Christianity itself binding him by the most solemn obligations to temperance.

'At every inn on this road we eat and dress in jig time as Welsh harpers seem always to be in full play, forming a very enlivening acquisition where they can be heard, and extremely unobtrusive in asking remuneration as they never beg though grateful for the merest trifle offered. The instrument has three rows of strings, or rather wires, but there is a great sameness in the music, which resembles a hornpipe and seldom exhibits any dignity or any volume of sound. The notes want roundness; but it is superior to the Irish harp, in which the key cannot be changed without retuning the whole instrument. Some harpers play a march to represent the advance and retreat of an army, beginning with scarcely an audible softness, afterwards swelling out to the fullest force of the instrument, and then dying away, as if they were five miles off, with so much management and effect that Bochsa himself might have been jealous.

'Our stage from Llanberris to Beddgelert was varied by several toilsome walks up hill, for travellers in the neighbourhood must lay their account with having occasion to pedestrianize frequently; and, could we have consulted a pedometer, it would certainly record our having achieved more miles of walking than we can venture to claim without an authority so unimpeachable. Timid persons might be inclined to walk down the descent also; for it required great reliance on the strength of our drag-chain to feel any satisfaction in rattling along these mountain paths, where I planned at least a dozen overturns which never took place and tried several times to guess how far we might have to send for a doctor.

'As travellers cannot live like camelions, it may be conjectured that after having completed two long stages among the mountains in a sharp appetising morning, breakfast became no unimportant affair; and seeing that tourists on the Continent still keep up the good old custom of recording their bill of fare at every inn, it ought to be a matter of at least as much importance to know what was achieved in a Welsh kitchen as in one more remotely situated in Italy. Accordingly it deserves commemoration that we sat down to a praiseworthy dejeune consisting of fish a moment before off the hook, eggs not laid above an hour since, mountain butter that tasted of the grass, and cream as rich as any in London. Fearing the description of breakfast may occupy more room, however, than that of Snowdon itself, the rest shall be left to fancy.'

Chapter Eleven

One of the most spontaneous tours ever printed is *A Journey due North Wales*, published anonymously in 1860 and giving a fine account of the journey from London:

'Released, for a short period, on the arrival of the ever-welcome "long vacation" from the books and the papers and their concomitants dust and dirt, with which we had been, as usual, overwhelmed during the previous twelve months; and prepared with a "ticket of leave" to peregrinate beyond the limits of the Lane of Chancery, the Temple, and the equally, at other times, legally busy locality of "Whetstone Park", alias Lincoln's Inn Fields; the important question suggested itself: "Where shall we go to obtain the purest air and the finest scenery, in conjunction with the best travelling (riding and walking), without necessitating any very large drafts upon our exchequer?"

'The advertisement sheet of *The Times* supplied an immediate reply to this "momentous question". We found that we could go by the Great Western Railway to Llangollen Road and back for eighteen shillings first, or eleven shillings second class, any Monday to Saturday inclusive.

'Llangollen eo instanti suggested Snowdon. We had long wished to climb the "'British Alps" and at once determined to put our project into execution. We arranged to go by the train to Llangollen Road and from thence to Snowdon, walking the latter part of the journey more for the sake of health than robbing the coach of a passenger and a fare.

'The first step was to procure a Guide Book for what true-born Englishman ever starts on a journey without one of these indispensables? In this respect we had no difficulty, a kind friend having volunteered the loan of one thus saving not only the expense but the difficulty of making a choice. Packing up a few requisites in a small leather bag which we could carry with the aid of a good strap without feeling encumbered, we retired to rest, slept upon our resolution; and soon after six o-clock the next morning we were wending our way across the parks to the Great Western Railway at Paddington; whence, after having procured a ticket to return the following Saturday from Llangollen Road, we were whisked away by the train, catching a glimpse of the noble castle of Windsor as we passed Slough; then a view of the towers and steeples of that most beautiful of cities, Oxford, with a few minutes' stay at Banbury to take in, not coals, but cakes. Then charming Leamington suggested thoughts of Kenilworth; then Warwick and its distant castle; until the everlasting smoke of Birmingham and the "black country" succeeding sent us back to our book, by whose aid we were striving to master a few of the household words of the principality whither we were bound.

'The general restlessness of our fellow-passengers and the continual peeping out of window now warn us that we are nearing our destination and we feel the exultant joy of the schoolboy home for the holidays as we reflect that business and care may for the present be flung to the winds and in a few minutes we shall be free amidst the beautiful scenery which already seems to invite and inspire us.

'Even the old gentleman in the corner, who all the way down has been so persistently reading his paper and grunting disapprobation at anyone who presumed to address him, seems to thaw and remarks, in the tone of an ill-used bear, that it is a fine day, a fact we had all discovered long since and as he might have done had not the leaders of "The Thunderer" possessed more charms for him than the beauties of nature.

'At length, about 3 pm, we arrive at the Llangollen Road station. Leaving those passengers who had wives, children or luggage with them, to gather their encumbrances together as best they may, we set out with our before-mentioned small leather bag for a five miles' walk to Llangollen, through one of the most charming of countries.

'Arrived at Llangollen, our hotel selected, our bed secured and ourselves refreshed, we start for a quiet evening stroll which we do not appreciate the less because we have been all day cooped in a close carriage and have so recently left the dust and noise of busy London behind us.'

The second day brings the writer and his companions 20 miles on foot through Corwen to Cerrigydrudion whence, on the third, they commence an exceedingly long walk through Betws and Capel Curig to the summit of Snowdon and a night very different from anything they could have anticipated:

'The next morning we settled our account [at the White Lion Hotel] which was more than reasonable and, bidding farewell to our kind entertainers, we strode about six or seven miles to Pentre Voelas which is a small hamlet, itself of little importance but a short distance from which are the Conway Falls. And here again we would fain linger for a while, to enjoy the beauties nature exhibits. But it must not be and we proceed for another six miles, when we arrive at Bettws y Coed, a small yet very pleasant village about a mile from which the river is crossed by a bridge of a single arch of 105 feet span, called Waterloo Bridge from its having been erected in the same year that the Battle of Waterloo was fought.

'As we move onwards, the objects that next attract our attention are the Swallow Falls and here again nature may be seen in all her grandeur. The water in its descent is broken into many streams· and dashes furiously over large rocks which impede its progress down a rugged chasm some fifty feet wide.

'Leaving this romantic scene, we soon arrived at Capel Curig in the immediate neighbourhood of Snowdon and of several of the finest lakes in North Wales. The spacious hotel here, which was erected by Lord Penrhyn, affords every accommodation to travellers; of which we take advantage, having walked about eighteen miles since the morning and having ten yet before us ere we reach our resting-place for the night.

'Refreshed by our short stay, we again set forth but the character of the scenery is entirely changed; we walk in the shadow of mighty mountains over whose tops the clouds in huge volumes are gathering and rolling downwards as though to overwhelm us. We feel a mysterious awe creeping over us and our thoughts take a solemn tinge as though to accord with the scenes through which we are passing. The solitude seems almost oppressive and we are not sorry when we catch a glimpse of the Pen y Gwrwd Inn, a short distance from which we find ourselves at the foot of Snowdon — the mountain Prince of Wales! and our point due N.W.'

Penygwryd, is in fact far from being at the foot of Snowdon. Pen-y-pass [the Head of the Pass] on the road from Llanberis to Penygwryd is 1,169 feet above sea level and so makes the Pyg Track and Miners' Track ascents theoretically easier than the paths from Rhyd-ddu, Beddgelert or Llanberis. The Miners' Track compensates for this deficiency by treating its explorers to an easy horizontal walk to Llyn Llydaw, a gentle incline to Glaslyn and then an exceedingly steep haul to join the Pyg Track before the latter in turn zigzags steeply up to the summit ridge. These zigzags were considerably tamed in the late 1980s and work was in progress in summer 1992 to cut a path out of the granite immediately below the ridge. The extraordinary sight of mountain bicycles being ridden along the Pyg Track in recent years must leave some walkers wondering how much more improved the mountain paths will become in future centuries. The gentle ascent from Capel Curig, meanwhile, does indeed make Penygwryd appear to be at the foot of Snowdon:

'Halting at the little inn here, we rest awhile and consider the best course to pursue. We had intended to make Llanberis (about five miles further) the termination of our day's journey; but ascertaining that it was scarcely so far to the top of Snowdon, and finding by one of his cards that "Philip Williams, of Summit House" contracted for bed and breakfast at his so-called hotel, for five shillings, we determined (having rested and refreshed ourselves and obtained all the information we could) to attempt the ascent at once and pass the night nearer to heaven than ever we had done before.

'It was a fine summer's evening, about 5.30, when we set out, without a guide, ambitious of making the ascent, if possible, unaided. For about two miles, the road was very good and we experienced no difficulty. We, however, came suddenly to a large lake [Llyn Llydaw] and had to make a wide detour in order to continue our route; but shortly after this we arrived at some copper mines and, being importuned by one of the miners, we consented to allow him to act as a guide.

'Ere long we began to enter the clouds and we here turned to take a last fond look at the earth which we seemed to be losing. The valley was now wrapped in a light mist and gave the view a most peculiar effect from the point where we stood; however, we did not pause long for a keen wind was blowing and we were glad to exert ourselves to keep up the circulation. A few steps further and the clouds have enclosed us, and we can see only a few yards around. We now congratulated ourselves on having a guide for the evening was drawing on and it would have been anything but pleasant to lose the way, which became more rugged every step, but on we go stumbling over small and climbing over large pieces of rock with which the mountain (there is no indication of any path) is plentifully strewed and at which we clutch every now and then as a fierce gust of wind nearly takes us off our legs — yet "excelsior" — after about an hour and a half of this sort of work we at length arrive at the termination of our journey due North Wales — "Summit House", Snowdon; a wooden building of no very prepossessing appearance on the very top of the mountain.

'We had become by this time thoroughly drenched by a driving rain and our passage through the clouds, and benumbed by the piercing wind, and after dismissing our miner-guide (who seemed to think nothing of these obstacles) we found ourselves about 8 pm comfortably installed by the fire, discussing a liberal supper of ham and eggs, bread and butter and tea, at a perpendicular height of three-quarters of a mile and completely embedded in the clouds and where, occasionally forgetful of our position, we fancied we heard the sound of church bells as though we had been still on the lower earth. Imaginary, as it must have been, it nevertheless served to cheer us in a cloudy prison. [It seems quite possible for the bells of St Mary's church in Beddgelert to be audible on the Snowdon summit given damp still air.]

'Our supper despatched, we began to consider how we should pass the long evening then setting in when we were agreeably surprised by the arrival of two gentlemen, and their guide who objected to be discharged in consequence of the boisterous weather which he said rendered it unsafe to descend and he was accordingly provided for in the kitchen.

'The wind was blowing great guns, everything seemed to promise a stormy night and we could not help congratulating ourselves upon being under shelter. The air had now become exceedingly cold and we felt it the more as all day we had been toiling under a burning sun; it was a sudden change from summer to the depth of winter. Fortunately we had a fire and we did not fail to appreciate the luxury (our host informed us his coals cost him £6 10s . . . six pounds ten shillings! . . . per ton). We drew our seats, not chairs, round it and, narrating our adventures to one another, the time passed quickly away until we all began to think of retiring to bed.

'But here a small difficulty arose; we were three in number and our host had but one bed, and that a small one. Our two fellow-travellers, however, in the most generous manner, insisted upon our being the occupant as we had walked about 30 miles that day and had besides arrived first at the summit.

After some little demur it was so settled and we separated. But not for long, for the wind, which had been steadily increasing, now blew with fearful violence and every moment we feared our frail house would be torn from its foundations and dashed to pieces or hurled into space. The rain, too, was pouring in at every crack and our hut (we beg pardon, "hotel") was plentifully supplied with these; indeed our host had found it necessary to nail a sheet over the door (which had been burst open once or twice) and this in some measure protected us from the wet.

'At last, finding sleep impossible, about twelve o'clock we returned to the company of our fellow-travellers, exchanging places with one of them who occupied the sofa. After racking our brains for every mode of which we were aware to woo coy sleep, we came to the conclusion that our case was hopeless and returned to our seats by the fire where we passed the remainder of the night in conversation with one (the last-mentioned) of our fellow-travellers; his companion apparently being more fortunate than we.

'It had long been apparent that we should neither see the sun rise nor obtain a view of the four kingdoms, which may be seen under more favourable circumstances; and so about 5 am we ordered breakfast, which was of the same description as our meal of the previous night. As we were finishing, two young gentlemen arrived, in whose favour we were only too happy to resign our places for they were drenched through by the heavy rain, having started about two am and had the full benefit of the rough weather which had now, however, somewhat abated.

'Our fellow-travellers having kindly intimated they should be pleased with our company in their descent (having settled with our host and purchased some of his mountain curiosities, the prices of which he did not dispute were high, consoling us by saying it was the "highest house in the kingdom") we at once set out and for some distance travelled, as on the previous evening, in nubibus, but after clearing these the views were magnificent and we finally reached Llanberis (we had come down by a different route) without incurring the slightest mishap or apparent danger.

'The difficulties to be encountered in the journey to the summit of this mountain have been much overrated. Tolerably fine weather, moderate health, a little labour and a little patience are the only necessaries. There have been, we regret to say, some fatal accidents within a comparitively recent period but we cannot help thinking that with a little care they might have been avoided. The only difficult or dangerous route is the "Bedd Gelert" and, generally speaking, the danger here may be reduced to a minimum by using ordinary precaution whilst, to a lover of nature, her beauties amply compensate for any slight risk that may be run.

'Arrived at Llanberis, we stroll about and admire some of its chief attractions pending the arrival of the coach from Caernarvon.

'This charming village is surrounded by immense rocks, the highest in the whole island, whose summits are buried in the clouds and are seldom visible at any period of the year. The lakes are very beautiful but we have only time to catch a glimpse at them for our coach appears at the Victoria Hotel. We soon mount up and proceed at a round trot for ten miles to Capel Curig where we determine to dismount and proceed on foot, for the want of our night's rest has several times during the journey made itself dangerously apparent. Here we parted from our mountain friends, with sincere regret, and were soon trudging on for Bettws y Coed, Pentre Voelas and Cerrig y Druidion, at which last place we arrived about 6 pm (we left the summit about 5.30 am) and proceeded to the White Lion thoroughly tired as our readers may imagine. The hospitable reception we again met with, however, cheered us up not a little; so after a most bounteous meal and some amusement we retired to our comfortable bed which seemed positively luxurious after our rough night on the mountain.

'Our fatigue had not entirely worn off the next morning so we determined to stay at our quarters until the evening and then walk to Corwen (10 miles, leaving 15 miles for the next morning to catch the train). However, "man appoints and the weather disappoints": it rained so hard in the evening, when we should have started, that we were constrained to postpone our journey until the morning. But, as we were in such excellent quarters, we did not regret this as we otherwise might have done. The morning came and still pouring with rain but we had no choice now — we must either go or lose our ticket. Our kind hostess had provided an excellent breakfast at a very early hour (soon after 5 o-clock) and a car in which we mounted after bidding farewell with many thanks for general kindness to a comparative stranger. Sheltering ourselves in some measure under a huge ancient umbrella that would have gladdened the heart of "Sairey Gamp" [Charles Dickens' fictional character], we jolted along through the pitiless storm (which, however, only seemed to refresh Dame Nature and make her appear even more charming) for twenty miles to Llangollen; from whence (our horse having a back journey of twenty miles and the driver and ourselves, particularly the driver, being anxious to avoid anything like cruelty to animals) we were reluctantly compelled to proceed the remaining five miles on foot with as much speed as possible and even then, had not the train been like your humble servant, behind, our early rising and uncomfortable ride would have been in vain. But "All's well that ends well"; we were soon installed in our carriage and, our thoughts still clinging to the mighty mountains we had left behind, we arrived in London about 6 pm without any further adventure, having in the space of six days (two of which were mainly occupied in the journey up and down between London and Llangollen) travelled from Llangollen Road to Snowdon and back, considerably over a hundred miles, nearly the whole of which distance was accomplished on foot and the whole of which might be done by coach without causing the total expenses incident to exceed a £5 note.

'Before taking leave of our readers we would remark that we feel certain those who have never travelled in North Wales and determine now to do so will not regret their experiment. For the pedestrian, the roads are excellent; and for those who do not care to walk, a daily coach runs from Llangollen Road to Carnarvon at threepence per mile; and cars can be obtained at the usual rate of a shilling a mile. For both pedestrian and "coachist", the scenery is equally charming; we are assured that it is not surpassed by anything abroad; and really it is time Englishmen generally should know a little more about the beauties of their native land. Indeed, so fashionable has foreign travelling been of late years, and so great are the facilities afforded by our powerful servant, steam, that we doubt not the Continent will be soon "used up" and Englishmen will be compelled to seek for novelty in their own country.'

Great effort has been expended over the centuries in unearthing wealth from the mountains of North Wales. Copper, lead, gold and asbestos have been extracted with varying degrees of commercial success, the most productive mining being at Parys Mountain in Anglesey where, by 1780, 3,000 tons of copper ore were being obtained each year. The atmosphere inside a working copper mine can be experienced at the Sygun site just outside Beddgelert on the road through Nant Gwynant. Abandoned in 1903, Sygun was re-opened in 1986 as a tourist attraction and appears to be thriving.

More profitable than any Welsh copper or gold mine, the slate quarries of Llanberis resemble the slices of an immense cake. The initial ugliness of these vast industrial relics becomes more tolerable with the realisation that the onlooker is seeing into the very heart of a mountain. Thomas Assheton Smith, a local land-owner, began developing the Dinorwig slate quarry with three partners in 1809 and acquired enormous wealth. Quarrying at Dinorwig continued for 160 years. A description of the enterprise was written in May 1859 by a Mr Millington, son of the then works superintendent, and is quoted in John Eardley-Wilmot's *Thomas Assheton Smith: Reminiscences of a famous fox hunter*:

'The Dinorwic slate quarries are situated on a mountain called the Elidir (one of the Snowdonian range, and contiguous to Snowdon), which rises about 2000 feet above the level of the sea: they derive their name of Dinorwic, or Dinorwig, from an ancient manor in which they are situated, and lie partly in the parish of Llanberris, and partly in that of Llandemilen, in the county of Caernarvon. The period at which slate was first found in these quarries is unknown, but the regular and systematic working commenced about sixty years ago and they have been gradually increasing in extent. The great increase, however, has taken place since 1828, when the late Mr Assheton Smith succeeded to the property at the death of his father. On entering into possession, he carried on the works in a most vigorous and enterprising manner, opened many fresh quarries, and extended those already in work, so that in the space of thirty years they have quadrupled in extent. There are now employed about 2,400 men and boys; and the amount expended monthly in wages and materials exceeds £9000.

'There are various descriptions of slates produced, varying in quality, as best or fine slate, seconds or strong slate; and also in the colour, as grey or light blue, dark blue or purple, red, and also green; the last named, however, being found in but small quantities. The body of slate rock is of very considerable extent. The present workings cover a space of not less than one square mile; the highest elevation of the quarries now open is about 1,500 feet above the level of the Llanberris lakes, and about 1,800 feet above the level of the sea. The depth of the slate rock has never been ascertained, but it is supposed to be between 1,500 and 2,000 feet. The rock in these quarries has been worked to the depth of 300 perpendicular feet. The roofing slates are split and dressed in numerous sheds, situated on the rubbish banks adjoining the quarries. The slabs are manufactured at powerful steam and water mills in the immediate neighbourhood. 'Convenient tramways, about twenty-three miles in extent, are laid along the various workings and quarry banks; upon these small waggons are run, into which the slates and slabs are loaded and taken to the inclines, whence they are let down by wire ropes to the railway terminus. The inclines are laid up the precipitous side of the mountain and are eighteen in number, averaging 600 feet in length. At the railway terminus adjoining the quarries, the small loaded waggons are placed upon large trucks (each holding four), and are then formed into trains, and drawn by locomotives to the shipping port. From the quarries to the port, the railway, called "the Padarn Railway", is rather more than seven miles in length, and was constructed by the late Mr Assheton Smith at a very considerable outlay about the year 1843, solely for the purposes of the works.

'The place of shipment is a commodious harbour, called "Port Dinorwic", a private port, used only for the shipment of slates from the Dinorwic quarries, and is situated in the Menai Straits, half-way between Bangor and Caernarvon. It was commenced on a small scale by the late Mr Smith's father, but was enlarged and extended to its present size by Mr Smith himself, who also added to it two commodious and convenient docks. About 120 vessels can lie alongside the quays and in the docks, securely sheltered from all winds. Slates are shipped largely from hence to most of the seaports of England, Ireland, and Scotland, to the Baltic and German ports, and extensively to the United States of America. A branch of the Caernarvon and Bangor railway connects this port with the Chester, and Holyhead, and London and North-Western lines, by which means slates are conveyed in large quantities to the manufacturing and midland districts of England.'

Several slate quarrying sites in Snowdonia were rescued from abandonment by switching their attention to the tourist industry, notably in Blaenau Ffestiniog and Llanberis. They exercised an equal fascination to travellers in the heyday of slate quarrying, encouraging a Bangor printer, A. R. Martin, to include in his 1856 guide to North Wales 'lines written by the late Judge Leycester':

'It has truly been said, as we all must deplore,
That Grenville and Pitt made peers by the score;
But now 'tis asserted, unless I have blundered,
There's a man that makes peeresses here by the hundred,
He regards neither Portland, nor Grenville, nor Pitt
But creates them at once without patent or writ;
By the stroke of a hammer, without the king's aid,
A lady, or countess, or duchess is made!
Yet high is the station from which they are sent,
And all their great titles are got by descent.
And where e'er they are seen, in a palace or shop,
Their rank they preserve, and are still at the top.
Yet no merit they claim from their birth or connection,
But derive their chief worth from their native complexion,
And all the best judges prefer, it is said,
A countess in blue to a duchess in red;
This countess, or lady, though crowds may be present,
Submits to be dressed by the hands of a peasant,
And you'll see when her grace is but once in his clutches;
With how little respect he will handle a duchess!
Close united they seem, and yet all who have tried them,
Soon discover how easy it is to divide them.
No spirit have they — they're as thin as a lath;
The countess wants life, and the duchess is flat.
No passion or warmth to the countess is known,
And her grace is as cold and as hard as a stone;
Yet I fear you will find, if you watch them a little,
That the countess is frail and the duchess is brittle;
Too high for a trade, yet without any joke,

Tho' they never are bankrupt, they often are broke;
And tho' not a soul ever pilfers or cozens,
They are daily shipp'd off, and transported by dozens.
In France, Jacobinical France, we have seen,
How nobles have bled by the fierce guillotine;
But what's the French engine of death to compare,
To the engine which Greenfield and Bramah prepare?
That democrat engine by which we all know,
Ten thousand great duchesses fell at one blow!
And long may this engine its wonders display
Long level with ease all the rocks in its way,
'Til the veil of Nantfrancon of slates is bereft,
Nor a lady, nor countess, nor duchess is left.'

Martin adds: 'These slates were whimsically named nearly a century ago by General Wharburton, duchess, countesses, ladies etcetera, to distinguish their size, colour etcetera.'

North Wales: How to See it for Four Guineas was published in Manchester in 1869 by John Bradbury. A companion volume would follow seven years later under the title *The Isle of Wight: How to See it for Six Guineas*. The proposed method of travel was mainly by rail, supplemented by walking, ferry and the occasional coach, using the following carefully costed itinerary:

	£	s.	d.
Return ticket, by excursion to Conway	0	8	0
Return ticket, Llandudno Junction to Llandudno	0	0	8
Tea at cottage on Great Ormes Head	0	1	0
Hotel Bill, Llandudno	0	16	0
Second class, Llandudno Junction to Bettws-y-Coed	0	2	2
Admission through Garden at ditto	0	0	1
Dinner at Bettws-y-Coed	0	3	0
Hotel Bill, Dolwydellan	0	4	0
Dinner at Pen-y-Gwryd Hotel	0	3	0
Second Class Llanberis to Carnarvon	0	1	0
Admission to Carnarvon Castle	0	0	4

Hotel Bill, Carnarvon	0	6	6
Coach to Beddgelert	0	3	6
Dinner at ditto	0	2	0
Hotel bill and sandwiches, Festiniog	0	8	6
Coach, Bettws-y-Coed to Bangor	0	5	0
Crossing Menai Bridge	0	0	1
Ferry to Garth Point	0	0	1
Ferry to Beaumaris and Returning	0	0	2
Hotel Bill, Bangor	0	7	6
Sandwiches, for luncheon at Penmaenmawr	0	1	0
Third class, Bangor to Penmaenmawr	0	0	9
Crossing Conway Suspension Bridge	0	0	1
Hotel Bill, Conway	0	7	6
Admission to Conway Castle	0	0	3
Sundries	0	1	10
	£4	4	0

Bradbury's description of Capel Curig is particularly pleasing:

'Capel Curig (pronounced Kappel Kerrig [kirrig]) is so called from a small chapel here dedicated to the British saint Curig. The proportions of the village are quite insignificant as it consists only of a few cottages which were stables in the "good old coaching days". A great number of horses were kept here to work the coaches plying between London and Holyhead en route for Ireland. It is scarcely possible to conceive a more retired or beautiful spot; and the tourist with time at his disposal should certainly spend a little of it in this charming place. He will find the Royal Hotel a most comfortable, homely and well-managed house. The prices are: breakfast and tea, 1s 6d, 2s, and 2s 6d; dinner, 3s; beds, 2s and 2s 6d; attendance, 1s 6d per day. These charges will be found most reasonable for the excellent accommodation received. The writer has spent some time here and strongly recommends all who can afford to make a stay at this hotel where they will find all the comforts of a home and receive every attention from the obliging host and hostess.

'The hotel was built by the late Lord Penrhyn and was a favourite place for coach travellers between Holyhead and London to pass the night. Its walls have sheltered the Duke of Richmond and numerous other dukes and members of the aristocracy. Our present Queen, when Princess Victoria, stayed here some time and behind the hotel is a small square pond in which she fished. Here they are compelled to breed fish for themselves in consequence of the isolated position of the hotel. The fish are bred in the two large lakes (called Mymbyr) near here and are at times netted and brought up to the small pond before-named where they are allowed to swim until required for the tea or breakfast of some hungry tourist, when they are lifted out by means of a small hand-net to be cooked; and very delicious they are I can assure you.'

Bradbury itemised his tours to the last penny though the prices he quotes make strange reading today. His recommendations for Llanberis:

'There are numerous well-conducted hotels here; the Royal Victoria is the principal and largest house. The Queen, when Princess Victoria, stayed at this hotel while visiting Llanberis Pass in 1832.

'The following are the hotels and their prices:-

'DOLBADARN HOTEL (proprietor R. Roberts):

'Breakfast or tea (plain), 1s. 6d.; with extras 1s. 9d. to 2s.; 3s.; bed (single), 2s.; double-bedded room, 3s.; attendance, 3d. per meal each person; chamber-maid, 6d. per night; boots, 4d. per pair.

'CASTLE HOTEL:

'Same proprietor and prices.

'GLYN PERIS HOTEL (proprietor, John G. Jones):
'Breakfast or tea (plain), 1s.; with extras, 1s. 6d.; dinners,

2s.; beds, 1s. to 1s. 6d.; attendance, 3d. per meal. (This hotel, being a little withdrawn from the village, is more moderate in its prices, so as to compete with those which are nearer Llanberis.)

'PADARN VILLA HOTEL (proprietor, J. E. Williams):
'Breakfast or tea (plain), 2s.; with extras, 2s. 6d.; dinners, 3s. 6d. to 4s.; beds, 2s.; attendance, 3d. each meal, or 1s. 6d. per night.

'GLYN PADARN, (proprietor, R. Williams):
'Breakfast or tea (plain), 1s.; with extras, 1s. 3d.; dinners, 1s. 6d.; beds, 1s. 6d. to 2s.

'And I must again recommend the reader, if he can spare the time, to stay awhile here. The best ascent of Snowdon is made from this village, the distance to the summit being only about five miles and a quarter. Ponies and guides, varying from 5s. to 7s. 6d. each, may be had at any of the hotels to take tourists to the top of the mountain. The track is quite available for ladies, and I know of nothing more enjoyable than a party ascending the king of Welsh mountains on a fine day. A guide is absolutely necessary to make the ascent, and on no account should the attempt be made without one. A diversity of opinion exists between the Llanberis, Pen-y-Gwryd, and Beddgelert people as to which is the best place wherefrom to make the ascent, each party claiming the preference; but, according to competent judges, Llanberis is by far the most preferable. About half a mile from the Royal Victoria Hotel is the waterfall of Cewnant Mawr; or, fall of the great chasm. It is about sixty feet high, and is formed by the descent of a mountain stream, called Cwm Brwynog, but would be worth a visit if you were remaining at Llanberis.

'The extensive Slate Quarries which are seen on the opposite side of the lake employ, it is said, about one thousand five hundred men. The blasting occurs every hour, and a horn sounds ten minutes before the time, to warn the quarrymen to leave the cuttings.

'Having spent a little time at Llanberis, we must reluctantly take train (second class fare, 1s.; distance, eight miles) to Carnarvon.'

The most notable feature of Caernarfon is its castle which, spiral staircases apart, affords welcome relief from a surfeit of mountain-walking. Bradbury gives an excellent sketch of its history:

'Carnarvon Castle was built by Edward I soon after his conquest of the Principality. The work began in 1283 and the building occupied about twelve years in erection. It is considered one of the finest ruins of its kind in the empire. The external portion is in a good state of preservation and almost entire. The Roman Segontium furnished materials for the building, the walls of which vary from eight to ten feet thick and enclose an area equal to about three acres. The first custodian was John de Havering who was probably succeeded by Sir Roger de Puleson.

'In 1294 the Welsh, ground down by excessive taxation, "revolushed" as the late Artemus Ward would say, and, led by Madoc, captured the castle, finally crowning their victory by putting the English inhabitants to death and burning the town. In 1402, Owen Glyndwr invested the town and castle but was beaten off by an English and two Welsh captains who gallantly defended the latter for Henry IV.

'During the civil wars it was taken and retaken several times by the Royalists and Parliamentary forces but in 1646 it yielded to the latter, commanded by a General Mytton. Two years later, Sir John Owen made an unsuccessful attempt to recover it for the king when a most determined battle was fought near Llandegai which resulted in Sir John's defeat and capture.

'Thirteen towers of different form adorn the castle walls, the principal being the Eagle Tower. A small dark chamber, twelve feet by eight feet, in this tower is shown as the room in which Edward II, the first Prince of Wales was born. But this is not true, simply from the fact that the tower was not then built and only finished when the second Edward was thirty years old and in the tenth year of his reign. Besides, the room is the most dungeon-looking apartment for such an interesting event to have taken place and has probably been the smallest and most ill-conditioned room in the castle. It is more likely to have been a prison or sentinel chamber. Tradition always assigns the smallest, darkest, most miserable and most unlikely corners in castles for royal births and important events. However, in this case tradition will have to "come down a cropper". The front entrance displays a fine bit of gothic. On the east side is the Queen's Gate, called after Queen Eleanor who is said to have entered the castle by this gate.'

Chapter Twelve

A popular route to the Snowdon summit is the Watkin Path which begins six kilometres north east of Beddgelert along the road to Capel Curig. The path was opened in September 1892 by the then prime minister, William Gladstone, and ran through land owned by the railway magnate Sir Edward William Watkin (1819 to 1901).

Quite apart from his love of Snowdonia, Watkin was a fascinating character. He was born in Salford and began his working life in the cotton trade with his father (Absolom Watkin) but in 1845 left to become secretary of the Trent Valley Railway. His management skills and his ability to unite competing railway companies attracted the attention of the Duke of Newcastle. In 1861, Watkin was sent to Canada to investigate the prospect of merging the five British provinces into a single dominion.

Watkin's ambition of creating an uninterrupted railway line between Manchester and Paris led him in 1881 to commence excavating a tunnel beneath the English Channel. A pilot tunnel was bored for a distance of nearly 2 km from a shaft at Shakespeare Cliff, Dover, and a similar distance from the French coast at Sangatte near Calais. Work was stopped very reluctantly in 1882 at the insistence of the British government, fearful of invasion, despite pressure from Watkin as member of parliament for Hythe. He turned instead to mining for Kentish coal. Watkin's later proposal for a railway tunnel between Scotland and Ireland came to nothing but his attempt to give Britain a rival to the Eiffel Tower succeeded as far as its first stage. The Watkin Tower was opened to the public in 1896 but further funds failed to materialise and the structure was demolished six years after Watkin's death. It is now the site of Wembley Stadium.

The ceremonial opening of the Watkin Path was performed on Monday September 13 1892 at what is now called Gladstone Rock, about 2 km from the start of the path in the valley of Cwm Llan. Eight 1 inch diameter bolt holes which secured a temporary wooden platform can still be seen near the top of the rock, three of them (in 1991) still retaining their bolts. The derelict remains of Watkin's chalet can also still be seen at the centre of a landscaped garden (now largely overgrown but still fascinating to visit) on the west side of the lower end of the path. David Erwyd Jenkins describes it in his book *Bedd Gelert, its Facts, Fairies and Folk-lore* which, despite the quaintness of its title, is one of the finest parish histories ever written:

'At the angle between the Snowdon path and the road to Hafod y Llan are Sir Edward Watkin's coach-house and stables, built from the stones of old ruins, like that of Bwlch Gareg, near Hafod y Llan Uchaf, and Mur Cryfaglach, the latter giving signs of having been a place of considerable importance.

'Sir Edward's chalet now looks down upon us from one of the choicest spots in Cwmllan, at an elevation of a little more than 100 feet above the main road. It is built on the ground of an old cottage called Ty'n y Coedcae but is made of a far more perishable material than the humble structure which it replaces. The appearance of the painted corrugated iron possesses no charm, and the retreat of the wealthy "Railway King"' of modern times depends entirely upon its situation for its external attractiveness. It is exceedingly comfortable within and Sir Edward visits his Eryrian home with intense delight whenever the season comes round, nestling within its peaceful seclusion as if weary of the weight of the crown which skill and enterprise have brought him and as if laying it down, unobserved by the world without, gave him new strength and energy for the busier life of Cheshire and Kent.

'The Chalet "is only one storey high but, occupying considerable space of ground, is a happy compromise between commodiousness and cosiness. All the rooms are panelled with light wood and every room is abundantly served with electric light. The service is ingeniously managed and is perhaps the cheapest in England [sic]". The never-failing reservoir constructed at Braich yr Oen, below the copper mine of that name, supplies "the motive power, which is concentrated upon a beautiful little engine in a shed just below the Chalet" (Pall Mall Budget, September 15, 1892).'

Jenkins then progresses to what was meant to be the formal opening of the Watkin Path:

'In the eyes of Welshmen, the most popular act of Sir Edward Watkin since his advent to Snowdonia was his bringing of Mr Gladstone to Cwmllan. The sturdy veteran [in his 83rd year] had been making a speech at Carnarvon on September 12 1892 on his way to Nant Gwynen and had made his route along the Narrow Gauge Railway from Dinas to Rhyd-ddu. On the 13th thousands followed the same route, seeking to reach a particular spot in Cwmllan in time for the meeting to declare Sir Edward's new path to Snowdon free for ever for public use. It little mattered to those enthusiastic admirers of the Grand Old Man that a drenching rain poured down upon them; their one concern was getting to Cwmllan. And who can describe their various methods of getting there?

'Shortly after mid-day the hanging clouds began to lift and it turned out a delightful afternoon such as we frequently get in these mountain districts after showery mornings. When the sun had come forth from behind the dense clouds, it came to cast its gleams upon the hundred cataracts of Cwmllan, which the morning rains had coloured and quickened. Nature, indeed, seemed to have come to a good understanding with the important occasion and vied with the two thousand people in the heartiness of its welcome. Between three and four o'clock, Sir Edward and Lady Watkin, Miss Gladstone, Mrs Drew, Mr Herbert Gladstone, Mr J. Bryn Roberts MP, Mr Thomas Ellis MP and Mr D. Lloyd-George MP had surrounded Mr and Mrs Gladstone on the rostrum which had been put up for the occasion on "a picturesque bluff" in the very centre of the valley. The hymn-singing, which had been interrupted by the enthusiastic cheers of the crowd, gave Mr Gladstone so much delight that he was loath to do anything except listen to the music; but an address from the Liberal Association of Festiniog, and another from the quarrymen of Llanberis, had to be heard read in the vernacular before the second hymn was given. The choirs of Carnarvon and Portmadoc were led by Mr W. J. Williams, of the former town, but nearly every member of the crowd swelled the strains along with the choirs from first to last.

'Mr Gladstone was in the best of spirits and made an excellent speech dwelling upon Disestablishment only for a brief moment and throwing the weight of the occasion into the vexed "Land Question in Wales". Mr Bryn Roberts MP proposed a vote of thanks and Mr T. E. Ellis MP, who came in for a well-deserved word of praise in the speech of his great leader, seconded the same. After Mr Lloyd-George MP had warmly supported the proposition, Sir Edward asked the gathering to show its favour by lifting up their two hands. The rocks resounded with the cheers which followed and the "Grand Old Man" replied by asking for "more of that delightful Welsh music". After several pieces had been rendered, the party returned to the Chalet amid the hearty strains of "Land of my Fathers".

'The amusing side of this gathering is that it was meant to open up the new path to Snowdon, and to declare it public property for ever more; but not a word was said of the new path from beginning to end. On the following morning, however, the host, hostess and guests started out of the Chalet, accompanied by Mr Edward Owen, the tried guide of Bedd Gelert, and some constables, on their way to Snowdon, or at least Bwlch y Saethau. This formally, or informally, opened up the path, though only Mrs Drew and Mrs Edgar Watkin climbed to the summit.'

In 1871, Swiss promotors had completed Europe's first

rack-and-pinion railway. This ran from Vitznau on the shore of Lake Lucerne to the summit of Mount Rigi. Plans for a similar venture on Snowdon were published in the *London Gazette* in November of the same year but foundered during the following year in the face of strong local opposition.

On August 15 1877, the North Wales Narrow Gauge Railway commenced carrying passenger traffic between Cwellyn on Snowdon's west flank and Dinas Junction where it met the main line to Caernarfon. The service was extended to a station appropriately called Snowdon Ranger on June 1 1878 and to Rhyd-ddu on May 14 1881. This line had little impact on the Llanberis-centered tourist trade until the railway managers had the bright idea of changing the name of Rhyd-ddu station to 'South Snowdon'. A contemporary advertisement issued by the line describes its route, much of which can still be seen and explored:

'This railway (the gauge of which is only 2 feet) passes through some of the most picturesque scenery in Wales.

'Starting from Dinas Station, 3 miles from Carnarvon, on the London and North Western Railway, the line ascends for 2 miles, at a gradient of 1 in 48, to Tryfan Junction, whence a branch goes up to Bryngwyn, rising for 2½ miles at an average gradient of 1 in 40.

'From Bryngwyn a magnificent view is obtained, extending over Carnarvon, the Menai Straits and Anglesey on the one hand, to the fine mountains known as the Rivals (Yr Eifl) on the other; and the access to the top of Moel Tryfan is easy. This mountain is of great interest from the prehistoric sea-beach deposited on its summit, now 1400 feet above the sea level.

'From Tryfan Junction the main line runs through the of Bettws Garmon, following from Wawnfawr to Rhyd-Ddu, the same route as that taken by the coaches from Carnarvon to Beddgelert. In this valley the mountains close in on either side. The scenery at this point becomes most picturesque; the line winds in successive curves between the river on the left and the mountains on the right. Soon the waterfall and the old bridge of Nant Mill, well-known to artists, come into view on the left; and running close to the foot of the Great Mountain (Mynydd Mawr) the line shortly after emerges into the open space in which lies Lake Quellyn [Cwellyn]. Close to the lake on the right hand is the sight of Wolf's Castle (Castell Cidwm). Here the peak of Snowdon comes into sight.

'Lake Quellyn is a beautiful expanse of water upwards of a mile in length and a quarter of a mile in width. It abounds with fish of all kinds; the fishing is free and boats can be hired for fishing or excursions on the lake at the Snowdon Ranger Hotel, which is close to Snowdon Station.

'On reaching the lake, the line runs along the side of the sloping ground at the foot of the mountains, rising gradually to Snowdon Ranger station. There a fine view of Snowdon and its rugged precipices is obtained. The ascent can be made from this place, the distance being about 3 miles to the summit.

'From Snowdon Ranger station to Rhyd Ddu, the terminus, the line ascends continuously. About a mile from Snowdon Ranger station, it crosses, by means of an iron bridge with a single span of 100 feet, a deep ravine, at the bottom of which there is a mountain stream, which descends in a cascade down the mountain side at the head of the gorge.

'From this point the line winds along the mountain side by rugged rocks and through wild scenery, not to be surpassed for its grandeur in Wales, until it reaches Rhyd Ddu. The view of the lake in the distance from this portion of the line is very fine and can only be obtained from the railway.

'The line is far above the level of the lake and of the Coach Road; and the scene before the traveller by the railway is grand and picturesque. Below lie the waters of Lake Quellyn; at its further end Mynydd Mawr stands boldly up and across, on the opposite side, are seen the sharp peaks of the mountains which rise above and behind the lower range of hills which fringe the further edge of the lake.

'From Rhyd Ddu the shortest ascent of Snowdon can be made, the distance to the summit being only 2½ miles.

'Rhyd Ddu is about 3 miles distance from Beddgelert. The road passes by the curious rock known as Pitt's Head from its likeness to the profile of that eminent statesman.

'Tourists by this railway will have ample time to visit Beddgelert (the grave of Gelert and Pont Aberglaslyn, returning by the same route, or they can proceed by coach to Llanberis and thence to Carnarvon by London and North Western Railway or proceed on to Portmadoc.

'Conveyances for Beddgelert meet the trains on arrival at Rhyd Ddu.'

Pitt's Head, incidentally, is still visible on the west side of the Caernarfon to Beddgelert road just south of Rhyd-ddu. It stares towards the Snowdon summit but can only be appreciated from its north side. David Jenkins explains its supposed origin in *Bedd Gelert, its Facts, Fairies and Folk-lore*:

'A heap of stones standing about fifty yards from the gate that leads up to the farm of Fridd Uchaf, on the left side of the road, is called in Welsh "Ceryg Collwyn" and in English "Pitt's Head". The latter name has been given to it by English-speaking tourists who, in looking from the Carnarvon side, see something in its outline like the profile of the great statesman Pitt. The heap is of artificial construction and was probably erected about the ninth century in honour of the Welsh chief Collwyn who was the head of one of the fifteen tribes of Wales, and who was lord of Eifionydd, Ardudwy and part of Lleyn. It is quite probable that this vale, in the middle of which stands this pile, is called after his name — in fact there can be little doubt of it.'

In 1906, a new company (the Portmadoc, Beddgelert & South

Snowdon) began constructing a railway from Porthmadog through the Aberglaslyn Pass and Beddgelert to join the North Wales Narrow Gauge Railway. The tight squeeze at Aberglaslyn was bypassed using the expensive option of blasting an 840 metre tunnel through granite. Before the line could be completed, the Dinas to South Snowdon service fell into bankruptcy, carrying its final passenger traffic in 1916. Work on the link continued and the complete line from Porthmadog to Dinas opened in 1923 as the Welsh Highland Railway. The service survived until 1933 and was sustained a further two years by the Festiniog Railway before being closed. In 1941, the track was lifted to contribute to the wartime need for scrap metal.

Adjacent to National Trust land, the route of the Welsh Highland Railway between Beddgelert and Pontaberglaslyn has become one of the most popular and beautiful walks in all Snowdonia, with the advantage for exhausted climbers of being almost entirely horizontal. The tunnel is sufficiently illuminated from each end to be quite safely walked without a torch and has undoubtedly been traversed by far more pedestrians than it would ever have carried rail passengers, even if the line had remained open.

The same railway mania which created the Dinas to South Snowdon narrow-gauge line encouraged the much more successful (and still very much alive) rack-and-pinion line from Llanberis to the Snowdon summit. In 1894, a syndicate of Llanberis and Liverpool promoters met to plan a line to the summit. In a letter to *The Times* of November 6 1894, the honorary secretary of the National Trust expressed his fears about these proposals:

'Sir, Considerable alarm has been caused by certain vague reports, in the Press, of a projected railway up Snowdon and an hotel on the summit. The enclosed correspondence on the subject may therefore be of interest to your readers. Having ascertained on reliable authority that the line had been surveyed, and that Mr Assheton Smith, the proprietor of part of Snowdon, had withdrawn his opposition and, though not a promotor of the scheme, was granting facilities to others, and knowing that he had on two other occasions successfully opposed Bills in Parliament for a similar project, I wrote to him as follows:-

"Tyn-y-Ffynon, Barmouth, North Wales, October 23 1894

"Dear Sir, I have hesitated to write to you till I had heard some certainty as to the railway so deplorably projected up Snowdon and I am the more emboldened to approach you because I know of your opposition, on former occasions, to the project. I write now — in the name of the National Trust for the Preservation of Sites of Historical Interest and Natural Beauty, which has lately been incorporated by charter of the Board of Trade — to ask if, at the eleventh hour, you would, in the best interests of the nation, reconsider the matter . . .

"Yours obediently, H. D. Rawnsley"

"Vaynol Park, Bangor, North Wales, October 24

"Dear Sir, In reply to your letter of this morning, I regret to say that I cannot take the same view of the matter as your association appears to do. You are right in saying that I was in former years opposed to the scheme; but times have changed and, if in many ways one does not advance with them, one is left alone. In trying to direct the tourists to Llanberis, and making things easy for them, I am consulting the interest of this estate and the neighbourhood in which I live, and I cannot recognise any outside interference in the matter.

"Faithfully yours, G. W. Duff Assheton Smith"

'It if be urged that the railway is necessary to give access to the mountain, we answer that it is easily accessible now from Capel Curig, Beddgelert and Llanberis, and that ample pony tracks go within a few yards of the summit. By day and by night, if need be, all but the infirm can ascend Snowdon. A friend aged 75 and his little grand-daughter aged nine made the ascent last summer without fatigue. The Arch-Druid, Clwydfardd, who has just died in his 95th year, ascended Snowdon when he was 84.

'If it be argued that more hotel accommodation is necessary, we rejoin that the little refreshment house on the summit, with its four beds, probably satisfies all the needs of those who wish to see the sun rise, and that neither the heat of the Welsh valleys or plains, nor the cloudlessness of the Welsh skies, will warrant any building of a health resort on the top of Snowdon.

'It is said that the projected railway will be good for trade and bring excursionists to Llanberis. We answer, Yes; and will destroy the trade of the ponies and guides that now exists, and impoverish the other villages from which the ascent is now often made, unless, as was the case on the Rigi, Capel Curig and Beddgelert, not to be outdone, at once promote rival railway schemes.

'It is asserted that such a railway will accommodate the thousands who come for a day trip. We believe we are right in saying that the cost of building such a line to the satisfaction of the Board of Trade is so great that the tariff must be prohibitive except to the well-to-do travellers. Cheap tickets on mountain railways are practically unknown, as the Swiss traveller can testify. It will not add to the cheapness of the Snowdon railway that the tourist season is a very short one, and the only way in which the passenger traffic management will probably be able to meet expenses is by the exploitation of the mountain and by mineral traffic. Those who remember what Llanberis was before the quarries existed are naturally not anxious to see the Llanberis experiment repeated from base to summit.

'What we protest against most, however, is the "commercialising" of scenery. Snowdon, unrailwayed, unvulgarised, and unexploited, is a better investment for Wales, for Llanberis, or any of the villages that cluster round its base, than Snowdon turned into a mixture of tea-garden and switchback. The love of natural scenery — hardly more than a century old in Great Britain — is working gradually downward into the mass of the people. To those who feel that mountain railways are the crown of our nineteenth century progress, we say, with Ruskin, "Yes, progress! but whither?"

'Yours obediently, H. D. Rawnsley, Hon. Sec. National Trust, Crosthwaite Vicarage, Keswick.'

Work on the line began on December 15 1894, Assheton Smith leading the ceremonials. His wife was unwell and was represented by their daughter Enid whose name is commemorated on one of the railway's engines. The service was opened on April 6 1896 under the banner of the Snowdon Mountain Tramroad & Hotels Company Limited but was marred by the loss of an engine and consequent death of a passenger . . . Ellis Griffiths Roberts, landlord of the Padarn Villa Hotel in Llanberis. He had been sitting next to the manager of the line, G. C. Aitchison, who was controlling the carriage-brake in one of the first trains to descend with a normal complement of passengers. As the train approached Clogwyn station, the two carriages suddenly lurched and began to accelerate. Aitchison shouted to his 83 passengers to stay in their seats as he applied the brake but two, including Roberts, jumped out while the carriages were still descending. Roberts suffered a severe leg injury and died the following day.

The brakes halted the carriages but the passengers emerged to find the engine, which for safety reasons was not coupled to the carriages, had vanished. The driver, William Pickles, and his nephew had jumped clear and explained that the engine had become disengaged from the rack while in the cutting above Clogwyn and, gathering speed, had left the curving track near the bridge where it crosses the path from Llanberis and plunged over a precipice. The line was closed a year for modifications and has since maintained an excellent safety record.

It is much to Sir Edward Watkin's credit that he neither

tunnelled through Snowdon nor built a rival railway to its summit though he was rumoured to be contemplating such a rival from the Beddgelert side. This might explain A. G. Bradley's confusion in his *Highways and Byways in North Wales*, 1898:

'The Wyddfa, the main peak of Snowdon, shows from time to time, and a faint white puff steaming along what looks from here like the edge of a mighty precipice marks the approach of Sir Edward Watkin's little train to its aerial terminus. People talk in somewhat exaggerated fashion, it seems to me, about these mountain railways, and indeed about all railways in their connection with scenery. By one's fireside, the size of a mountain is apt to dwindle and that of a locomotive to be magnified. But when it comes to the reality, what a tiny speck is this diminutive train on the wide waste of Snowdon, passing in and out of one's vision three or four times in the course a long summer's day in its tortuous journey of an hour and a half from Llanberis to the summit.

'There is a vague impression abroad, and I must confess to having once felt something of the kind myself, that the Snowdon railway would in some sort spoil the mountain, that its solitude would be desecrated and shaken by the perpetual roar and clatter of a noisy locomotive. If the main line of the South Western with four tracks, and trains following one another every ten minutes along each, ran over the top of Snowdon, it would be another matter. As for this little midget, it seems to me a trifle scarcely worth considering except for the pleasure it gives to innumerable people who are still possessed of all their faculties, have eyes and brains and every necessary qualification to enable them to enjoy the noblest view in Britain, but may perchance no longer be able to climb 3,560 feet without injury or discomfort.'

The Penygwryd hotel, at the far end of the road which climbs from Llanberis through Pen-y-pass, retains even today the charm which attracted Bradley:

'Pen-y-gwryd has memories of the Kingsleys who have celebrated it in prose and verse, and though universally patronised by passing coaches in the season, still belongs to the order of the snug and friendly Welsh inn as opposed to the caravansary under "English enterprise" where you become a number and are at the mercy of a young woman from Manchester, dressed in the height of second class fashion, to whom the neighbourhood of Snowdon is an intolerable exile to be counted by days.

'For my part I love these old Welsh inns. It takes a vast deal to spoil them. There are not many left, it is true, in the Snowdon mountains, but Pen-y-gwryd, if not precisely a type of those I am thinking of, has, hitherto at any rate, been of the genus. But I know them well, from Aberdovey to Flint and from Aberdaron to Montgomery. Now I do not like your chilly and pretentious coffee room, where you ring the bell for your modest requirements, and sit upon an anti-macassared chair looking at a print of Her Majesty's Coronation till a waiter in a white tie brings your change upon a silver tray. Give to me, ever and always, the snug parlour behind the bar, where the landlady, in the interval of her manifold duties, takes fitful snatches at her needlework and the local gossips foregather. And Welsh landladies, I may remark, are generally bright and often very clever matrons indeed. And the best of company. Here beneath the time-honoured and familiar prints of the old "Sir Watkin" [of the illustrious Wynn family, not Sir Edward] and the late Lord Penrhyn and the Old Maids of Llangollen and a stuffed trout or two, let me eat my noon-day crust and crack my bottle of Wrexham ale, while the metal horse that wants neither ostler nor food nor water waits patiently in the passage.'

Published in 1899, David Jenkins' *Bedd Gelert, its Facts, Fairies and Folk-lore* ranges far beyond the village confines and includes the following account of The Snowdon Summit:

'The excellent idea of providing refreshments on the summit of Snowdon is now over sixty years old and belongs to a miner who was at that time working in Clogwyn Coch copper mine. His name was Morris Williams, and his native place Amlwch, in Anglesey. It was while busily engaged in the mine that it occurred to him how large a number climbed Snowdon during the summer months, and that perhaps it would pay him to provide a small hut near the summit, where they might get something to refresh themselves. He tried the experiment once or twice without the hut, taking with him tea, coffee, butter, bread, and cheese, and was soon convinced that a living could be made there.

'The first hut was built about 1837 or 1838, and was situated below the summit cairn, on the property of Hafod y Llan. Its outer walls were of stone and its inner lining of neatly planed boards. Morris Williams could neither speak nor understand English, and his business suffered in consequence. In order to get over this difficulty he took one of the guides, William Williams by name, into partnership; and he, thinking to add to the attraction of Snowdon, dressed himself in a suit of goat-skin, consisting of cap, coat, and trousers, which made him appear like a savage from the land of perpetual snow. The strange dress did its part well, and the flocking visitors soon made the humble summit hut a paying concern.

'John Roberts, Blaen y Ddol, Llanberis, was a guide at this time, and was on the summit nearly every day. He perceived that the keepers of this hotel-in-miniature were on the high road to a solution of their own problem of "a living wage". He thought he would start an opposition, and as the mountain was then, just as it is at present, the property of three different people, he went to Sir R. W. Bulkeley, Baron Hill, to secure a spot for a hut, and succeeded in his errand. The tent was pitched on the spot where now stands a respectable structure, on the Llanberis side of the peak, and soon took away the greater part of the business done. There was nothing for it but to remove the prior structure to the top too; the wood lining the old hut was taken to build the new one, and the competition was placed on a fairer basis.

'Very soon afterwards, Morris sold his share to his brother, Phillip Williams, and the next thing we find is that Philip and John Roberts have united their interests by a formal partnership. We lose sight of William Williams all at once, and we cannot account for his disappearance, unless, indeed, it was about this time that he lost his life. He had been once a boots at the Dolbadarn Hotel, and was known by all as "William y Boots"; he lost his life in seeking for rare plants, and the gully into which he fell is known to this day as the Gully of William the Boots.

'Visitors now became more numerous every year and the partners determined to apply for a license to sell intoxicants. It was agreed that John Roberts should make the formal application and that the license should be in his name; but when Roberts had secured the license, he refused to let Williams have any advantage from it, and the partnership was dissolved. After a while Phillip Williams discovered that the summit was in the Bedd Gelert parish and that Portmadoc was the proper place to apply for a license. He made several applications, and was each time successfully opposed by Roberts; but his perseverance ultimately succeeded, and from that day to this two licenses are granted for the summit, one at Carnarvon and one at Portmadoc. The right of Carnarvon to grant a license for the summit is one of those obscure points with which British law teems.

'John Roberts died and left his interests to his nephew; Philip Williams died and his daughter kept his hut on after him, until Mr Robert Owen purchased the lease from her, in 1879. He and Thomas J. Roberts joined their business, and things went on smoothly until the Snowdon tramway was mooted, when these thriving men began to be harassed by notices to quit, and attempts to secure a license for another summit hotel. Assheton Smith, Esq., Vaynol, gave them notice to quit, in order to place the summit at the disposal of the Tramway Company, but he could only claim one-third of the area on which the huts were built, and so could not enforce the notice.

'The struggle ended by the company buying up Roberts' rights, and taking over Owen's lease for fourteen years. Owen having in the meantime built a good and commodious wooden structure, for which twenty tons of timber had to be carried up on men's backs and shoulders along the Rhyd-ddu path. Roberts' hut was only replaced at the beginning of last summer, after doing service for fifty-eight years, by a very excellent structure on the Llanberis side.

'At present the Tramway Company has handed over the management of the whole business to Miss Amos who opens out at Easter and closes for the winter about the last week in September. An average of about one hundred and fifty per day visit the summit from April to June, and of no less than seven hundred from July to the second week in September. Should anyone care to spend the night on Snowdon, in order to witness the sunrise, between fifteen and twenty can be accommodated with beds.

'A very great number of people prefer the climb to the ride up the mountain but the majority of those who ascend from Llanberis take the train. The finest day of last August induced no less than 2,200 to ascend, about 1,000 of whom had booked for the double journey; the 200 rode one way and the other 1,000 walked it up — the greater part along the Rhyd-ddu path. There is nothing so invigorating as mountain climbing, and where is there such a mountain for climbing as Snowdon?'

References in Chronological Order

c. AD 100	Cornelius Tacitus (c.55 - c.117) *The Annals of Imperial Rome*
AD 796	Nennius *History of the Britons*
1188	Gerald De Barri (c.1146 - c.1220) *Itinerary Through Wales*
1536	John Leland (c.1502 - 1552) *Itinerary in Wales*
1639	Thomas Johnson (d. 1644) *Itinerary of a Botanist*
1653	John Taylor (1580 - 1653) *Short Relation of a Long Journey*
1682	William Richards (1643 - 1705) *Wallography, or, The Briton Described, being a pleasant Relation of a Journey into Wales*
1698	Edmund Halley (1656 - 1742) *Philosophical Transactions*
1701	E.B. Probably Edward Bysshe *A Trip to North Wales*
1724	Daniel Defoe (1660 or 1661 - 1731) *Tour Through the Whole Island of Great Britain*
1732	John Macky (d. 1726) *A Journey Through England and Scotland*
1756	George Lyttleton (1709 - 1773) *Account of a Journey into Wales*
1774	Henry Penruddocke Wyndham (1736 - 1819) *A Gentleman's Tour Through Monmouthshire and Wales*
1774	Joseph Cradock (1742 - 1826) *An Account of Some of the Most Romantic Parts of North Wales*
1774	Samuel Johnson (1709 - 1784) *Diary of a Journey into North Wales*
1778	Thomas Pennant (1726 - 1798) *Tours in Wales*
1784	John Byng (1742 - 1813) *A Tour to North Wales*

1792	Nicholas Owen (1752 - 1811)
	Caernarvonshire. A Sketch of its History, Antiquities, Mountains and Productions
1795	Joseph Hucks (1772 - 1800)
	A Pedestrian Tour Through North Wales
1795	John Ferrar
	A Tour from Dublin to London
1797	Henry Wigstead
	Remarks on a Tour to North and South Wales
1797	Richard Warner (1763 - 1857)
	A Walk Through Wales
1797	John Henry Manners
	Journal of a Tour into Wales
1798	William Bingley (1774 - 1823)
	Tour Round North Wales
1798	John Evans (1767 - 1827)
	Tour Through North Wales
1798	Henry Skrine (1755 - 1803)
	Tours Through Wales
1802	William Williams (1739 - 1817)
	Observations on the Snowdon Mountains
1803	William Hutton (1723 - 1815)
	Remarks Upon North Wales
1805	William Mavor (1758 - 1837)
	A Tour Through Wales
1806	Antoine Philippe D'Orleans (1775 - 1807)
	Tour in Wales
1807	Edward Pugh
	Cambria Depicta
1810	Richard Fenton (1746 - 1821)
	Tours in Wales
1811	Edmund Hyde Hall
	A Description of Caernarvonshire (1809 - 1811)
1816	Samuel Heinrich Spiker
	Travels Through England, Wales and Scotland
1821	Robert Hasell Newell (1778 - 1852)
	Letters on the Scenery of Wales

1821	Anonymous *The Cambrian Tourist or Post-Chaise Companion through Wales*
1823	G. J. Freeman *Sketches in Wales*
1828	William Cathrall *History of North Wales*
1828	Peter Bayley Williams (1765 - 1836) *Tourist's Guide through the County of Carnarvon*
1833	John Smith *A Guide to Bangor, Beaumaris, Snowdonia and Other Parts*
1837	Joseph Onwhyn *Hints to Pedestrians, or How to Enjoy a Three-Weeks' Ramble Through North and South Wales*
1837	Thomas Turner *Narrative of a Journey with a Fly to North Wales*
1838	George John Bennett (1800 - 1879) *Guide to North Wales*
1838	Catherine Sinclair (1800 - 1864) *Hours in England and Wales*
1840	Emilius Nicholson *Cambrian Traveller's Guide*
1844	Carl Gustav Carus *The King of Saxony's Journey Through England and Scotland*
1845	Georg Johann Kohl *Travels in England and Wales*
1853	Thomas Roscoe (1791 - 1871) *Wanderings and Excursions in North Wales*
1854	George Borrow (1803 - 1881) *Wild Wales*
1856	A. R. Martin *Martin's Week's Wanderings in North Wales*
1860	John Tyndall (1820 - 1893) *Hours of Exercise on the Alps*
1860	Anonymous *A Journey due North Wales*
1869	John Bradbury *North Wales, How to See it for Four Guineas*

1891　　　John Askew Roberts
　　　　　The Gossiping Guide to Wales

1898　　　A. G. Bradley
　　　　　Highways and Byways in North Wales

1899　　　David Erwyd Jenkins
　　　　　Bedd Gelert, its Facts, Fairies and Folk-lore

1902　　　John Eardley-Wilmot (d. 1892)
　　　　　Thomas Assheton Smith

General Bibliography

Books relating to North Wales published prior to 1900

Aikin, Arthur, *Journal of a Tour through North Wales, 1797*.

Alsop, W., *A Descriptive Sketch of Bangor, the Suspension Bridge of the Menai, Snowdon, etcetera*. Shrewsbury, c.1830.

Ambrose, J.W., *The New Tourist Companion Through North Wales, 1856*.

Angus, J.W., *The Seats of the Nobility and Gentry in Great Britain and Wales in a Collection of Selected Views, 1787*.

Anonymous, *A Journey due North Wales, 1860*.

Anonymous, *A Short Account of Carnarvon*. Caernarfon, 1806.

Anonymous, *Gleanings of a Wanderer in Various Parts of England, Scotland and Wales, 1805*.

Archaeologia Cambrensis, 1846 to date.

B., E. [Probably Edward Bysshe], *A Trip to North Wales, 1701*.

Baker, James, *A Picturesque Guide Through Wales and the Marches, 1794-7*.

Barker, T., *Thirty-two Lithographic Impressions of Landscape Scenery, 1814*.

Batenham, A., *The Traveller's Companion in a Predestrian Excursion from Chester through North Wales, 1825*.

Batty, Robert, *Welsh Scenery from Drawings by Captain Batty*. London, 1823.

Bayne, James, *The Tourist's Guide to the Antiquities of Conway Castle, Town and Neighbourhood*. Conwy, 1852.

Bennett, George John, *A Pedestrian Tour through North Wales, 1838*.

Biden, H.B., *All round Snowdon*. London, 1877.

Bigg, W., *Ten Days in North Wales, 1862*.

Bingley, William, *A Tour round North Wales, Performed During the Summer of 1798, 1800*.

Bingley, William, *North Wales Including its Scenery, Antiquities, Customs and Sketches of its Natural History*. 1804.

Black, A.&C., *Black's Picturesque Guide through North and South Wales and Monmouthshire*. Edinburgh, 1851.

Blackwell, Henry, *Bibliography of Local and County Histories*. Brecon, 1886.

Borrow, George, *Wild Wales, 1854*.

Boydell, John, *A Collection of Views of Gentlemen's Seats, Castles and Romantick Places in North Wales, 1792*.

Bradbury, John, *North Wales, How to See it for Four Guineas, 1869*.

Bradley, A.G., *Highways and Byways in North Wales, 1898*.

Bransby, J.H., *Characteristics of the Snowdon Sheep, 1835*.

Bransby, J.H., *A Descriptive and Historical Sketch of Beddgelert and its Neighbourhood*. Caernarfon 1840.

Bransby, J.H., *A Sketch of the History of Carnarvon Castle*. Caernarfon, 1829.

Bransby, J.H., *A Description of Llanberis and the Snowdon District*. Caernarfon, 1845.

Bransby, J.H., *A Description of Carnarvon and the Neighbouring District.* Caernarfon, 1845.

Breese, Edward, *Kalendars of Gwynedd* (list of sheriffs, knights etcetera). London, 1873.

Brewer, J.N., *History and Antiquities of the Cathedral Church of Saint Asaph, with Engravings by J. & H.S. Storer, 1819.*

Bridge, William, *The Tourist's Guide to Llandudno and its Neighbourhood.* Conwy, 1858.

Broughton, B., *Six Picturesque Views in North Wales, 1801.*

Buck, S.&N., *Views of all the Castles in the Principality of Wales, 1742.*

Buck, S.&N., *Buck's Antiquities, or Venerable Remains of above Four Hundred Castles, Palaces etcetera. in England and Wales, with over One Hundred Views of Cities and Chief Towns, 1774.*

Buckler, J.C., *Views of the Cathedral Churches in England and Wales, 1822.*

Burke, J.B., *A Visitation of the Seats and Arms of the Noblemen and Gentlemen of Great Britain, 1852-3.*

Byng, John, *The Torrington Diaries, 1781-1794.* Published 1934.

Cambrian Directory, *The Cambrian Directory.* Salisbury, 1800.

Camden, William, *Britannia, 1695.*

Carlisle, Nicholas, *A Topographical Dictionary of the Dominion of Wales.* London, 1811.

Carus, Carl Gustav, *The King of Saxony's Journey Through England and Scotland, 1844.*

Catherall, Thomas, *Views in North Wales, c.1860.*

Catherall, Thomas, *The Stranger's Best Guide to Llandudno and the Great Orme's Head.* Bangor, 1855.

Cathrall, William, *A Guide through North Wales.* London, 1860.

Cathrall, William, *Wanderings in North Wales, a Road and Railway Guide Book,* 1851.

Cathrall, William, *History of North Wales comprising a Topographical Description of the Several Counties of Anglesey, Carnarvon, Denbigh, Flint, Merioneth and Montgomery.* Manchester, 1828.

Churton, Edward, *The Railroad Book of England/Scotland/Wales.* London, 1851.

Clark, Edwin, *The Britannia and Conway Tubular Bridges.* London, 1850.

Cliff of Worcester, *The Cambrian Tourist, or Post Chaise Companion,* 1814, 1821 etcetera.

Cliff of Worcester, *The Cambrian Directory, 1800.*

Cliffe, John Henry, *Notes and Recollections of an Angler, 1860.*

Cliffe, Charles Frederick, *The Book of North Wales, 1851.*

Clough, M.B., *Scenes and Stories Little Known, Chiefly in North Wales, 1861.*

Compton, Thomas, *The Northern Cambrian Mountains, 1817.*

Cooke, G.A., *The Modern British Traveller or Tourist's Pocket Directory.* London, 1802-10. Volume 21 contains Wales.

Cooke, G.A., *A Topographical and Statistical Description of Wales: Part 1, North Wales, c.1830.*

Costello, Louisa Stuart, *The Falls, Lakes and Mountains of North Wales, 1845.*

Cradock, Joseph, *An Account of Some of the Most Romantic Parts of North Wales, 1774.*

Cradock, Joseph, *Letters from Snowdon, 1770.*

Crane, W., *Picturesque Scenery in North Wales, 1842.*

Cuitt, G., *Etchings of Ancient Buildings in the City of Chester, Castles in North Wales and other Miscellaneous Subjects, 1816.*

Daniell, W., *A Voyage Round Great Britain undertaken in the Summer of the Year 1813, 1815.*

Davidson, J.B., *The Conway in the Stereoscope.* London, 1860.

Davis, W., *Hand-Book for the Vale of Clwyd, containing a Topographical and Historical Description of the Towns of Rhyl, Abergele, St. Asaph, Denbigh and Ruthin, 1856.*

de Barri, Gerald, *The Itinerary of Archbishop Baldwin Through Wales, AD 1188.*

Defoe, Daniel *Tour Through the Whole Island of Great Britain, 1724.*

Dineley, T., *Account of the Official Progress of His Grace Henry, the first Duke of Beaufort through Wales in 1684, 1888.*

Dugdale, T., *Curiosities of Great Britain.* England and Wales Delineated, 1854-60.

Eryri Hills (Anonymous) *A Panoramic sketch and a short description of the Eryri Hills or Caernarvonshire Mountains as seen from Anglesey.* Caernarvon, c.1850.

Evans, T., *Cambrian Itinerary, 1801* [republished in 1819 as 'Walks Through Wales' by T. Evans; later as 'Topographical and Statistical Description of the Principality of Wales'; later became 'The Cambrian Tourist and Post-Chaise Companion' (see Cliff).

Evans, John, *Tour Through North Wales, 1798.*

Evans, J., *The Beauties of England and Wales, 1801-15.* Volume 17 (1812) contains North Wales.

Fenton, Richard, *Tours in Wales, 1810.*

Ferrar, John, *A Tour from Dublin to London, 1795.*

Fielding, T.H., *British Castles, or a Compendious History of the Ancient Military Structures of Great Britain, 1825.*

Freeman, G.J., *Sketches in Wales, or a Diary of Three Walking Excursions in that Principality in 1823, 1824, 1825 (1826).*

Gilpin, William, *Observations of several parts of the Counties of Cambridge, Norfolk, Suffolk and Essex, also several parts of North Wales, 1809.*

Grose, Francis, *The Antiquities of England and Wales* (1776, 1783-7 editions. Volume 7: Wales).

Gruffydd, William John, *North Wales and the Marches.* London, 1851.

Hall, Edmund Hyde, *A Description of Caernarvonshire, 1809-1811.*

Halliwell, J.O., *Notes of Family Excursions in North Wales, 1860.*

Hanmer, Sir J., *Notes and Papers to serve for a Memorial of the Parish of Hanmer in Flintshire, 1872.*

Harwood, J. & F., *A Volume of Views in North Wales, c.1846.*

Hayward, J.W., *Guide to Trefriw and the Vale of Conway Spa.* London 1872.

Hayward, J.W., *The Vale of Conway Spa.* London 1872.

Hayward, J.W., *The Vale of Conway Spa.* Liverpool, 1865.

Hemingway, J., *Panorama of the Beauties, Curiosities and Antiquities of North Wales, 1839.*

Heywood, Abel, *Penny Guides: A guide to Carnarvon.* Manchester, 1870.

Heywood, Abel, *Penny Guide to Llandudno and The Creuddyn.* Manchester, 1868.

Heywood, Abel, *Penny Guides: Llanrwst, Bettws-y-coed, Capel Curig, etcetera.* Manchester, 1869.

Heywood, Abel, *Penny Guides. Bangor and Beaumaris with notices of Anglesey.* Manchester, 1868.

Heywood, Abel, *Penny Guide to Snowdon and the Glyders; with notices of Llanberis etcetera.* Manchester, 1868.

Heywood, Abel, *Penny Guide to Penmaenmawr and Conway.* Manchester, 1870.

Hicklin, John, *Llandudno and its Vicinity.* London, 1856.

Hicklin, John, *The Ladies of Llangollen, 1847.*

Hicklin, John, *The Illustrated Handbook of North Wales, 1853.*

Hicklin, John, *Excursions in North Wales: A Complete Guide to the Tourist, 1847.*

Hissey, J.J., *Round about Snowdon, 1894.*

Hoare, Richard Colt, *A Collection of 48 Views of Noblemen's and Gentlemen's Seats, Towns, Castles, Monasteries and Romantic Places in North and South Wales, 1795.*

Howson, J.S., *The River Dee, its History and Aspect, 1875.*

Hucks, Joseph, *A Pedestrian Tour Through North Wales, 1795.*

Hughes, H., *The Beauties of Cambria: 60 Views in North and South Wales, 1823.*

Hughes, Hugh Derfel, *Antiquities of Llandegai and Llanllechid, 1866.*

Hulbert, C., *The Parlour Book of British Scenery, 1832.*

Hulbert, C., *The History and Description of the County of Salop, 1837.*

Hutton, William, *Remarks Upon North Wales, 1803.*

Jackson, Thomas, *The Tourist's Guide to Britannia Bridge, 1854.*

Jenkins, David Erwyd, *Bedd Gelert, its Facts, Fairies and Folk-lore, 1899.*

John Price, *Old Price's Remains, 1863.*

Johnson, Thomas, *Itinerary of a Botanist, 1639.*

Johnson, Samuel, *Diary of a Journey into North Wales, 1774* (edited by R. Duppa, 1816).

Jones, O. *Cymru: Yn Hanesyddol, Parthedegol a Bywgraphyddol, 1875.*

Jones & Co., *Wales Illustrated in a Series of Views comprising the Picturesque Scenery, Towns, Castles, Seats of the Nobility and Gentry, Antiquities, etcetera.* London 1830.

Jones, W.H., *Old Karnarvon, 1882.*

Jones, William Basil, *Vestiges of the Gael in Gwynedd.* London, 1851.

Jones, Harry Longueville, *Illustrations of the Natural Scenery of the Snowdonian Mountains.* London, 1829.

Kohl, Georg Johann, *Travels in England and Wales, 1845.*

Lawson, W., *Collins' County Geographies: Carnarvon*. London, 1877.

Leigh, Samuel, *Leigh's Guide to Wales and Monmouthshire*. London, 1831.

Leland, John, *Itinerary in Wales, 1536*. 1710.

Leslie, C.H., *Rambles around Mold, c.1869*.

Lewis, Samuel, *A Topographical Dictionary of Wales, 1833*.

Lloyd-Williams & Underwood, *The Archaeological Antiquities and Village Churches of Denbighshire, 1872*.

Llwyd, Richard, *Beaumaris Bay, 1800*.

Llwyd, Richard, *A Trip to North Wales, 1832*.

Louis, M.L., *Gleanings in North Wales with Historical Sketches, 1854*.

Lovett, Richard, *Welsh Pictures, 1890*.

Lyttleton, George, *Account of a Journey into Wales, 1756* (published as an appendix to some editions of Wyndham and Bingley).

Macky, John, *A Journey Through England and Scotland, 1732*.

Manners, John Henry, *Journal of a Tour into Wales, 1797*.

Martin, A.R., *Martin's Week's Wanderings in North Wales, 1856*.

Mavor, William, *A Tour Through Wales, 1805*.

Mawe, John, *The Mineralogy of Derbyshire, North of England, Scotland and Wales*. London, 1802.

McLean, T., *A Picturesque Description of North Wales Embellished with 20 Select Views from Nature, 1823*.

Moore, J.&G.J. Parkyns, *Monastic Remains and Ancient Castles in England and Wales, 1792*.

Morris, F.O., *Picturesque Views of Seats of the Noblemen and Gentlemen of Great Britain and Ireland, c.1880*.

Nelson, Thomas, *Nelson's Pictorial Guidebooks. North-East Wales: Llandudno, Llangollen, Denbigh and Rhyl*. London, 1870.

Nelson, Thomas, *Nelson's Pictorial Guidebooks. Carnarvon and Snowdon*. London, 1869.

Newell, Robert Hasell, *Letters on the Scenery of Wales*. London, 1821.

Nicholson, George, *The Cambrian Traveller's Guide and Pocket Companion*. Stourport, 1808.

Nicholson, Emilius, *Cambrian Travellers' Guide, 1840*.

Nicholson, S.&G., *Plas Newydd and Vale Crucis Abbey, 1824*.

Onwhyn, Joseph, *Hints to Pedestrians, or How to Enjoy a Three-Weeks' Ramble Through North and South Wales, 1837*.

Owen, Nicholas, *Caernarvonshire. A Sketch of its History, Antiquities, Mountains and Productions, 1856*.

Parry, Edward, *Railway Companion from Chester to Holyhead, 1848*.

Parry, J., *Llandudno, Its History and Natural History, 1861*.

Parry, P., *The Llandudno Visitor's Handbook, 1855*.

Parry, Edward, *Steam-Packet Companion from Liverpool to Beaumaris, Bangor and Menai Bridge, 1843*.

Parry, J., *Trip to North Wales made in 1839, 1840*.

Parry, E., *The Cambrian Mirror, or the Tourist's Companion through North Wales, 1850 edition*.

Paterson, M., *Mountaineers Below the Snowline or a Solitary Pedestrian in Snowdonia and Elsewhere, 1886*.

Pedestres, *A Pedestrian Tour of 1347 miles through Wales and England. London, 1836*.

Pennant, Thomas, *The History of the Parishes of Whiteford and Holywell, 1796*.

Pennant, Thomas, *Tours in Wales, 1770-1773*.

Philippe d'Orleans, Antoinne, *Tour in Wales, 1806* (translated by Malcolm Hay in 'A Prince in Captivity'. London, 1960).

Pichot, A., *L'Irlande et le pays de Galles; esquisses de voyages, d'economie politique, etcetera*. Paris, 1850.

Poole, J., *Gleanings of the Histories of Holywell, Flint, St Asaph and Rhuddlan, with Statistics and Geographical Account of North Wales in General, 1831*.

Pratt, Samuel Jackson, *Gleanings through Wales, Holland and Westphalia, London 1795-1802*.

Price, John, *Llandudno and How to Enjoy it*. London, 1875.

Pring, Dr., *Particulars of the Grand Suspension Bridge erected over the Straits of Menai*. Bangor, 1826.

Provis, W.A., *An Historical and Descriptive Account of the Suspension Bridge Constructed over the Menai Strait*. London, 1828.

Pugh, Edward, *Cambria Depicta: A Tour Through North Wales illustrated with Picturesque Views, 1807, 1816*.

Pughe, D.W., *Humphreys' Series: An Historical Sketch of Conway Castle and its Environs*. Caernarfon, 1863 (3rd edition).

Pughe, D.W., *History of Caernarvon Castle and Town*. 4th edition. Caernarfon, 1863.

Ramsay, Andrew, *The Geological Structure of Merionethshire and Caernarvonshire*. London 1858.

Rhys, Gweirydd ap, *Hanes y Brytaniaid a'r Cymry, 1872-4*.

Richards, William, *Wallography, or, The Briton Described, Being a Pleasant Relation of a Journey into Wales, 1682*.

Roberts, John Askew, *The Gossiping Guide to Wales, 1891*.

Roberts, A., *Wynnstay and the Wynns, 1876*.

Rock & Co., Picturesque Views in North Wales, 1871.

Rodenberg, Julius, *Ein Herbst in Wales, Land and Leute, Marchen under Lieder*. Hanover, 1858.

Roscoe, Thomas, *Wanderings and Excursions in North Wales, 1836*.

Ross (M.) and Somerville (E.), *Beggars on Horseback*, a Riding Tour in North Wales, 1895.

Sael, G., *A Collection of Welsh Tours, or a Display of the Beauties of Wales, 1797*.

Sandby, Paul, *The Virtuosi's Museum*, containing Select Views in England, Scotland and Ireland, 1778.

Sandby, Paul, *A Collection of One Hundred and Fifty Select Views in England, Scotland and Ireland, 1781.*

Sheringham, W.L., *Sailing directions for the Coast of Wales.* London, 1843.

Simond, Louis, *Journal of a Tour and Residence in Great Britain During the Years 1810 and 1811,* by a French traveller. Edinburgh, 1815.

Sinclair, Catherine, *Hill and Valley, or Hours in England and Wales.* Edinburgh 1838.

Skrine, Henry (1755-1803), *Tours Through Wales, 1798.*

Smith, John, *A guide to Bangor, Beaumaris, Snowdonia, and other parts of North Wales.* 3rd edition. Liverpool, 1833.

Snowdon, *Snowdon: A Journey due North Wales, for Summer Excursionists by a Pedestrian Tourist.* London, 1860.

Society of Gentlemen, *England Display'd, being a New, Complete and Accurate Survey and Description of the Kingdom of England and the Principality of Wales by a Society of Gentlemen, 1769.*

Sotheby, W. (and J. Smith), *A Tour through Parts of Wales, 1794.*

Spiker, Samuel Heinrich, *Travels Through England, Wales and Scotland, 1816.*

Stevens, F., *Views of Cottages and Farmhouses in England and Wales, 1815.*

Storer, J.S.&J. Greig., *Antiquarian and Topographical Cabinet,* containing a Series of Views of the most Interesting Objects of Curiosity in Great Britain, 1807-11.

Tacitus, Cornelius, *The Annals of Imperial Rome,* 100 A.D.

Taylor, John, *Short Relation of a Long Journey, 1653.*

Taylor, H., Historic Notices of the Borough and County Town of Flint, 1883.

Thomas, D.R., A History of the Diocese of St. Asaph, 1874.

Torbuck, John, *A Collection of Welch Travels and Memoirs of Wales, 1741.*

Turner, J.M.W., *Picturesque Views in England and Wales, 1832-8.*

Turner, Thomas, *Narrative of a Journey with a Fly to North Wales, 1837.*

Tyndall, John, *Hours of Exercise on the Alps, 1860.*

Virtue, G., *The Tourist in Wales,* comprising Views of Picturesque Scenery, 1835.

Walcott, M.E.C., *Memorials, Archeological and Historical, of Chester, Manchester, St Asaph and Bangor.* Chester 1865.

Walford, Thomas, *The Scientific Tourist through England, Wales, Scotland etcetera. 1818.*

Waller, William, *A Description of the Mines in Wales.* London.

Warner, Richard, *A Second Walk Through Wales, 1798.*

Warner, Richard, *A Walk Through Wales, 1798.*

Welsh Tours, *A Collection of Welsh Tours.* London 1797-1798.

Wigstead, Henry, *Remarks on a Tour to North and South Wales, 1797.*

Williams, William, *Observations on the Snowdon Mountains, 1802.*

Williams, Peter Bayley, *The Tourist's Guide Through the County of Caernarvon.* Caernarvon, 1821 and 1828.

Williams, Robert, *The History and Antiquities of the Town of Aberconwy.* Denbigh, 1835.

Williams, J., *Ancient and Modern Denbigh*, A Descriptive History of the Castle, Borough and Liberties, 1856.

Willis, B., *A Survey of the Cathedral Church of St. Asaph and the Edifices belonging to it*, 1720.

Willis, B., *A Survey of the Cathedral Church of Bangor*. London, 1721.

Wood, John George, *The Principal Rivers of Wales Illustrated*, Consisting of a Series of Views from the Source of each River to its Mouth, Accompanied by Descriptions, 1813.

Worrall, John, *Worrall's Directory of North Wales*. Oldham, 1874.

Wright, G.N., *Scenes in North Wales with Historical Illustrations, Legends and Biographical Notices*, 1833.

Wyndham, Henry Penruddocke, *A Tour through Monmouthshire and Wales*, Made in the Months of June and July 1774, and in the Months of June, July and August 1777 (1781).

Wynne, Sir John, *History of the Gwydir Family*. Oswestry, 1878.

Y, H.B., *Humphreys' Guide to the Summit of Snowdon*. Caernarfon, 1850.

Index

- **THE BOTANISTS AND GUIDES OF SNOWDONIA**
  - Dewi Jones. *I SBN 0-86381-383-6; £6.95*

- **WALKS FROM LLANDUDNO**
  - Christopher Draper.
  ISBN 0-86381-559-6; £4.95

- **CIRCULAR WALKS IN MEIRIONNYDD**
  - Dorothy Hamilton.
  ISBN 0-86381-545-6; £4.50

- **WALKS IN AND AROUND THE BERWYN MOUNTAINS**
  - John Tranter.
  ISBN 0-86381-547-2; £4.50

- **CIRCULAR WALKS IN NORTH EASTERN WALES**
  - Jim Grindle.
  ISBN 0-86381-550-2; £4.50

- **THE NORTH WALES PATH AND TEN SELECTED WALKS**
  - Dave Salter & Dave Worrall.
  ISBN 0-86381-546-4; £4.50

- **LLŶN PENINSULA COASTAL WALKS**
  - Richard Quinn.
  ISBN 0-86381-574-X; £4.50

- **CIRCULAR WALKS IN THE BLACK MOUNTAINS**
  - Nick Jenkins.
  ISBN 0-86381-558-8; £4.50

- **WALKS IN THE WYE VALLEY**
  - Richard Sale.
  ISBN 0-86381-555-3; £4.50

- **CEREDIGION WALKS**
  Richard Sale;
  ISBN: 0-86381-602-9; £4.50

- **CIRCULAR WALKS IN THE VALE OF GLAMORGAN**
  Dorothy Hamilton;
  ISBN: 0-86381-603-7; £4.50

- **WALKS FROM COLWYN BAY**
  Chris Draper;
  ISBN: 0-86381-604-5; £4.95

- **A CAMBRIAN WAY**
  Richard Sale;
  ISBN: 0-86381-605-3; £6.90

- **CARMARTHENSHIRE COAST & GOWER CIRCULAR WALKS**
  Paul Williams;
  ISBN: 0-86381-607-X; £4.50

- **CIRCULAR WALKS IN THE WESTERN BEACONS**
  Nick Jenkins;
  ISBN: 0-86381-638-X; £4.50

- **WALKS FROM CONWY**
  - Christopher Draper
  ISBN 0-86381-695-9; £4.95

- **CIRCULAR WALKS IN THE DYFI VALLEY**
  - Dorothy Hamilton
  ISBN 0-86381-688-6; £4.50

- **OWAIN GLYNDŴR'S WAY**
  Richard Sale.
  ISBN 0-86381-690-8; £4.95

- **A MEIRIONNYDD COAST WALK**
  Laurence Maine.
  ISBN 0-86381-666-5; £5.50